VIOLENCE IN/AND THE GREAT LAKES

Thinking Africa is a series produced by the Department of Political and International Studies at Rhodes University and University of KwaZulu-Natal Press. For more information on the project, visit http://www.ru.ac.za/politics/thinkingafrica/ or write to:

Leonhard Praeg: Series Editor
Thinking Africa
Political and International Studies
Rhodes University
Private Bag 94
Grahamstown 6139
South Africa

Email: L.Praeg@ru.ac.za

Previous series titles:
The Return of Makhanda: Exploring the Legend by Julia C. Wells (2012)
On African Fault Lines: Meditations on Alterity Politics by V-Y Mudimbe (2013)
A Report on Ubuntu by Leonhard Praeg (2014)
Ubuntu: Curating the Archive edited by Leonhard Praeg and Siphokazi Magadla (2014)

thinking
africa

VIOLENCE IN/AND THE GREAT LAKES
The Thought of V-Y Mudimbe and Beyond

Edited by
Grant Farred, Kasereka Kavwahirehi and
Leonhard Praeg

UNIVERSITY OF KWAZULU-NATAL PRESS

Published in 2014 by University of KwaZulu-Natal Press
Private Bag X01
Scottsville, 3209
Pietermaritzburg
South Africa
Email: books@ukzn.ac.za
Website: www.ukznpress.co.za

ISBN: 978-1-86914-284-1

Managing editor: Sally Hines
Editor: Alison Lockhart
Proofreader: Christopher Merrett
Typesetter: Patricia Comrie
Indexer: Ethné Clarke
Cover design: MDesign
Cover art: Luc Tuymans, *Speech*, 2010 (206.4 x 138.4 cm, oil on canvas)

Printed and bound in South Africa by Interpak Books, Pietermaritzburg

CONTENTS

To V-Y Mudimbe: Friend, Colleague, Thinker

Both the seminar, hosted at Rhodes University, South Africa, and the publication that emerged from it, *Violence in/and the Great Lakes: V-Y Mudimbe and Beyond*, would not have been possible without the support of the Africana Studies and Research Center at Cornell University and the Thinking Africa project at Rhodes University. As editors, we would like to thank the Africana staff at Cornell – Ms Renee Milligan for her tireless, diligent work on arranging the logistics, all conducted in the best possible spirit; Ms Treva Levine for her keen oversight and the interim director, Salah Hassan, for providing subvention support – and the Thinking Africa staff at Rhodes – Siphokazi Magadla, Sally Matthews and Phumlani Majavu – for working through the winter break to organise the colloquium. We also acknowledge the generous financial support provided by the office of Peter Clayton, deputy vice-chancellor of research at Rhodes University.

We are grateful to V-Y Mudimbe's assistant, Mr Trip Attaway, for liaising among three institutions and two continents. It could not have been easy, but Mr Attaway always, it seems, had a smile at the ready, no matter what the logistical issues were to be resolved.

University of KwaZulu-Natal Press was encouraging and supportive from the first. We are grateful for the work they have done to make this publication possible. As has been the case in the preceding volumes of the Thinking Africa book series, we would like to acknowledge the support and dedication of Debra Primo and Sally Hines. In particular, we would like to thank our editor, Alison Lockhart, for her close and insightful reading of the manuscript.

Grant Farred would like to thank Richard Pithouse, who first welcomed him to Rhodes University. His engagement with the Thinking Africa project at Rhodes University began with Richard.

Thinking Africa would like to thank Grant Farred from Cornell University for initiating and funding the lion's share of this collaboration.

Lastly, we want to thank the participants/contributors for their commitment to the project. Our colleagues travelled great distances to attend the seminar and they kept, as nearly as can be expected, to the publication schedule; moreover, they did so in good cheer. All of which, we suspect, can be ascribed to their deep regard for the thinking of V-Y Mudimbe and the pressing questions his work provokes, as well as the intellectual example he has established over several decades.

Through his work, our friend, colleague and, above all, our teacher, Valentin-Yves Mudimbe has inspired many generations of scholars, all across the world, to take up the difficult issues he raises. He does so in the most learned, generous and serious way imaginable. We are all immensely pleased and, indeed, honoured to have been able to share the colloquium experience with him. This publication is the acknowledgement of our relation (one that he will deny, as is his wont) of intellectual and ethical debt, a debt we are all too happy to assume, to underwrite, to him. So much of our work would not be possible without him, without the *oeuvre* he has created – for us and for those who will surely take up this responsibility after us.

Our metaphysical faculty is paralyzed because actual events have shattered the basis on which speculative metaphysical thought could be reconciled with experience. Once again, the dialectical motif of quantity recoiling into quality scores an unspeakable triumph.

— Theodor Adorno, 'After Auschwitz'

Introduction
Silhouette of the Unknown Woman

Grant Farred

> . . . mustn't responsibility always be expressed in a language that is foreign to what the community can hear or understand only too well?
> — Jacques Derrida, *The Gift of Death*

> Here is a nightmare of my wearing black for more than ten years.
> — V-Y Mudimbe, *'Debitores Sumus . . .'*

V-Y Mudimbe's essay, *'Debitores Sumus* . . . On Ways of Exhausting Our Question on Violence' (Chapter 9), grounds this volume. It does so only in part, it must be said, because *Violence in/and the Great Lakes* derives from a conference, of the same name, assembled in Mudimbe's honour. *'Debitores Sumus'*, a 'statement about the deaths of millions of people. For sure, between seven and ten, by now. The statement is grave', is the central essay because it sets the terms for this thinking of violence in Mudimbe's native region. Violence in the Great Lakes region is the 'nightmare', the number of dead so shocking as to exceed any other in history, that compels Mudimbe to wear only black 'for more than ten years'. In its oral presentation, at the conference at Rhodes University, in Grahamstown, South Africa, there was a signal moment in which Mudimbe – a bespectacled man, almost hunched over his papers, dressed all in black, only the grey in his whiskers providing any contrast – presented his audience with another, now long-forgotten nightmare. Mudimbe's oral presentation – possessed of the authority of delivery, the authority of physical presence – was the defining moment of the conference and as such it, rather than the published version in this volume, provides the philosophical basis for this introduction.

The ending of Mudimbe's presentation was, like his choice to forswear any colour other than the most sober one, unmistakably a political event. It was poignant, too, possessed of an ethical conviction and a singular rhetorical and symptomatic force. It was strategically placed, designed to unnerve, to throw everything that had gone before – most of which is recounted in this volume – into stark, and starkly troubling, relief. It apprehended the audience, it made itself – Mudimbe's 'revelation' (I will offer other articulations of it shortly) – the object of thought that reverberated; Mudimbe's ending pointed back, it would seem, to the very beginning of the colloquium, but not only to the conference proceedings that had gone before, coming as it did in the final session of a gathering organised to honour Mudimbe. The last words of his presentation reached back chronologically to an act of violence that long preceded the conference. It was the very elocution of the last word that could not stand as such; instead, it demanded a response, as any 'final' remark is apt to do. The process of engaging with the last word that is, of course, never the last word, began in Grahamstown and finds its most recent articulation here – this time as the 'first word' in this collection, a first word that birthed the philosophical terms in which *Violence in/and the Great Lakes* is conceived.

The ethical force of the Grahamstown presentation derived from the haunting image with which Mudimbe concluded his argument. One night, in a convent, a woman was dragged off by some unidentified forces of repression (we have no idea exactly who committed this act), we know not where the Unknown Woman (there is no other way to name her, a fact that must itself trouble us) was taken but we suspect the worst, as we should when people are disappeared in the dead of night. (The Argentine name for those disappeared is, of course, *los desaparecidos*, the name made into a portentous political term because of the extreme violence of the *Guerra Sucia* (Dirty War), the civil war that pitted the brutal *generalissimos* against the leftist opposition.) Mudimbe is a silent observer to this event, a silent observer shaken to his core. That it is a woman who is disappeared is, of course, of significance, given the particular violence endured by women in the Great Lakes region, as Ngwarsungu Chiwengo and Laura Kerr make clear in Chapter 5 and Chapter 6 of this volume. It is a recurring nightmare, holding Mudimbe firmly in its grasp. The death of the Unknown Woman is strangely reminiscent, as scholars of Mudimbe's novels – such as Olga Hél-Bongo (see Chapter 4) – know, of Marie-Gertrude in Mudimbe's fourth novel, *Shaba deux: Les carnets de Mère Marie-Gertrude*.[1] These many decades later, Mudimbe is still captive to both hauntings, as he must be, this man who mourns – and in so doing, protests, visibly – the dead, seven million or ten, publicly; this man in black who mourns and protests and speaks out against the violence, for all of us to see, is a thinker haunted by death, by one death above all others, the one death that makes him mindful of (all) the others.

There are at least two (related) ways of understanding the conclusion to the oral presentation of 'Debitores Sumus . . .': (1) it might be labelled testimony: Mudimbe is present (the presence that birthed Shaba deux, where the haunting continued, found new articulation, assumed a new, but no less phantasmagoric form), at the beginning of what would become the catastrophic violence in the Great Lakes, speaking to the (kernel of the) event; in Grahamstown, he said so, in simple, self-incriminating terms: 'I was there. I saw it'; Mudimbe bearing witness and, in so doing, (2) finding now, several decades later, a moment to expiate, to express, through this observation, his Schuldigkeit – his guilt, to publicly stipulate his implication in the beginning of the violence.[2] 'Debitores Sumus . . .' stands as Mudimbe's St Augustine moment: his Schuldigkeit stems from his event of original (or originary) sin, making of the ending of his presentation the first statement of his own rueful, but philosophically and politically critical, 'Confessions'. There are Augustinian echoes in Mudimbe's testimony; like the Bishop of Hippo, Mudimbe 'bears about him his mortality, the evidence of his sinfulness' (Augustine 2006: 3). 'Sinful', Mudimbe may be (is betrayal his chief sin? Did he betray the Unknown Woman? Or is it in inaction, the fact that he did nothing? Is it this that haunts him more than anything? Does betrayal always bear on a certain mode of inaction? Even Judas, arch-betrayer, does 'nothing' – a gross misnomer, of course – after revealing the place where Jesus-the-Christ can be found), yet he 'bears about him' not only his own 'mortality', but also that of the many millions who perished because of the 'sinfulness' (extreme violence) of others.

In this way the Unknown Woman stands as an evocation (she provokes questions about the living and the dead, which raises the issue of representation) that cannot be disengaged from a crisis of nomenklatura. That is, the Unknown Woman must at once instantiate herself (claim her political necessity) and warn against herself, against her own hypostatisation.[3] As the figure for thought in Mudimbe's presentation, it is necessary to remember that the effect of the violence in the Great Lakes has been to produce millions of Known Women, even if in their being named as casualties of violence they are as quickly forgotten. In this way, the Unknown Woman is critical because in her figuring is included the known (named), the unknown (unnamed, not yet named) and the un–nameable. By resisting valorisation, Mudimbe's Unknown Woman remains political, insistently so and, as importantly, a figure that is always operative well in excess of her–self, a self that we must, out of ethical and philosophical necessity, speculate about in order to think her. We speculate about her because it is only through her that some notion of truth about the violence becomes available. The effect of the Unknown Woman's haunting is that it demands its own speaking, a speaking that, as taken up by Mudimbe, is simultaneously singular (in her spectrality on that historic night she cannot be emulated; the exceptional force of the singular is that it forecloses the possibility of repetition) and multivalent ('contemporary' voice of the Known, the Unknown and the un–nameable).

It is only through the Unknown Woman that any path to truth is opened up, which makes it possible to see how in sinfulness (Augustine's, Mudimbe's) there is also, there always is, as recent Augustinian critics are quick to point out, the desire and determination to 'affirm the truth of Christianity' (Burrus, Jordan and Mackendrick 2010: 35). In his Augustinian speaking, Mudimbe uses his presence – he *was* there – at the event to 'affirm' the truth of an originary violence, a violence for which he now knows (as he might always have known) he bears an (unshakeable, singular) responsibility. It is a responsibility that he cannot forswear, a historical burden that he cannot shift. No one else can assume this responsibility, which Mudimbe knows, and yet he is also intensely aware (it is an ethical matter for him) that part of his responsibility is to be responsible to the secret of the event, which means that he must speak the secret. Mudimbe must speak of his haunting, the Unknown Woman, so that it becomes possible to give the Known Women an antecedent, so that the violence is dated with an im–precise spectrality; so that the violence is historicised and made visible in its *longue durée*. The violence in the Great Lakes is structural, even if it seems episodic and fitful, which is what ensures that it will always be intensely bloody.

Mudimbe must give the secret of the event to history and, in so doing, he makes all who are party to its dissemination responsible for the event. All responsibility begins with a Self that understands that it must act in the cause of establishing a relation to the Other, a relation that is entirely capable of emerging, of articulating itself, in situations, under conditions, that hardly seem hospitable to its enunciation or dissemination. The Self's responsibility, as will be discussed shortly, begins in ir–responsibility. The secret born in the Congo during the 1960s (after Patrice Lumumba's assassination) comes into its own, makes a new demand under the sign of responsibility, in post-apartheid South Africa. Like the secret, the event of the Unknown Woman knows its own time. And, apparently, its own place, a place that brings that 'first' place directly back into view, the object of a new thinking, a thinking that the event itself could not have known.

It is Mudimbe's originary presence, the consequence of pure accident, which allows the spectre of the Unknown Woman to emerge. Philosophically and ethically, however, the Unknown Woman must be accorded a singular status because she is not only (as Many as there are of her, she is the first One; so, she retains to herself, to the violence done to her, her Oneness – the singularity of the singular), as has been discussed, symptomatic or prescient; she is not only the sign of things to come. She inscribes herself as an anti-Kurtzian figure (possessed of the moral core that Joseph Conrad's Kurtz so patently lacks, or has rather happily shed) who, through a quiet, steadfast resilience, allows for no historical amnesia. Having been present, Mudimbe is now made her writer, her Marlowe, but she is a figure for thought (for thinking violence), not a muse (or, if she is a muse, she belongs to the Adorno school, which challenges us to make 'poetry after Auschwitz'); besides, it is no quiet, murky Thames from which Mudimbe writes. It is, rather, a post-apartheid South Africa riven with its own tensions, faced with its own (intractable) problems. In Mudimbe's Grahamstown presentation, the Unknown Woman is the first sighting of 'the horror, the horror' to come. She is neither Kurtz's naive betrothed nor the Amazonian woman of the heart of darkness, but a truly historical figure, a figure whose historicity is first recognised – attested to, if not immediately spoken of – by Mudimbe. In her turn, she is the one who sows the first ethical seeds of Mudimbe's sartorial severity. It is her originality (he was there, there where she endured her fate), in all senses of the term, which enables her to present Mudimbe with such philosophical and political difficulty. However, the Unknown Woman instantiates more than the putative (and figurative) 'first' victim of Great Lakes violence, as important as her originary/singular status is in itself, a status that must, of course, be acknowledged as such.

The Unknown Woman's real salience, however, derives from her standing as 'Debitores Sumus' figure of responsibility. In the precarity of her life and in the horrific expectation of her death, she introduces and incarnates responsibility. The Unknown Woman explicates responsibility for the Other as the only way to think responsibility – the Gospel of Matthew and the philosophy of Jacques Derrida and Emmanuel Levinas make this clear. Responsibility is only possible, responsibility begins, when the Self understands that it must be ir–responsible to itself, that it can only be responsible when it acts in the cause of establishing a relationship to the Other; that is, when it 'gives' itself to the Other, without any expectation of reciprocation, but remains steadfast in its commitment to act for the Other, when it takes up the Other's cause with no expectation that the Other will, at some point, behave similarly – ir–responsibility forswears, from the very first, reciprocation. Responsibility to the Other is, then, an asymmetrical relationship but not a Self–less one. The Self acts not out of abnegation, but out of a political commitment to exceeding it–Self, while not negating the Self. The Self is ir–responsible to it–Self. There is, furthermore, as Mudimbe recognises, something inexplicable – something mysterious, something that cannot be explained – about responsibility and the relationship to the Other that it establishes: 'The incomprehensible cannot meet analytical categories,' is how he put it in his presentation. There is indeed something 'incomprehensible' about the decision to commit politically to the Other without expecting (a similar) fealty in return. All responsibility is responsibility to, beginning with an ir–responsibility to (the Self).

In this regard, Derrida's work in *The Gift of Death*, which turns on a reading of Jan Patočka's *Heretical Essays*, is instructive. Derrida argues that the 'coming of Christian subjectivity' (an 'arrival' that is of no small consequence to Mudimbe's *oeuvre*) derives from Patočka's notion that, after the *mysterium tremendum*, 'responsibility resides henceforth not in an essence that is accessible to the human gaze, that of the Good and the One, but in the relation to a supreme, absolute and inaccessible being that holds us in check not by exterior but interior force' (in Derrida 1995: 93). The Unknown Woman is, in Mudimbe's rendering, the face of the 'interior force': or, responsibility exteriorised – responsibility, that is, come into its own; it is also an act of ir–responsibility, of course, because the Self is the first 'interior force', the force of interiority that endures through and into, that is subsumed into and (subjugated by) the relation (responsibility) to the Other. Traces of the Self remain politically visible in the exteriorisation of responsibility. Responsibility to the Other (Christ's responsibility to all of humanity requires that God condemn his Son to death; the Samaritan's decision to assume responsibility, entirely unprompted, without prospect of acknowledgement, or any form of reward, as recounted in the Gospel according to Luke, to the unknown, but intensely symbolic victim) is the only way in which the interior force can be made visible – brought (in)to its exterior self, despite Christ's (all too mortal) fears, because the Samaritan is fully responsible to his interiority, to the force of the political ('ethical', Mudimbe might label it) that is palpably his own and demands that he act towards the Other. This interior force is lacking in the priest and the Levite who will not so much as acknowledge the victim. Like the Samaritan who comes to the traveller's aid, the Unknown Woman allows us to 'see', to grasp viscerally (in our shock at the recognition that the event has been made opaque to us, is made to happen before our very eyes; in 'seeing' her our eyes are also drawn, unfailingly, to the known, to the other victims), Mudimbe's responsibility to the Other. Mudimbe's responsibility must stand, take a stand against the necropolitics of the Great Lakes region: 'What is negated in the Great Lakes violence is not only human dignity, but might be the mysterious and unique humanity of the gift of life,' says Mudimbe in his presentation. There was, on that long ago night, no regard for the 'mysterious and unique humanity of the gift of life', a violent process that seems to have continued ever since. There was no outrage expressed that night and so it is that Mudimbe now makes himself responsible to the life of that woman. In presenting her to us, he is making us all responsible for the violence that would negate the gift of life.

Clearly, then, the gathering that produced *Violence in/and the Great Lakes* is owed entirely to the event of the Unknown Woman; in particular to what it is that the event makes known. Because of the Unknown Woman, all our thinking on responsibility, from the woman (women: subjects disproportionately vulnerable to the region's violence) to the gathering in Mudimbe's name and to the devastation that is Great Lakes life (as argued so persuasively by Kasereka Kavwahirehi in Chapter 1) begins spectrally. With a shadowy figure, in the dark of night, that is where our thinking of how violence demands (an especial) responsibility to the Other finds its first address. What interior forces compel us towards (the exteriority of) responsibility? These interior forces that demand that we speak, take action, that we undertake our work in the cause of the Other's safety in the face of superior force? Like the superior force she faced on that night, rendering her unspeakably vulnerable, as the Known Women continue to be.

The effect of the spectre of the Unknown Woman is to make legible (it is now possible to write her, to write of the violence and then to understand the violence of that writing) – and audible, too, to give the woman a voice that speaks through, because of, Mudimbe, making of Mudimbe an ethical ventriloquist post *ipso facto*. After the fact, responsibility installs itself at the core of Mudimbe's Latinate title, '*Debitores Sumus*': 'we are all debtors'. All the thinking that takes place in *Violence in/and the Great Lakes* is indebted to the Unknown Woman because that is the voice to which Mudimbe is, before all else, responsible. It is, we might say, the Unknown Woman who makes Mudimbe responsible because that is the voice, we might call it 'conscience' (not acting in the moment of record; this is, as Shakespeare knows, Hamlet's critical failing – the Prince of Denmark has so many opportunities to act; he never does so), or the voice rooted in fear or concern for the fate of the Unknown Woman, that has troubled Mudimbe ever since. The Unknown Woman is a figure of ethical perturbation for Mudimbe because the terms of indebtedness, his and ours, each in their own way, are of a different order, an order intuitively present in Patočka's insistence upon the subservience of the 'exterior' to the 'interior'. We know this from the verse in Romans 8:12 that gives Mudimbe's presentation (and essay) its title: '. . . we are debtors, not to the flesh, to live after the flesh'. It is in the cause of living 'after the flesh', of making it possible for all of humanity to live after the flesh, that Jesus-the-Christ accepts his fate. The Samaritan rescues the traveller and cares for him so that his caring is not only in the cause of the flesh, but because he is acting in the spirit of life 'after the flesh'.

It is for this reason, this recognition that the call in Romans issues from a 'mysterious' but eminently recognisable place, that Mudimbe knows the voice will not leave him in peace. It is a voice that has not, since that moment, given him any philosophical rest (a point that relates to Leonhard Praeg's argument in Chapter 8). He is bound to, by, that voice. It is the voice that returns to him, again and again, it is the voice – or the terrified visage, if the optic is preferred to the metaphoric – in which Mudimbe's ethics, his Patočkian 'Good', manifests itself. Mudimbe, from that day to this, continues to hear that voice; he continues to see the Conradian horrors that will befall the Unknown Woman. To be gathered in the name of violence, in this instance, means that we are brought together by – in the name of – a responsibility that precedes us and, yet, a responsibility to which we are in debt (we have a relationship to the Other): it is not simply a matter of exchange, of being indebted to some economy. Christian debt, on the order of Abraham (and Isaac) and the Crucifixion, makes us responsible.

Because responsibility establishes a relationship to the Other, it cannot be prematurely foreclosed. It cannot be foreclosed at all. The Samaritan, more than anyone, knows this; he cannot simply leave the traveller at the inn and be done with it. He must pay for the traveller's stay and his keep, especially the medical attention that will be required. In Mudimbe's case, this means that the debt cannot be discharged until the Unknown Woman has been spoken for: until the Unknown Woman has been afforded justice. Moreover, justice, given the enormity of the horror that faces us, that Mudimbe came to see when he saw not her face, but her silhouette before she was taken away, can only be achieved in life 'after the flesh'. This is the uncompromising demand of responsibility to the Other to which the Self subscribes.

Responsibility in silhouette

It is the nature of responsibility to address itself generally. It is never only you or I who are called upon to address the Other, but all of us. It is, then, not only Mudimbe who is charged with responsibility, although it is he who opens us to the call of responsibility. Present at the event, the call comes through him. It is through him (and his relation to the Unknown Woman, which is begun in silence, yet weighed down with surreptitious expectation – or responsibility) that the call is issued. In this instance, responsibility makes of all who are (now) in its ambit, a polis: gathered together by the Unknown Woman (the parable's traveller), possessed of no proper name, bound by the silhouette to a surreptitious responsibility (a responsibility that is nevertheless unyielding because we are, none of us, exempted from it). Responsibility comes to us in the figure of the Unknown Woman whom we can now only properly understand as a symptomatic All who stands for all the dead (known and unknown and un–named) and for all the dead to come; the All asks us to recognise their names and, most importantly, to intervene in their name; the dead promise that they will haunt us, and they invariably do, making us ir–responsible because they know that we can never speak properly – that is, with the necessary authority and experience – in their name; but that is our charge and we must give ourselves to it if any of us is to 'live after the flesh'. And, for anyone to 'live after', it is imperative that life is lived properly in the now. The first requisite of living properly is to safeguard the 'mysterious and unique humanity of the gift of life'. In order to 'live after', life itself must first be possible here. The wanton negation of life must itself first be negated.

We are, all of us who were present at the colloquium and who later contributed to the publication of those proceedings, made to assume responsibility for someone we do not know; do not know as Mudimbe knew her, even as he did not know her. Who could be more Other than the woman who has neither name nor profile, the woman who breaks the political economy of exchange? Who exists only in silhouette? Who is so possessed of, so full of, Conradian spectrality? (What is it Marlowe says of Kurtz's 'going native'? 'His name, you understand, had not been pronounced once. He was "that man"' (Conrad 1979: 46). When will we learn – to say – her name? How is it that her name will come to us so that she will no longer be our 'Unknown Woman' but – made – Known to us?) Who takes us so relentlessly out of our time? Or, who takes us fully into the time of responsibility? What is it that the Lacanians say, the letter always arrives where it should? At its proper address? In this way, all responsibility comes, directly, from the Other: addressing itself to us – the letter of responsibility finds us at the historically appointed address. We are made responsible by the violence done to her and, paradox of paradoxes, we are all made responsible – a prospect entirely unimaginable until just now – by the unknown violence she endured, a violence that we now cannot forswear, let alone escape. It is, to phrase the matter (perhaps incorrectly, no doubt hubristically) in terms of messianicity, it is through her sacrifice – to a violence that we do not know, but that has now, already after we first heard it, come to haunt us – that we can learn how to be responsible to and for the Other. It is death that makes us responsible, that makes us unmistakably present to ourselves. We are responsible to death, which makes us responsible for inveighing against the violence committed against the Unknown Woman. In this way, the Unknown Woman can be said to have at least two names, both of them proper to her, one inextricably bound to the other: Death and Responsibility. One must not, of course, treat these two 'impostors' – as Rudyard Kipling's 'If' might have it – 'just the same', but it is now (after Mudimbe's Augustinian revelation) possible to see – to think – how Death makes us Responsible. The responsibility of death; all responsibility begins in death. How are we to be in the world if we cannot be responsible to death? All that is left to us if we cannot be responsible to death is to act like Marlowe and vaguely point in the direction of 'that man' and refuse, as Mudimbe says, 'to face the unspeakable'; to act, that is, as if we do not know the gift-destroying violence that emanates directly from 'that man'.

The accomplishment of 'Debitores Sumus . . .' is, then, disturbingly obvious. Having brought us face to silhouette with the Other, Mudimbe leaves us no choice but to assume responsibility for the Other. Culpability, which begins in Mudimbe's unforgettable, irrepressible *Schuldigkeit*, is no longer an option; it is, we can say with confidence, the last possible moment for or of ir–responsibility. 'Debitores Sumus . . .' has given us a figure through which to think our responsibility to the Other. We must not say that it is Mudimbe's 'gift' to us and yet it is because the Unknown Woman is the gift of a trope that at once echoes and resists Conrad's, a literary trope that takes us into the heart of an entirely different, but still hauntingly evocative darkness. The Unknown Woman, disappeared under the dark of night. Or, the Un–Known Woman: *la desaparecida*, a different haunting, a continent away; we are never free of the Unknown Woman, or the Unknown Soldier, for that matter. Under circumstances such as these, we know that it is impossible to avoid Conrad and his writing, or any writing, about violence in the Great Lakes.

It is now, more than ever, possible to see how that any thinking of responsibility must begin in and from ir–responsibility, a responsibility that understands that in order to be responsible to the Other it must at once recognise the Self (act in that Self's name) and forswear, abjure, it–Self as the first order of responsibility. Ir–responsibility begins with the Self inclined toward a relation to that which is not Self; ir–responsibility is thinking in the direction away from the Self. Ir–responsibility is not martyrdom.[4] It is the political act of the Self that makes the Self responsible for acting in relation to.

In the meanwhile, we are left to question why it took Mudimbe so long, these many decades, to give us the Unknown Woman? Why did he give her to us just now? Or, does the Other know when we are most prepared, most likely, to come properly into/as our ir–responsibility? Or, was she always there, in his fiction (here Justin K. Bisanswa's Chapter 3 and Hél-Bongo's Chapter 4 might have something to say), in his philosophical tracts (see Praeg's Chapter 8 and Zubairu Wai's Chapter 7), in his repeated turns to Scripture (Grant Farred's Chapter 2)? We simply did not recognise her? To make the Unknown Woman ours, to take full responsibility for her (an impossibility, but still), it is imperative to understand that we are never done with the work of responsibility. It is like politics of the Trotskyist (permanent revolution) or the Derridean (all politics is *l'avenir*) variety, the struggle that must be taken up: again, and then again. There is no end to responsibility; responsibility begins again, as if for the first time. Mudimbe's refusal to give up his memory, his determined sharing of his debt, philosophically alchemised into a gift of thought, is given to us through his Unknown Woman, who is now also our Unknown Woman. We have been made a gift, what a gift we have been made, 'mysterious and unique'.

And therein lies yet one more haunting. Mudimbe's gift is like Edgar Allan Poe's purloined letter. Given what we now know (the Known and the Unknown, the un–named), given how Mudimbe has presented the legacy of the gift (of death) to us, how will we think our responsibility? At stake is, then, both who the Un–known (we know her, we can even sometimes name her, but, still, we cannot know the violence she – and all like her – have endured) Woman of our time is and, as importantly, what violence she is enduring without our intervention. Can we now face the Other for whom we are responsible, who teaches us responsibility, who makes us learn responsibility and who, in turn, learns a certain mode of political possibility from us, face to face rather than face to silhouette? In Poe's terms, can we bring the force of Detective C. Auguste Dupin's intellect – that is, our thinking – fully into the open? Mudimbe's charge, in this regard, is singular and memorable: we must now be responsible to our own thinking; we must begin to think our responsibility. Our moment demands responsibility as never before because it understands the need for responsibility as never before.

Mudimbe, because of the gift he has made us, is equally uncompromising in his demand. It is not enough, he states, to suggest that it is 'unspeakable that religious systems seem to have failed us'. There is a pressing interrogation that follows hard on the heels of this statement, the final line in his presentation: 'Have we failed the systems?' Can we look into the face of our ir–responsibility, look into the horror, look directly on Kurtz and those acts of Great Lakes violence that are heirs to his colonialist legacy?

In some way or other, every essay – but Bisanswa's, Kerr's and Wai's especially – in this collection is a response to Mudimbe's injunction. Responsibility to the Other is, sometimes in entirely unexpected ways, the shared project, the shared political understanding of *Violence in/and the Great Lakes*. As such, responsibility to the Other turns here, firstly, on the willingness to begin with our failure, our own culpability; technocratically, we have lived with and continue to live with the failure of postcolonial democracy; or, to simply make the state function and properly serve its citizens, to make the state do its technocratic work.[5] Responsibility to the Other is, to phrase this in Conradian terms, the antidote (responsibility) that might well be discerned in that famous, terrified, guttural uttering, 'The horror, the horror'. 'The horror, the horror' is the inevitable outcome of the political subject whose first, and most enduring allegiance, is to the Self (the colonial or the colonised Self) that cannot recognise her or his ir–responsibility. This is the horror of our failure that Mudimbe cannot and will not countenance; this is the horror of failure that instils a profound fear in him, a fear that is institutionally grounded as much as anything else. This is a fear that Jacques Lacan might be impatient with or unsympathetic to, but it is a real one for Mudimbe: the fear that responsibility will not find its proper address. Mudimbe's *oeuvre* is a stringent rejection, as the essays in this collection show, of any thinking that will not take up responsibility at its political core, that will not seek to identify the spectre that provokes us to thought.

This is why, although the silhouette of the Unknown Woman emerges only at the end of the presentation (what are we to make of her second disappearance in the published version? Where has she gone? Why has she gone? Or, is it now impossible for her to be absent, so entrenched is she as a symptomatic haunting?), she is in truth the kernel of the event, located at the centre of Mudimbe's thinking. Without her, what kind of intellectual life would Mudimbe's have been? Without her, what questions, those structured either by guilt or the determination to bear witness, would have been possible? Without her haunting, her reminding him of his debt to her, to all like her, then and now, Unknown, Known and un–named, in the many intervening decades, how would he have been able to tolerate his work? Mudimbe is, always, in one form or another, writing through her, to responsibility. More than any other figure, she points him, relentlessly, without sympathy (without mercy, dare we say?), in the direction of responsibility.

Mudimbe's responsibility to responsibility finds its articulation in every essay in *Violence in/and the Great Lakes* because every author seeks to think her or his responsibility to the figure of the Un–known Woman, or to some figuring of responsibility in Mudimbe's work. This is the first responsibility of many of the contributions in this collection; this is the signal accomplishment of this volume: responsibility to the thinker who calls for responsibility. *Violence in/and the Great Lakes* is a commitment to thinking responsibility in terms that derive from, but do not necessarily seek to find consonance or commensurability with, Mudimbe's because the principal – and principled – call for responsibility issues not from Mudimbe, but from the figure of the Unknown Woman, made Un–Known in our apprehension of her. This is the figure in whose name Mudimbe thinks, the figure that makes, above all, every writing in this collection ir–responsible. Appropriate, of course, that the Un–known Woman should function in this way because all responsibility must begin with the Other. In keeping with his fidelity to responsibility, Mudimbe's '*Debitores Sumus . . .*' stands as the first argument in this volume to show us how the Un–known Woman's silhouette, now more clearly defined, making her haunting all the more acute, is the only place from which thinking our responsibility can begin.

The ending of Mudimbe's presentation is, of course, by no means an attempt at closure (he is not attempting to pronounce on the matter with any finality). It is, instead, a calling forth of all the Un–known Women (and men and children who have endured violence, from the Great Lakes and far beyond) who haunt us so that we might think, with very few moments of pause or in the hope of cessation, how we are – and always must be, will be – responsible to them. It is our debt to them that, in binding us to them, makes us not only responsible to them, but also the kind of 'Christian subjects' Patočka (and Søren Kierkegaard, too, we must add) could have envisaged. 'Christian subjects' who understand that the political demands the making visible – making manifest in the world – of the 'Good' of the 'interior force'. To be in debt, then, and to act in and according to those terms, is to bring the force of the interior to bear on the world. It is, above all, to know how the event of Un–known Woman dis–articulates the political by refusing, in the moment of record (bearing witness, acknowledging the Self's implication, acting as the Self in the direction of the Other, helplessness, *Schuldigkeit*), to uncouple the interior from the exterior. To be a fully articulated Christian subject means nothing less than recognising what is at stake in declaring responsibility to the Other: the figure of the Samaritan who understands, in the most telling ethical moment (the moment that promises absolutely no political reward; the moment that promises the possibility of the 'life after'), ir–responsibility. Ir–responsibility is the Christian subject who acts in the direction of establishing relationship to the Other, an acting that is made all the more imperative when the Other bears no name except the 'generic victim' of St Luke's Gospel – making the figure all the more symptomatic because it is this victim who is used to instruct the priest and the Levite about the 'mysterious and unique humanity of the gift of life'). Or, as we have now come to know, the other name that ir–responsibility inscribes is that of Mudimbe's Un–known Woman.

Notes

1. If *Shaba deux* inscribes the Unknown Woman in an–other form, then, in a strange way, Mudimbe's persistent (we dare not say 'eternal', though we are close to it) figure invokes, of all characters, the 'Unknown Soldier' of 'I Knew the Unknown Soldier!', the comic written by Robert Kanigher and drawn by Joe Kubert. The comic 'Unknown Soldier', a disfigured, seemingly indefatigable protagonist, has the capacity to be able to assume the identity of any man; a feat that can be achieved with nothing, but latex masks and make-up. Mudimbe's Woman/Women possess, in their relentless return(s), a similar indefatigability.
2. The phonetics of *Schuldigkeit* are, in the context of South Africa, interesting. In Afrikaans, 'guilt' translates as '*skuldig*' – '*skuldigheit*' – so that Mudimbe's 'guilt' resonates uncannily in South Africa.
3. Of course, the counterpoint – or, the illumination, the 'other side' of the Unknown Woman's shadow (the shadow, strictly speaking, has no other side) – is the Unknown Soldier, that figure of violence, slain by violence, who must stand in for all the dead. For both these figures, there is the impossible burden of representation to bear.
4. This definition of ir–responsibility acknowledges Michel Foucault's important admonition about the self-sacrificial act because it insists that a certain mode of Selfness – ipseity – is critical to ir–responsibility. In this regard, it is of course Foucault's notion of care of the self that is being invoked.
5. See Olúfémi Táíwò's *Africa Must Be Modern: The Modern Imperative in Contemporary Africa*, a sobering critique that speaks precisely to this point.

References

Augustine, St. 2006. *Confessions*. Translated by F.J. Sheed. Indianapolis: Hackett Publishing Company.

Burrus, Virginia, Mark D. Jordan and Karmen Mackendrick. 2010. *Seducing Augustine: Bodies, Desires, Confessions*. New York: Fordham University Press.

Conrad, Joseph. 1979. *Heart of Darkness*. London: Penguin.

Derrida, Jacques. 1995. *The Gift of Death*. Translated by David Wills. Chicago: University of Chicago Press.

Kanigher, Robert and Joe Kubert. 1966. 'I Knew the Unknown Soldier!' *Our Army at War* 168 (June).

Mudimbe, V-Y. 1989. *Shaba deux: Les carnets de Mère Marie-Gertrude*. Paris: Présence Africaine.

Táíwò, Olúfémi. 2014. *Africa Must Be Modern: A Manifesto*. Bloomington: Indiana University Press.

CHAPTER 1

For a Common Ascension in Humanity
The Intellectual's Mission in the Great Lakes Region

Kasereka Kavwahirehi

> Whatever the case, no boundary is worth a human life.
> — V-Y Mudimbe, *Cheminements*

I

In *Living in the End Times* (2010), Slavoj Žižek relates that the main headline of *Time* magazine, 5 June 2006, was 'The Deadliest War in the World'. *Time* gave details about how approximately four million people died in Congo amidst the political violence that had been raging for the last ten years (1996–2006). However, as surprising as it might be, this front-page headline did not trigger any wave of humanitarian protests, as one might have expected. Only a few readers wrote to the editor. How do we explain this situation? Was it indifference or blindness? For Žižek, it is simple to explain: '*Time* had picked the wrong victim in the struggle for hegemony in suffering – it should have stuck to the list of usual suspects: Muslim women and their plight, oppression in Tibet, and so forth.' He continues:

> Congo today has effectively re-emerged as a Conradean zone: no one dares to confront it head on. The death of a West Bank Palestinian child, not to mention an Israeli or an American, is mediatically worth thousands of times more than the death of a nameless Congolese. But why this ignorance (2010: 162)?

From an ethical point of view, we cannot fail to stress the troubling semantic and moral value of the expression 'bad victim', which suggests the existence of a 'good victim'. To this we need to add the value of death by the media markets, as referred to by Susan D. Moeller in her meticulous analysis in *Compassion Fatigue: How the Media Sell Disease, Famine, War, and Death* (1999). The trouble worsens when one understands that the opposition between 'good' and 'bad' victims can echo the opposition between a 'valuable life' and a 'non-valuable life', a distinction that seems to have been produced by neoliberal securitarian policy.[1] Moreover, knowing that the situation described by Žižek does not only concern America, but also the 'international community' in general, which is strangely indifferent to the human tragedy that hit Congo, we can effectively ask: why such ignorance? However, another question arises: is it really ignorance? Were the readers of *Time* and members of what we call the 'civilised world' simply seeing these millions of deaths as the trivial results of a new explosion of dark passions of primitive tribes with whom they have nothing in common? This is not the place to address these serious questions. Suffice to say that we fear this blindness, or indifference, might be a symptom of a world that, to borrow the words of Jean-Luc Nancy, is 'de-worlded' (*se dé-monde* in French) by shirking what makes it meaningful, namely a common world, which is essentially a place for existence and human solidarity. In this regard, we can remember that a similar event occurred in 1994. Under Bill Clinton's administration, the international community refused to use the word 'genocide' in order to avoid the moral obligation to intervene and save human lives in Rwanda as it did, some years before, in the Balkans.

But, as suggested by Žižek, it would be hazardous or simply a denial or a gross overshadowing of reality to think that the millions of deaths in Congo can be justified by the dark passions of savage tribes, for:

> Beneath the façade of ethnic warfare, we . . . discern the workings of global capitalism . . . Each of the warlords has business links to a foreign company or corporation exploiting the mostly mining wealth in the region. This arrangement suits both parties: the corporations get mining rights without taxes and other complications, while the warlords get rich. The irony is that many of these minerals are used in high-tech products such as laptops and cell phones – in short: forget about the savage behavior of the local population, just remove the foreign high-tech companies from the equation and the whole edifice of ethnic warfare fuelled by old passions fall apart . . . There is a great deal of darkness in the dense Congolese jungle – but its causes lie elsewhere, in the bright executive offices of our banks and high-tech companies (2010: 163–64).

However, Žižek does not stop there. He points to a paradox, which, if exposed, could enable us to ask important questions concerning the conditions of human cohabitation in the Great Lakes region, deeply immersed in turmoil since the Rwandan genocide. We know that neoliberal missionaries in the Great Lakes region have the tendency to reduce these conditions to the simple sharing of Congolese resources with the country's neighbours. However, can a simple sharing of wealth constitute the foundation for a community of life, a sphere of civilisation and humanisation? Before we address this question, let us continue with Žižek. For Žižek, the paradox concerning the Congolese tragedy is that 'in among the predominant exploiters [and criminals] are Rwandan Tutsi, victims of the horrifying genocide over fifteen years ago' (2010: 163).

This paradox raises many fundamental questions. If one agrees with Régis Debray that 'physical death is only a raw material, it is the task of the group to convert it into instrument of policy production. Death is in principle a force that produces order, but there are unused forces as there are lost deaths' (1981: 337), the question becomes: what has been done politically about the grief and the feeling of vulnerability provoked by the absurd loss of thousands of victims in the genocide that affected the entire Great Lakes region? Are Congolese men, women and children who were massacred, raped, wandering around like phantoms from one makeshift camp to another, in order to escape from an absurd death, so faceless (in the Levinasian sense) that their tragedy leaves the whole of humanity unmoved? Don't they have something in common with those whose security and well-being justify invasion, war and the illicit exploitation of Congo's resources?[2] In sum, are Congolese lives merely bare lives exposed to death, as Giorgio Agamben would say?

II

For survivors of genocide, the vulnerability that was experienced or felt in its pure nakedness can found at least two political attitudes. It 'can [firstly] become the basis of claims for non-military political solutions, just as [secondly] the denial of this vulnerability through a fantasy of mastery (an institutionalized fantasy of mastery) can fuel the instrument of war' (Butler 2006: 29). However, if the first possibility is those who succeed in transforming the 'narcissistic preoccupation of melancholy . . . into a consideration of the vulnerability of others' (Butler 2006: 31), with whom they share humanity, we must admit that the second possibility is simply a senseless solution for at least two reasons.

The first reason is related to the limits of all military domination and the hatred that wars and their unjustified atrocities generate and exacerbate. This hatred can grow in a very subtle form in the lives of victims until a devastating explosion that will reveal the illusion of immunisation against others through military omnipotence. The domination or the humiliation of a particular human group, as the reduction of one's life to its barest biological level, is far from being a humanising protection. Worse, as Roberto Esposito puts it, when we reach a certain point, the immunity we need for protecting our lives can end up negating life:

> That is, immunity encages life such that not only is our freedom but also the very meaning of our individual and collective existence lost: that flow of meaning, that encounter with existence outside of itself that I define with the term *communitas*, which refers to the constitutively open character of existence. Heidegger would call it the *ex* of *existentia* (2013: 62).

The second reason is related to the human condition, which is unchangeable by military power. Indeed, our condition as human beings who are always handed over to people we have not chosen, but on whom we depend and with whom we cohabit the earth, makes it impossible to surpass corporeal vulnerability. As Judith Butler puts it: 'We cannot . . . will away this vulnerability. We must attend to it, even abide by it, as we begin to think about what politics might be implied by staying with the thought of corporeal vulnerability itself, a situation in which we can be vanquished or lose others' (2006: 29). Rethinking politics from this vantage point of vulnerability, which is constitutive or co-essential to us, and reorienting relations amongst nations or human groups through the mindfulness and lived experience of this corporeal vulnerability that puts us in a permanent state of interdependence and mutual exposure, is an imperative task in Central Africa in particular and sub-Saharan Africa in general. It is a necessity if we want to put an end to the cycles of violence and revenge that bring us back to a state of nature and if we want to revive the hope for our continent or the world as a common space where everyone can live and unlock their potential for the well-being of humanity.

The truth is that 'to forclose that vulnerability, to banish it, to make ourselves secure at the expense of every other human consideration is to eradicate one of the most important resources from which we must take our bearings and find our way' (Butler 2006: 30) to make of the earth a world full of meaning. This path is not yet the sharing of what is quantifiable and calculable as neoliberals, thoroughly opposed to the ideas of no-gain, immeasurability or transcendence, believe.[3] In fact, before any new political economy, most fundamental is to acknowledge that sharing is our condition and that war or violence that divides human beings, in whatever form or location, is simply a denial of existence, the intensive phase of the negation of what gives us meaning and makes us human beings: building bonds, exchanging, proximity, togetherness. It renders impossible the 'community of existence, a community without limit of what has been thrown into existence' (Nancy and Bailly 2007: 23). A community that is not built around property, undivided inheritance, an atavistic myth or a will to power, that would at the same time join and dis-join such a community is 'the submission to an injunction (order)', to 'a law above the Law', an 'imperative' that creates 'obligations' and 'makes us obliged beings' (Nancy 1983: 139 ff.), *always already* exposed to the responsibility to 'make [of the planet] a world'. In other words, it is a 'community which exceeds every aspect of politics [and whose] togetherness [the fact of being together] precedes all forms of associations or gatherings' (Jandin 2012: 77). Only then are we able to think a new political economy and begin to offer a vision of the future other than one that perpetuates violence in the name of denying it.

In fact, what has collapsed due to politics, which has for so long forgotten its condition of possibility and lost sight of its purpose, is the meaning of the *with* (or *to come into being with*) 'in which we have our existence' and that is the structure of being.[4] As suggested by Nancy, this sense of our existence as coexistence (*cum-eksistere*) is perfectly expressed by the French verb *comparaître* (from the Latin *cum*, with and *pareo, parere*, to appear, show up), which 'puts us in front of each other . . . delivers us over to each other . . . risking us against each other'. In short, what we have lost sight of is the *cum*, which brings us to the experience of existing necessarily together with and constitutes and defines our being-in-common (*notre être-en-commun*), not to be confused with 'a common being [*un être commun*]' conceived as a *donné*, as a 'common property [*propriété commune*]' (Nancy 1999: 201), in whose name communities engage in the work of death and commit massacres (2000: 8).[5] It is truly this *cum*, this ontological *being-with or existing commonly with*, that exposes us and makes us sensitive to a body dying of hunger, a tortured body, a bruised will, a war mass grave, a migrant's wandering, an insidious deprivation of being and so on and makes us take hold of them as a denial of existence. 'This denial, wherever it happens, reaches all existence, for it touches the "In" of "In common" [*l'en, de l'en-commun*]. And this is the way it makes us appear and answer of him, that is of us' (Nancy and Bailly 2007: 103). It attests to our humanity, our sense of being human, of being members of the human community, a community of shared humanity and vulnerability.

III

It is at this fundamental level of the community of existence, exceeding all politics and free from all ideological reification, all nationalism, patriotism and ethnicism, as well as from all forms of boundaries instituted socially or religiously, that we need to think of the future of the Great Lakes region by reconsidering politics as a problem of meaning and, within these politics, the place of ethnic groups. Instead of assuming the right to mobilise the members of a community around an exclusive, unique memory, to which an ideological institution has given a common meaning, justifying all that it does, a national policy (which, for a long time, has had the tendency to impose itself as an order of meaning) should be considered now as a humble service of a (plural) community that exceeds it. From this excess also emerges the requirement for us to dare to change the way we think, no longer making reference to a nation-state or an ethnic group, but to the measure without measure – *la mesure sans mesure* (Glissant 1996: 90–91) of the world: that is, to dare to think of what can sustain a world and bring people together without sacrificing plurality, giving ourselves over to uncovering hidden bonds amongst people, ethnic groups and continents, whose forces mutually oblige us. On the whole, as Nancy suggests, 'if "politics" has, once more, to say something, and say something new' today, it cannot limit itself to regulating

> the exercise of power – of political economy – by the continuously threatened and modified end of a 'law' whose necessity cannot hide the fact that it cannot yet reach the 'essence' of the 'common [*du commun*]'. For this 'essence' – which is not an essence and falls in the ontology of the in-common (*en-commun*) as an *existence* – pertains to a pre-existing law, to the law of what is right without law (Nancy and Bailly 2007: 98).

However, this law without law is what makes possible the Law as an institution of life in a society, irreducible to its coercive dimension, because it takes us to the meaning of human vulnerability and, hence, to the responsibility we collectively have towards all human lives. This responsibility cannot but condemn war as 'an effort to minimize precariousness for some and to maximize it for others' (Butler 2010: 54). This is what could define, at best, our globalised world with its so-called 'preventive' wars against an enemy often wrongly located or identified, the omnipresence of security plans in governments' programmes and all sorts of immunisation devices against attacks from outside. This is paradoxical, in the sense that through their implementation and the consequent efforts at protection against outside, it is the human being who ends up protected from not only him/herself, but also from all that determines him/her as a being whose existence is always a coexistence (*cum-ek/sistere*) and whose habitation of the world is always a cohabitation (*cum-habitation*).

Rethinking community or the conditions of a life policy in Central Africa is of paramount importance after the recognised or unrecognised genocides, massacres and massive and repetitive human rights violations that make the destruction of life rampant in this region. In order to carry out this fundamental task, which ultimately consists of reimagining or refounding, politically and socially, the African Great Lakes region to make it an area of humanisation and civilisation (that is, a world of meaning), our imperative starting point is vulnerability, which goes beyond national and ethnic boundaries. In other words, the requirement here is to look for a way to represent the grief and vulnerability as a 'point of departure for a new understanding' and, as indicated earlier in this chapter, to move the 'narcissistic preoccupation of melancholy . . . into a consideration of the vulnerability of others' (Butler 2006: 31). It consists of acting such that a meditation on our exacerbated vulnerability takes us to the 'apprehension of our common human vulnerability', arouses in us a commitment to 'protect others from the kind of violence we have suffered' and, finally, allows us 'begin to think about what politics might be implied by staying with the thought of corporeal vulnerability itself, a situation in which we can be vanquished or lose others' (29). In this way, solidarity between victims and non-victims can be strengthened and can catalyse an effort 'to produce a public culture and different public policies', whose priority is to recreate viable social and economic environments for the survival of all. As Butler points out, the strength of such solidarity based on vulnerability comes from crossing through identity categories or belief-defined contexts:

> Precarity cuts across identity categories as well as multicultural maps, thus forming the basis for an alliance focused on opposition to state violence and its capacity to produce, exploit, and distribute precarity for the purposes of profit and territorial defense. Such an alliance would not require agreeing on all questions of desire, or beliefs or self-identification. It would be a

movement sheltering certain kinds of ongoing antagonisms among its participants, valuing such persistent and animating differences as the sign and substance of a radical democratic politics (Butler 2010: 32).

This requirement is inseparable from our capacity to carry the mourning of those who have been lost. Indeed, without this, we lose the acute meaning of life, which we need to oppose violence. Moreover, as Butler writes: 'As long as we haven't learnt that other lives are equally grievable and require to be mourned – in particular, lives we contributed in eliminating – [it is not certain] that we are really on the way to overcoming the problem of dehumanization' in order to start building a space of humanisation and civilisation (2005: 86). This is where the intellectual, whose voice has not been heard enough in the Great Lakes region during this tragic period, must play a crucial role in the reconfiguration of imaginations and identities or, better, of thinking, first, our being-together-in-the-world and, second, policy that gives to that thought of being-together-in-the-world a chance to develop (Nancy 2008: 62).

IV

Edward Said has written that the intellectual is very often asked by members of his/her community to represent them, speak on their behalf and testify on their sufferings. The intellectual can hardly escape from this solicitation. However, as pointed out by the Palestinian-American thinker:

To this terribly important task of representing the collective sufferings of your own people, testifying of its travails, reasserting its enduring presence, reinforcing its memory, there must be added something else, which only an intellectual, I believe, has the obligation to fulfill. After all, many novelists, painters, and poets, like Manzoni, Picasso, or Neruda, have embodied the historical experience of their people in aesthetic works, which in turn become recognized as great masterpieces. For the intellectual the task, I believe, is explicitly to universalize the crisis, to give greater human scope to what a particular race or nation suffered, to associate that experience with the sufferings of others (1996: 44).

Fundamental for us in Central Africa, Said adds:

It is inadequate only to affirm that a people was dispossessed, oppressed or slaughtered, denied its rights and its political existence, without at the same time doing what Fanon did during the Algerian war, affiliating those horrors with the similar afflictions of other people. This does not at all mean a loss in historical specificity, but rather it guards against the possibility that a lesson learned about oppression in one place will be forgotten or violated in another place or time. And just because you represent the sufferings that your people lived through, which you yourself might have lived through also, you are not relieved of the duty of revealing that your own people now may be committing related crimes on *their* victims . . . It is always easy and popular for intellectuals to fall into modes of vindication and self-righteousness that blind them to the evil done in the name of their own ethnic or national community (1996: 44–45).

This task is certainly difficult to assume in a world where people dispute who has the monopoly on suffering. What is happening in the Great Lakes region, where intellectuals, when they do not choose silence, rally behind the cowardly positions of their community leaders, is proof enough. Certainly, the terrible accusation of betraying the cause of his nation or her people falls upon any intellectual who refuses to fulfil the role of ideologist that is expected of him/her. However, the risk of being treated as such is what characterises intellectuals. For authentic intellectuals, there is no solidarity without criticism, no sense of belonging that is not, at the same time, an openness to other communities, such that all marks of belonging carry the possibility of a *dis-sensus* when truth and ethics require it: being a member of a national or ethnic community does not mean allowing yourself to be possessed and limited by it. This mode of belonging is tantamount to the betrayal of the intellectual and the death of the community whose dynamism depends on the openness to the exteriority that defines it. There is reason to think that it is through accomplishing this difficult task that the intellectual reveals the full scope of the cry, 'Never again'. This cry, both an obligation to memories and a hope for another future, can reach the fullness of its meaning only by being universalised, in other words, by worrying about others and showing concern and compassion towards others. As Butler says, 'remembrance does not restrict itself to my suffering or the suffering of my people alone' (2011: 89–91). This is also the meaning of Theodor Adorno's reformulation of the Kantian categorical imperative:

'Thinking and acting so that Auschwitz doesn't repeat itself, that nothing similar to that occurs' (1978: 283). In fact, for the intellectual, universality

> means taking the risk in order to go beyond the easy certainties provided
> us by our background, language, nationality, which so often shield us from
> the reality of others. It also means looking for and trying to uphold a single
> standard for human behavior when it comes to such matters as foreign and
> social policy. Thus if we condemn an unprovoked act of aggression by an
> enemy we should also be able to do the same when our government invades
> a weaker party (Said 1996: xiv).

The memory of my loved ones I unjustly lost, of the ones lost without any reason by the community to which I belong, cannot justify amnesia or indifference when it comes to the sufferings of others, who appear from then on as stricken by insignificance or an absolute strangeness, denying any closeness or excluding them from the community of a shared humanity or vulnerability. The unbearable is such only when it is acknowledged and lived as such, as well as when it touches my own people or when it touches others whoever they may be and wherever they are, simply because beyond the fact that they form another group, maybe rival or even opposed to mine, they *are* human beings and, like me, *are* subject to pain and vulnerability. We therefore understand why Butler could write the following, which is essential, because it touches on the thorny, disgusting relationship between Israel and Palestine. We will agree that this relationship is a thorn in a pretentious world that calls itself civilised, claiming commitment to human rights and democracy whose characteristic is to 'prom[ote] and prom[ise] freedom of all human beings in the equality of all human beings' (Nancy 2009: 78):

> If we are to allow the memory of dispossession to crack the surface of
> historical amnesia and reorient us toward the unacceptable conditions
> of refugees across time and context, there must be transposition
> without analogy, the interruption of one time by another, which is the
> counternationalist impetus of the messianic in Benjamin's terms, what some
> would call a messianic secularism . . . It may be that the very possibility
> of ethical relation depends upon a certain condition of dispossession
> from national modes of belonging, a dispossession that characterizes our
> relationality from the start, and so the possibility of an ethical relation. We

are outside ourselves before ourselves, and only in such a mode is there a chance of being for another (Butler 2011: 88).

Furthermore, she adds, which harmonises her thought with Nancy's:

> We are, to be sure, already in the hands of the other before we make any decision about with whom we choose to live. This way of being bound to one another is precisely *not* a social bond that is entered into through volition and deliberation; it precedes contract, is mired in dependency . . . Thus, it is even from the start, to the stranger that we are bound, the one, or the ones, we never knew and never chose. *If we accept this sort of ontological condition, then to destroy the other is to destroy my life, that sense of my life that is invariably social life* (Butler 2011: 88, emphasis added).

By somehow displacing the concept of *ex-posure* as used by Nancy, we can say that before any contract, before any foundation of Law and before any foundation of politics, the human being is exposed to responsibility and to the sense that consists in coexistence, in *l'avec*. In other words, what is expressed by *ex-*, as in existence (*ek-sistence*), does not indicate an accident that, as Pierre-Philippe Jandin suggests, would affect a being already there, suddenly thrown into ecstasy. The existent is not simply 'thrown into the world [*jeté-dans-le-monde*]', as suggested in the formula that has now become a classic; it is at the same time and by so doing, 'trusted to others'. It is from the mutual exposure to each other that arises the community as a space for our existence, or for our *co-ek-sistence*. In other words, *ex-* is as fundamental as *with* [*l'avec, le cum*]; it is openness and spacing. 'It is *within* the world, in other words, between us, that we have the sense of existence'; 'between us' meaning 'we with each other and distinct from each other' (Jandin 2012: 44). It is in the service of such a community that politics and economy should be oriented.

In this sense, the intellectual should not aim at consolidating the position of his/her community, especially if it has the tendency to banish or exclude the stranger or what does not allow it to keep its claimed substance or essence. The intellectual needs to constantly seek to break the consensus based on atavistic mythologies and excluding any call for openness to others, to another type of community that acknowledges that the human sphere goes beyond its borders. The first principle of this intellectual is, as the epigraph from V-Y Mudimbe puts it at the beginning of this chapter: 'no boundary is worth a human life'. Better yet, the intellectual should help his/her fellows to recognise that human existence has its meaning in the *bond with* others, in '*le renvoi ou le rebond de proche en proche*, through which a world becomes a world, something other than a heap or a worthless point' (Nancy 2000: 9). In other words, the intellectual's task is, by opening the inside onto the outside like a bridge or hinge, to prevent his/her community from folding back on itself against the Other and protecting it against all forms of closure that contain within them the threat of totalitarianism.

This means that, for the intellectual, the sense of belonging to a community must be inhabited by a critical distance, a vigilant openness to the outside and to the event to come, which will break the frontiers of what has already occurred as well as the institutionalised, in order to engage the community in the adventure of becoming, of what in it is still to come. The community can be humanly viable only as far as it is always *en puissance d'être*, ready to welcome the Other in all his/her otherness and singularity. It is irreducible to any form of institutional status quo. In other words, in so far as its vitality is related to the uprooting of petrified certainties of past figures (founding myths, ancestral words, genealogy) that protect against the advent of the stranger, of she/he who comes from another territory (but, for sure, not from another world or planet), the community must constantly be prepared to receive a new name, which comes from somewhere else and which means a new situation in common, or a new common in situation (*un nouveau commun en situation*). Believing that we have nothing in common with the stranger is to close ourselves against the constitutive otherness of what we are or, as Nancy says, 'to close up to *the being with* – or to *the in-between* [*à l'entre*] – in which we have our *existence*, that is, at the same time, our place and environment, and in which and by which we *exist* in the strong sense, that is that we are *exposed*' (2000: 8).

In this regard, beyond macroeconomic equilibrium or a growth index without palpable social or human impact, what is fundamentally needed in the Great Lakes region is a new sense of community, a new conscience of the *common*, 'which is actually the global regime of the circulation of meanings' (Nancy 2009: 91). It is a matter of moving from a community lived as a property, a fullness, a territory to defend, to extend and to protect against contagion of those who do not belong, into one understood as 'an emptiness, a debt, a gift (all meanings of *munus*) towards others', which also reminds us of 'our constitutive otherness with ourselves' (Esposito 2000: cover page). It is very important that the community recognises that alterity or otherness is fundamental and beneficial. It is indeed the force that decentres the subject of ownership, forcing it to come out of itself and open itself to those who are not part of the community, though they are, as others, equally constitutive. This way of understanding and living a community can be rich in meaning in a world where communities are dominated by the will to immunise themselves against the danger represented by the stranger.

Here lies the fundamental stake of our democracy or, rather, of our democracies: the reimagining of a new way of living together or the rediscovery of what maintains a world by holding men and women together in respect of their singularity and dignity. Otherwise, it means reinventing or repurposing fundamental acts and symbols that found a community of civilisation. It is equally a matter of refounding politics as a capacity to live, think, act and undertake together for the well-being of the community. It is not pointless to recall that democracy, in its modern inauguration, aims to be an integral refoundation of politics. However, as Nancy puts it: 'He who wants to found must descend deeper than the foundation itself. [Thus] democracy gives birth to a new figure of human being . . . It once more opens the human being's destination to that of the world' (2008: 59–60). This means that the choice for democracy is a choice for an entire civilisation to invent, a choice for common thought and action, and finally a choice that engages us in the construction of a democratic existence that is meaningless without the existence of equal subjects. In this sense, democracy in Africa cannot be identified with the 'unlimited power of wealth' (Rancière 2005: 85) nor with good governance, though this is necessary. It must be conceived first as *new regime of being-with or meaning*.

Here is a sketch of the intellectual's responsibility in the Great Lakes region, which may be summarised in this sentence from Adorno's *Minima Moralia*: For the intellectual, 'it is part of morality not to be at home in one's home' (1974: 39). This is an ethical position that reminds us of 'exilic' intellectuals such as Michel de Certeau, Hannah Arendt and Said, whose first task was to put their ties, their ideological affiliations and their national belonging behind them in order to let the criteria of truth prevail on every occasion. 'Inside outsider,' as Paul Ricœur (2000: 254) writes, speaking of De Certeau, the intellectual must be the one who highlights the existence of bonds between people and communities, bonds of mutual obligation. Refusing the comfort of those who have the politics of memory in their hands, of those who decide what or who is memorable and what or who is not, this intellectual will ask questions that destabilise and restore the memory of occult or forgotten realities in the rush for action and collective judgements – for example, the memory of thousands of Hutu women and children who were chased, pursued and massacred in Congo by Alliance des Forces Démocratiques pour la Libération du Congo-Zaïre (ADFL) soldiers during their march into Kinshasa. Rejecting closure, the intellectual will develop a thought of thresholds, of bridges, of sharing or of relation, as Édouard Glissant would say. In addition, as the latter insists, the intellectual will not forget that his/her task is to contribute to the changing of the imagination and of the mentalities at the base of present tragedies. For, as Glissant writes in a passage deserving of meditation, as long as we allow ourselves to be locked up in ethnic or national identities, as long as we 'live with the idea of unique rooted identity [*une identité racine unique*], there will be Rwandas, there will be Burundis, and, every time, we will be facing the same impossible'. Glissant adds:

> I was speaking with my Tutsi friends from Rwanda and I was perfectly convinced that they were victims of a Hutu plot; but I am also persuaded that if there were five hundred Tutsis and ten Hutus, the ten Hutus would be dead . . . In other words, there is no solution. There is no solution within an identity context of system thought . . . We should never hesitate in defending the oppressed and the offended, but the issue is to change the notion, the deep of the experience that we have of our identity and to conceive only the imaginary of All-world [*Tout-monde*] (that is the fact that I can live in my place while still in relation with *la Totalité-monde*) . . . [that] can help us overcome these types of fundamental limits which no one wants to overcome. The *Tout-monde* is an immoderation [*une mesure sans mesure*] and if we do not take appropriate measure in this immoderation, we risk . . . dragging, and dragging, and dragging old impossibilities that still determine intolerance, massacres and genocides (1996: 90–91).

As Esposito suggests, re-enacting a Nietzschean metaphor, it is through the displacement of our eyes from the land of our ancestors or of our fathers towards our children's land, towards the country coming (*le pays qui vient*), that resides 'the only way of recognizing that community, which land still tries to conceal in the closing of its borders: to return to that great sea that surrounds the earth – and crosses it – as its fatal truth' (2000: 140).

In order to avoid misunderstanding, I must make a last observation here. For some, my sketch of the intellectual may reflect an elitist vision. If I insist on the ability of intellectuals to escape social and political determinations, when necessary or, better, when required by the search for truth, it is to emphasise freedom as a condition of critical thinking, without which intellectuals cannot 'hold in respect nations and traditions' (Said 1996: 25). This does not imply that intellectuals should not be involved in social movements or should be a class apart. In our countries, where many intellectuals have become mere servants of the powers that oppress the people, it is important to rethink the concept of the intellectual paying attention to how the task of the intellectual is assumed today in our societies. One might then realise that film-makers, photographers or painters, popular musicians, artists and writers assume important aspects of intellectual activity. They challenge the hegemonic discourse and dominant ideology and express better than anyone the suffering and hopes of the oppressed. In sum, they constitute what Grant Farred, rethinking the Gramscian concept of organic intellectual, calls the 'vernacular intellectual' (2003). Political violence and social crisis in Congo since 1996 has seen the emergence of young artists who can rightly be considered vernacular or local intellectuals. For them, far from being mere entertainment or a means to escape from daily political and social violence, rap, reggae and sometimes religious songs are spaces where social and political consciousness of the masses is articulated and expressed, spaces where the experience of suffering is articulated in the language of the vulnerable and precarious masses. By so doing, they affirm their ability to act and open spaces of political struggle. Moreover, as Farred suggests, it should be noted that the conventional intellectual can vernacularise him/herself. In this sense, 'vernacularity marks that sociopolitical occasion when the conventional intellectual speaks less as a product of hegemonic cultural-economic system than as a thinker capable of translating the disenfranchised experience of subjugation as an oppositional, ideologically recognizable, vernacularized discourse'. In other words:

Vernacularity signals the discursive turning away from accepted, dominant intellectual modality and vocabulary and the adoption of a new positioning and idiomatic language . . . The vernacular is defined by its immersion in the language of the popular, the particularities, idiosyncrasies, and distinctness of vernacular resistance and popular culture to power (Farred 2003: 11–12).

V

Finally, intellectuals cannot escape the vital task of deconstructing the political, legal, religious and ideological, colonial and postcolonial set-ups or devices that are structurally at the base of recurrent violence in the Great Lakes region, nor the founding myths that fuel the imagination of the conqueror and a desire for domination of one over the others.[6] This deconstruction must show that groups living in the region are not natural entities decided or created by God, but constructed entities, manufactured and, in some cases, invented, with a background made up of a history of fighting, conquest and domination. And if they were once constructed, they can be reconstructed, so as to face new challenges.

We need to deconstruct and reconfigure memories and antagonists' narratives, which perpetuate hatred from one generation to another, by aiming at their convergence. This, on the one hand, makes it necessary 'to learn to narrate otherwise', while paying 'a particular attention [with kindness] to founding events which are not mine and to life accounts which are those of the other party' and, on the other hand, to be 'willing to understand these others whose history has made enemies' (Ricœur 2000: 618). In this sense, it is important to update, in order to deconstruct and reconstruct these 'founding events' in a different manner, events whose ambivalence nurses hatred: if they are reasons of glory for some; for others, they are, on the contrary, sources of great humiliation and 'symbolic wounds requesting healing' (86).

Even conflict resolution and peace-building models applied to Africa should not escape critical analysis. In fact, as Patricia O. Daley (2008) suggests, a liberal peace plan that entrusts victims of violence to humanitarian agencies and leaves political negotiations to representatives of political parties may not favour the emergence of a new political culture and a new African subject. The fate of the liberal peace-construction model will not be different from aid programmes, which, if 'they have done something to relieve the conscience of privileged ones . . . [have] done very little to reduce distress' or to initiate a true development dynamic owned by local people (Galbraith 2007: 946). The peace and reconstruction that African people need must be capable of 're-humanizing physically, materially, and spiritually the African body', which has been submitted to violence and objectification since slavery and colonisation (Daley 2008: 232). As Daley suggests, the Eurocentric and liberal concepts of peace and development cannot give rise to the social transformation needed for the elevation of African humanity. This is for two inseparable reasons: on the one hand, the African context requires a human-centred approach and not a market-centred approach and, on the other hand, the 'culture of impunity in the African Great Lakes region is imbricated in global economic development structures and the role of the African in them'. Therefore, addressing the culture of impunity requires the creation of new relations, which, first and foremost, recognise the intrinsic value of African lives – that is, the human in the African and 'the responsibilities or the *ubuntu* that connects every human being' (238). Globalisation, in the specific meaning of the becoming world of a *de-worlded world*, is the price to pay. But, as Žižek suggests, for this to happen, we have 'to truly awaken from the capitalist "dogmatic dream" (as Kant would have put it)' (2010: 164) and its sacrificial religion.

Notes

All translations, unless otherwise indicated, are the author's.

1. See Judith Butler, *Frames of War: When Is Life Grievable?* (New York: Verso, 2010) and *Precarious Life: The Powers of Mourning and Violence* (New York: Verso, 2006).

2. On this topic, see United Nations, *Report of the Security Council Committee Established Pursuant to Resolution 1533 (2004) Concerning the Democratic Republic of the Congo* (10 February 2005), available at http://www.un.org/ga/search/view_doc.asp?symbol=S/2005/81; United Nations High Commissioner for Refugees (UNHCR), *Democratic Republic of the Congo, 1993–2003*, report of the mapping exercise documenting the most serious violations of human rights and international humanitarian law committed within the territory of the Democratic Republic of the Congo between March 1993 and June 2003 (August 2010), available at http://www.ohchr.org/Documents/Countries/ZR/DRC_MAPPING_REPORT_FINAL_EN.pdf; and the final reports of the United Nations Security Council Experts of the Illegal Exploitation of Resources and Other Forms of Wealth of Democratic Republic of the Congo (2001, 2002, 2003, 2008), available at http://www.un.org/News/dh/latest/drcongo.htm; http://www.pcr.uu.se/digitalAssets/96/96819_congo_20021031.pdf; http://reliefweb.int/report/democratic-republic-congo/final-report-panel-experts-illegal-exploitation-natural-resources and http://www.friendsofthecongo.org/pdf/un_report_dec_08.pdf.

3. This does not mean that this proposition makes no sense, but that it cannot be presented as the foundation of human cohabitation. Before being a material, economical problem, it is a problem of relation between one and the Other, a problem of meanings or of recognising the Other as a human being.

4. At the beginning of *Qu'est-ce que la politique?* Hannah Arendt writes: '*La politique repose sur un fait: la pluralité humaine*'. And later, she adds: '*La politique prend naissance dans l'espace-qui-est-entre-les hommes, donc dans quelque chose de fondamentalement extérieur-à-l'homme . . . La politique prend naissance dans l'espace intermédiaire et elle se constitue comme relation*' (Politics is based on a fact of human plurality . . . Politics arises in the space that is between human beings, thus in something fundamentally external to the human being . . . Politics starts in the intermediary space and constitutes itself as relation) (1995: 39, 42).

5. In the same way, in order to mark the importance of the '*cum*' at the heart of Roberto Esposito's *Communitas* (2000), Nancy writes: '*Le* cum *est ce qui lien (si c'est un lien) ou ce qui joint (si c'est un joint, un joug, un attelage) le* munus *du* communis *dont Esposito a si bien repéré et développé la logique ou la charge sémantique . . . le partage d'une charge, d'un devoir ou d'une tâche, et non la communauté d'une substance. L'être-en-commun est défini et constitué par une charge, et en dernière analyse il n'est en charge de rien d'autre que du* cum *lui-même. Nous sommes en charge de notre avec, c'est-à-dire de nous*' (The *cum* is what links (if it is a link) or what joins (if it is a join, a yoke, an attachment) the *munus* of *communis* for which Esposito so well identified and developed the logical or semantic load . . . the sharing of an office, an obligation or a task, and not the community of substance. The being-in-common is defined and constituted by a responsibility, and ultimately it is in charge of nothing but of the *cum* itself. We are in charge of our with, that is to say of us) (Nancy 2000: 8).

6. See V-Y Mudimbe, *The Invention of Africa: Gnosis, Philosophy, and the Order of Knowledge* (Bloomington: Indiana University Press, 1988) and *Parables and Fables: Exegesis, Textuality, and the Politics in Central Africa* (Madison: University of Wisconsin Press, 1991); Mahmood Mamdani, *Define and Rule: Native As Political Identity* (Cambridge: Harvard University Press, 2012) and *When Victims Become Killers: Colonialism, Nativism, and the Genocide in Rwanda* (Princeton: Princeton University Press, 2002); Patricia O. Daley, *Gender and Genocide in Burundi: The Search for Spaces of Peace in the Great Lakes Region* (Bloomington: Indiana University Press, 2008); Josias Semujanga, *Les récits fondateurs du drame rwandais: Discours social, idéologies et stéréotypes* (Paris: L'Harmattan, 2000).

References

Adorno, Theodor W. 1974. *Minima Moralia: Reflections from Damaged Life*. Translated by E.F.N. Jephcott. London: NLB.

———. 1978. *Dialectique négative*. Translated by Le groupe de traduction du Collège de Philosophie. Paris: Payot.

Arendt, Hannah. 1995. *Qu'est-ce que la politique?* Edited by Ursula Ludz. Paris: Seuil.

Butler, Judith. 2005. *Humain, inhumain: Le travail critique des norms; Entretiens*. Paris: Editions Amsterdam.

———. 2006. *Precarious Life: The Powers of Mourning and Violence*. New York: Verso.

———. 2010. *Frames of War: When Is Life Grievable?* New York: Verso.

———. 2011. 'Is Judaism Zionism?' In *The Power of Religion in the Public Sphere*, edited by Eduardo Mendieta and Jonathan Vanantwerpen, 70–91. New York: Columbia University Press.

Daley, Patricia O. 2008. *Gender and Genocide in Burundi: The Search for Spaces of Peace in the Great Lakes Region*. Bloomington: Indiana University Press.

Debray, Régis. 1981. *Critique de la raison politique*. Paris: Gallimard.

Esposito, Roberto. 2000. *Communitas: Origine et destin de la communauté*. Paris: PUF.

———. 2013. *Terms of the Political: Community, Immunity, Biopolitics*. Translated by Rhiannon Noel Welch. New York: Fordham University Press.

Farred, Grant. 2003. *What's My Name: Black Vernacular Intellectuals*. Minneapolis: University of Minnesota Press.

Galbraith, John K. 2007. '*Voyage dans le temps économique*'. In *Economie hétérodoxe*, 773–1030. Paris: Seuil.

Glissant, Édouard. 1996. *Introduction à une poétique du divers*. Paris: Gallimard.

Jandin, Pierre-Philippe. 2012. *Jean-Luc Nancy: Retracer le politique*. Paris: Michalon.

Mamdani, Mahmood. 2002. *When Victims Become Killers: Colonialism, Nativism, and the Genocide in Rwanda*. Princeton: Princeton University Press.

———. 2012. *Define and Rule: Native As Political Identity*. Cambridge: Harvard University Press.

Moeller, Susan D. 1999. *Compassion Fatigue: How the Media Sell Disease, Famine, War, and Death*. London: Routledge.

Mudimbe, V.Y. 1988. *The Invention of Africa. Gnosis, Philosophy, and the Order of Knowledge*. Bloomington: Indiana University Press.

———. 1991. *Parables and Fables: Exegesis, Textuality, and the Politics in Central Africa*. Madison: University of Wisconsin Press.

———. 2006. *Cheminements: Carnets de Berlin (avril–juin 1999)*. Québec: Humanitas.

Nancy, Jean-Luc. 1983. *L'impératif catégorique*. Paris: Flammarion.

———. 1999. *La communauté désœuvrée*. Paris: Christian Bourgois.

———. 2000. '*Conloquium*'. In *Communitas: Origine et destin de la communauté* by Roberto Esposito, 3–10. Paris: PUF.

———. 2008. *Vérité de la démocratie*. Paris: Galilée.

———. 2009. '*Démocratie finie et infinie*'. In *Démocratie, dans quel état?* by Giorgio Agamben, Alain Badiou, Daniel Bensaïd, Wendy Brown, Jean-Luc Nancy, Jacques Rancière, Kristin Ross and Slavoj Žižek, 77–94. Paris: La Fabrique.

Nancy, Jean-Luc et Jean-Christophe Bailly. 2007 [1991]. *La comparution*. Paris: Christian Bourgois.

Rancière, Jacques. 2005. *La haine de la démocratie*. Paris: La Fabrique.

Ricœur, Paul. 2000. *La mémoire, l'histoire, l'oubli*. Paris: Seuil.

Said, Edward. 1996. *Representations of the Intellectual: The 1993 Reith Lectures*. New York: Vintage.

Semujanga, Josias. 2000. *Les récits fondateurs du drame rwandais: Discours social, idéologies et stéréotypes*. Paris: L'Harmattan.

Žižek, Slavoj. 2010. *Living in the End Times*. London: Verso.

CHAPTER 2

Life, 'Life' and Death

Grant Farred

In the beginning was the Word, and the Word was with God, and the Word was God.

— John 1:1

. . . history is ultimately not a political but an 'administrative 'and 'governmental' problem, is nothing but a logical consequence of economic theology.

— Giorgio Agamben, *The Kingdom and the Glory*

I would tend to hypothesize that it is with the arrival of Christianity that things change: God begins to speak.

— V-Y Mudimbe, *Parables and Fables*

The tralatitious

It is possible to argue that Christianity is nothing other than the promise of fulfilment to come. Christianity promises that the Logos of the Gospel will come into itself; that John's Word, the Word that precedes John, of course, is nothing other than the foundational Word. The promise of Christianity is that the Word will be: will be made flesh (with the Eucharist promising the transubstantiation – *transsubstantiatio* in Latin; μετουσίωσις or *metousiosis* in Greek – of that flesh into the body and blood of Jesus-the-Christ). Christianity promises the coming of the Kingdom upon which the Word of the Gospel is founded. Christianity, as John the Evangelist knew better than almost anyone, is premised on the now–Coming of the Word, the Word that is always both immanent and transcendent. It is, after all, John who was not only one of the three disciples – together with James, his older brother, and Peter – who were with their master at Gethsemane and who stayed close to Mary during the entire ordeal of the Crucifixion, but it is also John who was the first to believe that Christ had risen from the dead.[1] The Word, then, can be said to mean at once both more to John and to mean something to John before anyone else. In this way, the Word is John's, even as it is given, without question and before all else, to everyone by God – from whom it derives, who gave it in the beginning.

The Word, the Logos that it inscribes, that the apostle John preaches at the very beginning of his Gospel, bears the same philosophical weight that V-Y Mudimbe assigns it in its (Central) African context. There can be no doubt that for both John and Mudimbe the Word is the event. Framed as it is by John's Gospel, how could it not be? 'In the beginning was the Word, and the Word was with God, and the Word was God.' However, coloniality lends Mudimbe's proposition – 'it is with the arrival of Christianity that everything changes: God begins to speak' – a historical specificity and 'freightedness' that John's catholic pronouncement lacks; in truth, Mudimbe's proposition supersedes John's pronouncement because it is the literal speaking of the Word: 'God begins to speak'. What could be more freighted than that? Nevertheless, Mudimbe's assertion stands as a deliberately philosophical understanding of the event. The event, as we well know, changes everything, both in its happening and, following Alain Badiou, its supplementarity; that is, when the event 'comes into its own' (after – when) we understand it as an event. Mudimbe understands this transformative force of the event – with the 'arrival of Christianity', things change – and how it changes things, beginning with the very ground of being.

For Mudimbe and John, the event is also the 'invention' – the first speaking – of language. In Mudimbe's case, it is the event of language in colonial Africa: 'God begins to speak.' No less than with John's beginning, this act of language – God speaking, which superannuates, liquidates, everything that went before – institutes history through disruption, through disrupting the silence that had heretofore prevailed; God's speaking, in Mudimbe's terms, is a momentous intervention into the history of humanity, amounting to what Jacques Derrida names the 'becoming-historical of humankind' (1995: 6). The silence that prevailed before the speaking was not silence, but a human history incapable of hearing God speak. Do humans only learn to hear and listen after God speaks for the first time? The silence before God's speaking, which was not really a silence, but a coming into history, a silence for which we have no proper name, was a constitutive lack because it could not attune itself to God's speaking. In Mudimbe's rendering, the event is the moment that God 'achieves', that moment He claims, a voice, His own singular voice, for Himself. God's is a speaking that must be attended to because it is God's intention to make himself heard: God speaks the Word, as the Word of God, no less. God brings everything into language with His speaking.

Everything derives from the Word because without the Word there is no possibility for thinking God; that is, God Himself derives from the Word. God is Logos and John's Gospel is, of course, inconceivable without the Word. Mudimbe's argument for such an understanding of God's speaking traces its origin to a tralatitious position. Its (having a) character, force or significance is transferred or 'derived from something extraneous' – one of the two meanings of 'tralatitious' (according to the second, biblical critics refer to a *tralatitious* interpretation as one received by expositor from expositor – in our case, from John's exposition to Mudimbe's). The extraneous force is borne of the challenge – issued by African theologians in their transition from the theory of 'adaptation' (Christianity must accommodate itself to African realities) to a more indigenised understanding of Christianity in Africa, or what Mudimbe names *'praeparatio evangelica . . .* an awaiting of the Gospels' – to recognise that 'African traditions and cultures contain facts and beliefs, signs and symbols' that enable the Gospels to assume a 'new form', an African one (Mudimbe 1991: 37). When the Gospels arrive in Africa, they emerge in a distinctly African form; in addressing the condition of the African Church, Mudimbe reveals the fundamental transformations that colonialism has wrought. For Mudimbe, thinking African theology must always begin from the premise that it is a tralatitious exercise. It is a praxis never distinct from thinking philosophy, for thinking philosophically *à la* the Heidegger of *Was heißt Denken?*

Shifting to the second meaning of tralatitious, in *Parables and Fables* (1991), Mudimbe asks: what happens in the theological act of thinking the Church from expositor to expositor; thinking the *African* Church from, say, Placide Tempels to Alexis Kagame to Vincent Mulago? What biblical discourse does thinking tralatitously open up, open on to? First and foremost, much of Mudimbe's work turns on the history and effect – as well as the affect – of Christian thought in colonial Africa, what he names the 'discourse of belief' in *Tales of Faith*: 'looking for illumination and in this very process bearing witness to it and thus to a revelation, an uncovering and its foundation' (Mudimbe 1997: 4). The value of thinking conjunctively the relation between Christianity and colonialism, faith and politics, Church and State, resides for Mudimbe not simply in the act of thinking two concepts, conditions or notions together. Here Gilles Deleuze's definition of the 'conjunction AND' is instructive and, as such, useful for explicating Mudimbe's project. Deleuze's (putative) conjunction is not 'a union, nor a juxtaposition, but the birth of a stammering, the outline of a broken line which always sets off at right angles, a sort of active and creative line of flight. AND . . . AND . . . AND' (1987: 7). In this instance, the repeated 'AND' serves not to join (to bring together), but to qualify, introducing nothing less than the conditional. The work of Deleuze's 'AND' is to undermine, to make us think again about the function of the conjunction – to pause and enquire after the work of putting together. So much so, that Deleuze's 'AND' is virtually indistinguishable from a series of 'BUTs': it is philosophical self-apprehension, reservation and hesitation. There is no conceptual or rhetorical coming together, no resolution, in the act of conjoining; rather, what emerges is a philosophical force that makes visible, that clarifies – edifies – the disruptive, disjunctive thought that composes the 'broken lines'. (Deleuze evokes here the Romantic inclining of William Wordsworth's 'Lines Composed a Few Miles above Tintern Abbey'. At the end of a poem remarkably free of conjunction – 'That after many wanderings, many years / Of absence, these steep woods and lofty cliffs, / And this green pastoral landscape, were to me / More dear, both for themselves and for thy sake!' – what emerges most powerfully in the poet's thinking is a brilliantly obvious insight: what is 'dear' to the self is equally so to the Other; thinking the self's relation to the Other begins, in this poem, with Dorothy Wordsworth, the poet's sister, who is frequently referenced in the poem.)

The Deleuzian conjunction derives its interrogative capacity, its thought, from its refusal to deal in forced or conventional couplings or extant 'juxtapositions'. In its place, there is the commitment, however tentative (there is always the constitutive element of uncertainty in a commitment; an unspeakable trepidation in giving oneself over to something, be that another human being or an idea), to following a 'broken line' flight, to be open to sudden or sharp ('right angle') turns, to divergences and hesitations. In Mudimbe's case, the Deleuzian conjunction translates as the activation – activating – of Christian thinking that will not rest with the archive as it exists; or, for that matter, the archive's ability to catalogue, to accommodate, a figure such as Tempels. (Mudimbe has a deeper regard than most scholars for the plethora of knowledge that can be gained in the archive; he is a careful and generous reader of the archive who finds much of value there, much to stimulate his thinking.) Instead, Mudimbe's work is marked by the capacity to apprehend and approach the coming 'AND' (Christianity and colonialism, in this instance) with caution, diligence and assiduousness. Such an approach requires following the 'line of flight' that leads, to phrase this propositionally, from Christianity to colonialism, all the while also understanding Christianity as

(a) colonial force. The colonial force of Christianity 'conjoins' an encounter of Church and Other, a conjoining that produces an encounter (laden with historic tensions) amongst Church, State and Other.

Saliently, the Deleuzian conjunction 'isolates' (rather than polarises) the critic into singular thought: to follow the lines of thought that lead to, however vertiginously, theology or philosophy in Africa. The conjunction works against the domination of 'union' or of 'bringing together' and is, because of that refusal, ever alert – in that space, that aporia, that interval, that *archē*, even – to the 'order of relations', what and how things mean in relation to each other and, as such, the pivotal concept – that interval or nodal point, produced under theoretical pressure – where thought must be confronted. In Giorgio Agamben's *The Kingdom and the Glory*, this concept is '*oikonomia*', which means 'administration of the house' (2011: 17), where 'the *oikos*, is not the modern single-family house or simply the extended family, but a complex organism composed of heterogeneous relations, entwined with each other'. For Agamben, the primary relations that are 'entwined with each other' are those between the Kingdom and the Government and, specifically, the place of God in the Trinitarian relations.

The Kingdom and the Glory is Agamben's reversal of Carl Schmitt's notion, in *Political Theology* (2005), that the model of political power derives from the theological. For Agamben, and here *oikonomia* is central, the theological struggle between the argument for the unity of the Trinity and its impossibility (there can only be one sovereign; if it is God the Father, then Jesus-the-Christ cannot be his equal) 'culminates' – if that is the correct term – in the division of powers. 'There is something lacking in spiritual power,' Agamben insists, 'in spite of its perfection, and that something is the effectiveness of the execution' (2011: 102). God does not know how to govern and neither, without the model of the political, does the Church. In order to obtain the technique necessary to govern, the Church must look outside itself. God does not know how to govern. God, too, must look outside Himself in order to understand what it means to govern. Consequently, the Church must turn its gaze towards that social institution that is best at practising *oikonomia*, Government. Contra Schmitt, it is not the theological (God, the Church) that grounds – founds, Agamben might go so far as to say – the political, but the political (Government) that serves as the model for the theological. *Oikonomia* instructs the theological in the political art of 'administration'. According to the terms of *oikonomia*, God and the Church learn to govern tralatitiously; it is a political skill that does not begin with the Church; governance is not ontological to God or the Church. The question about the beginning of governance is first addressed by Aristotle in *Politics* and has occupied theological thinkers such as the Gnostics, the Stoics, Augustine and Gregory, among several others. In our moment, it is perhaps recognised less as Aristotle's dialectic between immanence and transcendence than, from Martin Heidegger (its finest twentieth-century exponent) through Michel Foucault and Agamben, as the issue of biopolitics.

The ontotheology of bare life

> *Den Eigensinnigen ist Leben nur Leben* [For those who are stubborn, life is merely life].
>
> — Martin Heidegger, in Jacques Derrida,
> *The Beast and the Sovereign*

> Jesus Christ, our Lord, through whom we have received grace and apostleship to bring about the obedience of faith among all the Gentiles for the sake of his name.
>
> — Romans 1:4–5

> . . . what is primarily at stake in the division between the two powers is guaranteeing the possibility of the government of men.
>
> — Giorgio Agamben, *The Kingdom and the Glory*

Between them, the two epigraphs from Paul and Agamben above delineate the problem that Mudimbe identifies in the administration of the Church in (Central) Africa. It is, furthermore, not a problem of Mudimbe's making, or even Africa's making, for that matter. At the very moment that the notions of *zoē* (bare life) and *bios* (political or contemplative life) are brought into public, we are returned to the theological – revealing as much the political force of the theological as the theological kernel of the political.[2] Bare life, especially (and it is, of course, impossible to hold absolute, if at all, the distinction between *zoē* and *bios*), articulates nothing so much as the utter vulnerability of the human. In a singular way, Christianity, in and through the figure of the Samaritan, destroys – or at the very least, seriously dilutes – the Us versus Them dialectic. Nowhere is grace, God's love (because only God is capable of grace, so that we must approach grace as love beyond love because it is love itself, love that we as humans are incapable of), more scripturally evident than in that encounter between the man who has been robbed and the Samaritan who comes to his rescue. The event of the Samaritan is made memorable because the Samaritan offers help, going so far as to pay for the victim's lodging and care after he has deposited him safely in a nearby town – after the priest and Levite have left the helpless victim to his own fate. To show love ('Love thy neighbour as thyself' is the lesson of this parable from the Gospel of Luke) as the Samaritan does, to care for the Other, is a politically radical first step in that it begins to destroy the distinction between Us and Them, between Self and Other. (To care, solely out of love, for the Other, as the Samaritan does, is to know what Emmanuel Levinas means when he talks about, affirmatively, the sheer political power of the face-to-face encounter with the stranger.)[3] By following the example of the Samaritan's mercy (love), Jesus's injunction to his adherents is bracing in its simplicity and uncompromising in its demand: 'Go, and do likewise.' In order to know love as God does, in order to know God's love, in order to love as God does, all this begins with understanding the parable of the Samaritan. The Samaritan's act sets a political precedent. It stands, from the very beginning, against the foundation of Schmitt's argument on sovereignty, which is grounded in the distinction between friend and enemy. The Samaritan parable rejects this distinction in its privileging of the Other, its establishing the base condition for loving the Other in the time (the aftermath) of violence, its determination to attend to the needs of the Other; in Levinas's terms, this act reaches its apogee in the act of welcoming the stranger (who might, of course, be Jesus-the-Christ since neither the time of his coming nor the guise in which he will come is known).[4] In the terms of Luke's Gospel, it means giving up your own donkey so that the injured one might be able to travel in (relative) comfort; tending to the victim (Other) and assuming responsibility for his well-being (by paying the innkeeper for the Other's care and promising to make further restitution). In any state, for any government, this is the Law's first obligation: to adjudicate between friend and enemy – to order, if and where possible, those relations.

This is the colonial Church's problem. If the colonial government's administrative role is clear (it must rule), then the colonial Church's is less so. Can the Church, assigned the task Paul so zealously took up, namely to evangelise (conceived in – and made possible by – grace), produce a 'faith' capable of grace? To whom will this Church be faithful? How, in Agamben's terms, will it conduct its domestic affairs? What strategies will it employ to keep its house in order? Christianity, Mudimbe argues, 'has thus been culturally marked by its integration into various European cultures, and those Christian customs and feasts which are genealogically linked to immemorial pagan traditions bear silent witness to this fact' (1991: 57). What this suggests is precisely the struggle of the colonial Church, a struggle derived from *oikonomia*, in so far as the theological derives its mode of governance from the political. The question, however, retains its pertinence and directness. In thinking the Church in Africa, the question 'Whence does its power come from?' is one of the most important for critics such as Mudimbe.

In some ways, of course, the question about to whom the Church owes its powers is a simple and straightforward one: to the colonial regime, with whom the Church has been enmeshed from the beginning. It was/is, after all, the (post) colonial government that safeguarded and continues to safeguard the Church in the (post)colonies and this affects – or subjects, it would also be possible to say – the Church's ability to execute its mission, especially – and Mudimbe is a keen student of this – its evangelising mission: 'to bring about the obedience of faith among all the Gentiles for the sake of his name'. The Word, in Paul's teachings and through his rather fearsome (fearless, some would say) and unrelenting example, asks of the faithful to spread the 'obedience of faith' and to spread it among, not only 'all the Gentiles', but also, in this instance, the Africans, 'for the sake of his name'. What does it mean to execute the power of faith when the colonial government retains for itself (as a mark of its sovereignty) the power over both *zoē* and *bios*?

Proselytisation presents itself, then, from the beginning as *the* politico-theological problem, maybe even as *the* onto-theological problem. In whose name does the Church convert since the colonial Church is caught in what Agamben names the 'conflict between two swords'? Whose aims does the colonial Church advance? Whom does the Church serve? These are questions of unparalleled significance. What is the *oikonomia* of the colonial Church? That is, according to which administrative terms does the Church govern itself? More saliently, is the question of 'administration' even pertinent if we remember the direct structural simplicity of Jesus-the-Christ's teachings (the famed, all-encompassing eleventh commandment, 'Love one another as I have loved you'; 'Go, and do likewise' – Luke 10:25–37) and his anger at the maladministration of the Church (his throwing the moneylenders out of the temple – 'Stop making my Father's house a marketplace' – John 2:13–22)?

In this regard, one cannot ignore Derrida's disagreement – a significant and irrevocable one – with Agamben's distinction between *zoē* and *bios* in *The Beast and the Sovereign* (2009) and the implications this has for the latter's claims regarding biopower. Taking issue, firstly, with Agamben's distinction between *bios* and *zoē* (for Derrida it is not a 'reliable and effective instrument, sufficiently sharp' for distinguishing one from the other), Derrida, supported by Aristotle, offers a critical qualification: 'sometimes *zoē* designates a life that is qualified, not bare' (2009: 326). Derrida's refutation of the 'airtight frontier [between *zoē* and *bios*] along which Agamben constructs his whole discourse' has implications, at least one of them foundational, for thinking the colonial Church.

The limit of the Church's theological, spiritual and philosophical horizon cannot ever be *zoē*. Bare life is, in all ways that matter theologically and as a basic tenet of faith, an untenable position for the Church. Under no circumstances can the Church be committed to mere 'instrumentality'; there can be no such thing as the 'bare life' of the Church – nor any countenancing of the 'bare life' of the Church's members, more specifically. The life of the Christian Church, based as it is on the promise of everlasting life, can never be reduced to the minimalist materialism of *zoē*. The promise of life everlasting makes *zoē* entirely incommensurate with the mission of Christianity. Bare life is not only an impossible, but also a theologically impermissible position for the Church. (Here, Agamben's argument is troubling because he fails to draw into question the theological grounds of what he names the 'conflict between two swords,' between the Kingdom and the Government. Agamben thinks their political incompatibility; that is, the tension that marks the relation between Church and State, but without ever attending to the status or meaning of spiritual work, the very lifeblood of Christianity. The life of the Church is Jesus's Life, we might say, which can never be conceived as bare life, bared to extreme violence as his life may have been in relation to the political of his day.) The Church's proper mission, as the invocations from John and Paul make clear, is life beyond life, the Life that gives life to the Word. This dedication is redolent in Christianity, though perhaps nowhere more so than in the 'Profession of Faith' (the *Nicene Creed*): '. . . and the life of the world to come. Amen.' All life, which is to say all thinking (Logos), begins with the Word and the Word, as Paul all too enthusiastically insists, writes within itself, promises in and by itself, Life – what Agamben configures as the 'Kingdom'. It is this evangelical charge that always – as Mudimbe reminds us at almost every turn – informs, haunts and (whether the charge is heeded or not, whether it is rationalised away or not) shapes, not only the colonial Church, but also the Church itself. Christian life, then, cannot countenance *zoē* in any articulation. (Except, of course, as the exception – Jesus-the-Christ's bare life – that proves the foundational status of the exception.)

The Church must always stand opposed to bare life, especially as rendered by Heidegger's figure of the 'stubborn' (which we might also understand as the unthinking), which is nothing if not a cipher for governmentality of the Agambenian – and maybe Foucauldian – variety. 'For the stubborn,' Heidegger says, 'life is merely life' (*Den Eigensinnigen ist Leben nur Leben*) (in Derrida 2009: 305). If life were merely life, there would be neither a struggle between the Kingdom and the Government (the Government would long since have emerged victorious and declared itself so) nor the prospect of a Pauline 'apostleship'. Moreover, if life were the limit of Life, that would be tantamount to, firstly, denying God and, secondly, as a consequence, denying God the possibility, the opportunity, to exercise, to offer, 'grace'. Out of this condition would arise the impossibility of love. And that life would be bare life itself. What kind of life is that? What kind of Government would underwrite – that is, write against, legislate against, offer its word against – a life that is 'bared' or (one could also say, more poetically) 'pared' of love? What kind of violence might emanate from such a Government; what kind of violence would such a Government provoke? What kind of Government would that be but violence itself?[5]

And yet there is something, the Derridean demurrals notwithstanding, to be said for following the line of flight – for a brief moment and, of necessity, strategically – offered by the concept of *oikonomia*. Through insisting upon the 'division' between the Kingdom and the (colonial) Government, *oikonomia* reveals itself as the moment in which thinking the doubleness of power – the sacred and the profane, if you will – becomes at once inescapable and immanent. The strange and difficult (or troublesome) – for theological purposes – interplay between the two *archēs*, *auctoritas* (power that lacks executive power, for example the sovereign/king who reigns, but does not govern, or God in his im–potence, the im–potence of the omnipotent) and *potestas* (the power that can be exercised, the power that constitutes, at its an–archic core, the government) makes opaque the absolute reach of biopower. In Foucault's terms, the biopolitical is writ in the power of the state to discipline its citizens or, for Schmitt, it is the core of sovereignty – in the power to decide the exception, which turns on the power over bare life. The very foundation of Christianity, of course, rests upon one such bare life: *zoē*, if that is not too profane a term for it, at its most elemental and exceptional. Derrida, in his reading of Jan Patočka's *Heretical Essays in the Philosophy of History*, casts this life as the '*mysterium tremendum*: the terrifying mystery, the dread, the fear and trembling of the Christian in the experience of the sacrificial gift' (1995: 6). This is a life that, as Luke's Gospel attests, demands that the Christian, following the lead of the Samaritan, understand that the 'sacrificial gift' of Christ's death imposes a particular responsibility on the Christian in relation to the Other. The 'gift of death [*de la mort donnée*]' assigns Christians a historic role, a responsibility that cannot be forsworn: to act like Christ; to bear the name of Jesus-the-Christ is to know the 'dread, the fear and trembling' – but also the unparalleled promise of the 'life of the world to come' – that is the Christian inheritance; the gift of death demands living a Christian life, living like Jesus-the-Christ.

If the parable of the Samaritan introduces itself as the inaugural figure of the Other and poses in itself questions about what founds the Other, what founds the Self – questions that provide, as we have said, the philosophical basis of Levinas's work (and inform Jean-Luc Nancy's, as Kasareka Kavwahirehi argues in Chapter 1) – then here Agamben's figure of the sacred man, '*homo sacer*' (1998), returns as a figure at once more disconcerting and promising. In fact, nothing, no figure, could be more promising because here the Gospels offer the prospect – something, the very possibility of Life beyond life, to look forward to (still, it retains its force as an overwhelming mystery: '*mysterium tremendum*') of Eternal Life; that is, the founding negation of *zoē*, the liquidation, through a violence wrought by (the Father's) love, of death – the gift of death is grounded in a terrifying, fear-inspiring promise. (It is all the more terrifying because it raises the prospect, as Patočka (1996: 105) argues, of an 'individual mortality' that is 'different from the immortality of the mysteries'.) Here is the Life that follows death, that puts to rest all life 'that is merely life'; the Life that shows that life is not 'all of life': 'the life of the world to come. Amen.'

In *Homo Sacer*, a work ordered by the spectre of the camp, Agamben – fully engaged throughout as he is with Schmitt in this dissertation on the 'sacred man' – locates the effect of the exception in the fact of exclusion. Specifically, he thinks its effects in relation to the 'limit figure': 'What emerges in this limit is the radical crisis of every possibility of clearly distinguishing between membership and inclusion, between what is outside and what is inside, between exception and rule' (1998: 25). The figure of the 'sacred man' who is at once conceptually sacred (protected by the Law, made vulnerable by the force of sovereign exception) and sacrificable (the sacred man has no protection in the face of the sovereign's decision, the sovereign's power over life and death; a different, and yet similar, kind of overwhelming mystery) provokes a thinking of many difficult questions, not least of which is human vulnerability. (A vulnerability, of course, that begins with the '*mysterium tremendum*': how do we think such a mystery? How are we to live overwhelmed by it? How could we not live in fear of it? How can we not tremble before its sheer conceptual force? What kind of thinking, what kind of mind, conceives of such a mystery?)

And this is where the effect of Christian eschatology comes fully into its own. In Christian eschatology, love and vulnerability, the sacred and the profane, God and human, theology, ontology and the political, are all eminently on display. They all demand a thinking, a conjunctive thinking, no less. The Christian 'limit figure', who is also the figure of infinite possibility and love, is, of course, Jesus-the-Christ. Here we have the figure promised by the Gospels, the most sacred of men, because He is the Son of God who is made to endure the most harrowing and public death. He is condemned to die, irrevocably and without argument; His fate is tied to all of ours and, as such, is inescapable; He is subjected (and He must submit, a radical subordinating of the Self to the wishes of the Father) to a fate he can only articulate in painfully hopeless dialectical language, recited here only through vernacular Roman Catholic memory: 'Lord, let not my will but Thy will be done.' In the face of the Father's command, the Son's plea, heartfelt, honest, is utterly impotent and without the possibility of reprieve: it is outside the realm of possibility that the Father will allow 'this cup to pass him by' (Matthew 26:39: 'My Father, if it is possible, let this cup pass from me; yet not what I want, but what you want'). Here we have submission, to the end that is not the end, but the beginning of the yet-to-come, the beginning that fulfils a promise. This most sacred and therefore sacrifice–able of men, this Son of God, is made vulnerable by the Father's love and His love of the Son and of all those on earth who have come before and will come after, is subjected – the Law, Pontius Pilate, which knows him to be innocent, will not intervene on his behalf; clemency is denied him when he is utterly deserving (this brings before us again, violence, justice and love, the life-affirming mystery of the sacrifice, an event unthinkable without a thinking of death) – to a death that is visible to all, the most common of deaths, hung on a cross. In the hour of his execution, he is explicitly denied any symbols of sanctity. Surrounded as he is on the cross by common thieves, he is anything but sacred, eminently sacrifice–able. He must be given up, given to us, as a gift: death as the highest order of the gift.[6] In the light of the Crucifixion, what Slavoj Žižek names the 'radical kernel of Christianity' (for, without the Crucifixion there can be no Resurrection and without the Resurrection, no prospect of Eternal Life), how are we to think '*homo sacer*'? What is sacred about life that clings 'stubbornly' to life in the face of the most brutal assault on life? Is it possible to think (for) Life under these conditions of life? Or, conversely, are there any conditions – where life is immanently threatened – when the thinking of Life could be more urgent? In light of the conceptual difficulties that Mudimbe's work presents us with, it is clear: thinking this Life, thinking life/Life under these philosophical imperatives, is the work that Mudimbe's *oeuvre* compels us to undertake.

'The presence . . . of the Idea'

> The church does not possess Jesus Christ nor eternal salvation. Essentially, the term salvation is synonymous with the Kingdom. That is to say, it expresses the presence of God the Savior who acts through Christ in the cosmos and throughout history, particularly within the secret of each human's desire for God.
>
> — Alphonse Mushete Ngindu, in V-Y Mudimbe,
> *Parables and Fables*

Parousia, in the Greek sense, is the presence of any thing of the idea after which it was formed, the presence of any thing that inspired the idea. It denotes a being present. *Parousia* also means, theologically, the second coming or a coming of the original Word so that the secular (philosophical) and the theological meanings are always, simultaneously, informing and complicating each other. Mudimbe assigns the Word's coming an originary status or meaning (Derrida, as we have seen, follows a similar line of thought): it makes possible a speaking that invites, even necessitates, disputation. The Word is never passive; it is never simply received because even in its being given, exactly *because* it is given, it must be struggled over. The coming into presence of the Word is the ontological birth of politics. Mudimbe is concerned with the facticity of things, with the fact that things change and the effects of that change – every 'arrival' signals itself as a potential event, none more so than the coming of the Word, all the more so because 'God anthropologizes himself' and, importantly, 'by his incarnation God proclaims himself as the culmination of the sacrifice' (Mudimbe 1991: 25). Articulated as such, we might wonder – especially since we are familiar with the history of the sacrifice and are never permitted to lose sight of the eventfulness of the sacrifice – about the arrival of the Word. Does the Word arrive, in the process breaking the silence, breaking into the silence, to instruct us about this 'culmination'? After all, as Mudimbe declares, 'God always precedes his messengers', so that the Word is both the beginning and the after–thought – the Word is the Logos that comes, in Mudimbe's reasoning, after God – the Logos follows God, can begin only when God has spoken (21).

Pointedly phrased, is the Word only revealed – only spoken – in order that the 'sacrifice' might be fully comprehended? Does the Word find itself, come fully into itself, *as* the 'sacrifice'? Is this John's promise? Is it, for this reason, in the Word that *zoē* and *bios* encounter their philosophical limit? Is it possible to 'administer' life – which implies that we can grasp both *oikonomia* and the economy of the sacrifice? Or is an entirely different order of thinking – thinking for the Word that begins with absolute regard for the Word – required in order to apprehend Life as the 'culmination of the sacrifice'? In that case, is the Word of John's Gospel the *parousia* of the Word? John's Word must be taken as a prophetic truth. It is that rare thing: at once the promise of the Word and the Word itself because it inscribes – no, it gives us immediate access to – the presence of the idea after which it was formed. There is no choice then but to 'anthropologize' John: 'In the beginning was the Word, and the Word was with God, and the Word was God.' There is no choice but to take John at his word because it is the Word. In Mudimbe's poetic phrasing, in Africa God 'becomes talkative once Christian missionaries arrive. This is a decisive event. Before the arrival of Christianity in Africa there is really no such thing as prophetism, religious renewal decided by God, or the divine direct message for the transformation of societal structures' (1991: 24). We know the event, it is possible to argue, not only by its historic effects – 'Before the arrival of Christianity in Africa there is really no such thing as . . .' – but also by its philosophical force. In its having happened, we have the event of the Word as an unprecedented event. After the Word, to not think the event is 'unthinkable'.

It now becomes possible to understand God's speaking as, following Mudimbe, a 'major conversion', 'unthinkable out of Christianity' (1991 25). With God's speaking comes a circumscription: the Word and its effects pertain (only) to Christianity.[7] In turn, this very circumscription 'converts' 'delimitation' into thinking. To be 'unthinkable out of Christianity' reinforces the notion of beginning – lending Christianity a certain autochthony that borders on ontology, which inscribes Christianity as a unique philosophical force – that makes the thinking of Christianity's 'unthinkability' a political necessity. What is pronounced 'unthinkable' must, before all else, be thought. It must be thought in precisely the same way that Christ's coming, his Crucifixion and Resurrection and the event of His sacrifice (which means that all conversations about life and Life originate in death, in *that* death) were once understood as beyond thought. Nothing is unthinkable. The first effect of the event is to make everything thinkable.

Mudimbe's invocation of Ngindu is, in this regard, a salient one. It reveals the ways in which Mudimbe takes up the question of life, both in Agamben's and Heidegger's senses. This is Mudimbe's rendering of *parousia*. The question of life (and Life), and not always in that order, is the prevailing presence in his thinking. Mudimbe's *parousia* – in part anthropological, in a telling measure theological and, always, insistently political, in that it charges us to understand, to never lose sight of the power of the Word – begins in and through the presence of the idea of life. Mudimbe's *parousia* is alert to the signal ways in which the theological archive left by colonialism has been put to use. Mudimbe traces for us, in *The Invention of Africa, Parables and Fables* and *Tales of Faith* (the title leaves us in little doubt), the effects, conscious and unwitting, of not only that body of knowledge that composes – and potentially de–composes; 'difference' is the name Mudimbe gives it in *Parables* – but also the ways in which (colonial–theological) the archive writes the Word. And Mudimbe always understands conjuncturally the relationship between the colonial archive and the Word.

Or, as Mudimbe puts it, perhaps understating matters through his reading of Ngindu, the 'question of salvation complements that of interpretation of the world' (1991: 23). (There is something hermeneutically mischievous about this phrasing, as though Mudimbe were gently mocking Karl Marx, a figure of standing in *Parables*. Marx, as we well know, insisted that the first order of philosophical business was to understand the world in order that we might change it. Mudimbe privileges interpretation.) In truth, however, Mudimbe is deadly serious about the work of interpretation, about the power of the Word, about the effects of the Word since God 'first' spoke or spoke His presence for a second time.

Parousia and Valentin Mudimbe

Violence in/and the Great Lakes derives from a gathering in the name of 'Valentin Mudimbe' – as much as that name, that body of thought, bespeaks the struggle Valentin Mudimbe presented against organising in his name, to honour his name. The conference 'Violence in/and the Great Lakes' was organised for one purpose above all others: Mudimbe asked that he and his interlocutors think in the name of violence in/and the Great Lakes, the very place from which his work derives, the very site of his theological struggle, the very place that provokes the philosophical difficulty his work takes up, because it turns directly on the question of life.

Mudimbe's injunction is *parousia* itself, in all its subtlety (there are moments when it could be described as a kind of 'dissembling', but the unrelenting respect for the idea, always discernible in Mudimbe's thinking, militates against that), its Heideggerian meanderings, its determination to pursue every thinking. Present in Mudimbe's demand is the idea itself – not named as Agamben or Derrida do, but immanently present nonetheless – of how to think life in its full political possibility and precarity. Present is the presence of life, of how it must be thought, of how Life – in John's sense – is assigned a critical urgency when life itself seems 'unthinkable'. Mudimbe's injunction is a demand to announce thinking present in such a way that the silence of thought before God's speaking is broken, that the disruption wrought by thinking irrupts. Mudimbe's thinking irrupts a little like he presents God's nineteenth-century speaking in colonial Africa, to colonial Africa: God speaks directly to colonial Africa so that thinking might find its voice, again.

Within the Church, the nineteenth-century struggle in colonial Africa was one that would be waged between indigeneity and 'adaptation'. It was, of course, a historic moment in Christianity's making itself present in Africa. However, the kind of presence that forms Mudimbe's thinking (his making present of that nineteenth-century speaking) is such that, for our purposes, will not be satisfied with a 'mere' attesting. Testimony, what might be unfairly rendered as the announcing of a presence to the event and a notion already contained within *parousia*, will not suffice.

Parousia, as the injunction issued by Mudimbe, can only be understood as the presence in the idea of our making that demands that the very idea of life – of Life – begin with an argument against the violent sacrifice of life because the Heideggerian stubbornness of life, all that resilience, fortitude and even faith in life, has shown itself incapable of ensuring – let alone sanctifying – life itself. (Not even *the* sacrifice is able to secure life. What standing would the sacrifice have if all life were already secured? The sacrifice can only come into its historic role if life is precarious.) For this reason, the questions persist: what happens when there is no name for those lives that have been taken without a moment of reflection? It might help, of course, to assign such life a name, but it matters more that such a life is brought into thinking. The W/word 'life', as struggled over by Derrida, Agamben, Nancy, Levinas, Judith Butler (especially in her thinking on precarity) and others, is the word with which the project of thinking the violence that afflicts life in the Great Lakes must begin.

'Life' is the word that lends Mudimbe's thinking (and his forthright challenge) its philosophical depth and urgency. As figured in Mudimbe's thinking, *parousia* is the mark of a very particular responsibility: to work not in Mudimbe's name, but to work towards making life and Life possible in the Great Lakes region. The nineteenth-century event of God's speaking the Word made thinking possible. The responsibility of thinking in our moment is to secure life itself, to ensure against the sacrificing of lives. After all, what is the value of *the* sacrifice if the magnitude of *that* death is not properly apprehended? To borrow a phrase from Patočka: all thinking of life must begin with a 'concern for death': *that* death institutes a concern for all death (1996: 105). The only way to understand the place of death in philosophy is as fundamental, to approach it as *'meletē thanatou*, care for death' (109). In order to secure life, it is necessary to first learn how to 'care about death'. In asking for a conversation about life, Mudimbe has led us to a fundamental scriptural, philosophical and political conjuncture – death: the key to understanding how life ('individual immortality') and Life (the immortality upon which the Word is founded) issue from the *mysterium tremendum*.

Notes

1. There is considerable dispute about the identity of John the Evangelist. It is assumed that he is the younger brother of James, son of Zebedee and Salome of Galilee, but there is greater doubt as to whether the apostle St John, author of the Gospels and of Revelations (written in Patmos, where John is presumed to have been in exile) is the same as John the Evangelist or, for that matter, whether it is John of Patmos, a different figure entirely, who wrote Revelations. Then there is, to further complicate the matter, the issue of John the Presbyter and whether or not these are all separate figures or a single one.
2. I am, of course, invoking Slavoj Žižek's rendering of the Crucifixion as the 'radical kernel' of Christianity. See *Fragile Absolute: Or, Why Is the Christian Legacy Worth Fighting For?* (London: Verso, 2000).
3. Levinas is also alert to the violence that can emanate from the face-to-face encounter; the violence that is at the core of intimacy. The violence that took place in Bosnia and Rwanda, where neighbours killed neighbours, makes this point sufficiently.
4. See, in this regard, Jane Juffer's recent work, *Intimacy across Borders: Race, Religion, and Migration in the U.S. Midwest* (Philadelphia: Temple University Press, 2013), which uses Levinas's figure of the stranger to critique contemporary immigration politics in the United States.
5. Is this not what we have been witnessing in Egypt since the takeover of the democratically elected government by a military headed by General Abdul Fattah al-Sisi on 3 July 2013? In Egypt there has unfolded the most bizarre struggle for democracy; democracy of one kind or another. The Muslim Brotherhood proclaim, with good reason, their electoral triumph

in June 2012; the secularists condemn the Brotherhood for using their victory to impose a fundamentalist agenda on the nation. In Egypt, the 'secularists' have declared their love for their country by protesting, both violently and peacefully, the Muslim Brotherhood; on the anniversary of President Morsi's election (30 June 2013), some 14 million Egyptians took to the streets to militate for his ouster. After an intensification of unrest, with protesters ransacking the Brotherhood's national headquarters in Cairo, protesting Egyptians implored their military to replace the Morsi government. These 'secularists' asked the military to act against the 'terror' – or, the 'terrorists' – that is the Muslim Brotherhood; or, the secularists asked the military to act against a Morsi government that proved, in its year in office, to be inept at statecraft. In their turn, the Brotherhood, under siege, under threat of arrest and imprisonment and, worse, of course, repeatedly declare their devotion to Allah, calling for an Islamic state. The Brotherhood's logic is aggressive in its opposition to the secularists and the military and sacrificial in that they deem their commitment to Islam worthy of their very lives.

6. As James Shirley's seventeenth-century poem, 'Death the Leveller', reminds us, death is, because of its universal inevitability, a necropolitical force: 'Sceptre and Crown / Must tumble down, / And in the dust be equal made / With the poor crookèd scythe and spade' (1968: 30). Shirley's poem is often read as a riposte to John Donne's 1610 sonnet, 'Death, Be Not Proud,' the tenth of Donne's posthumously published 'Holy Sonnets'. An Anglican minister, Donne ends his poem with that memorable rhyming couplet: 'One short sleepe past, wee wake eternally, / And death shall be no more; death, thou shalt die' (2004: 207). Shirley's poem ends with death as a finality, but if death is the last justice, it is not without discrimination: 'Only the actions of the just / Smell sweet and blossom in their dust.' In death, the just 'blossom'.

7. Taking up Patočka's work on the particular force of Christian conversion, much of Derrida's thinking in the essay 'Secrets of European Responsibility' in *The Gift of Death* (1995) addresses itself to this question in ways that find echoes in Mudimbe's approach.

References

Agamben, Giorgio. 1998. *Homo Sacer: Sovereign Power and Bare Life*. Translated by Daniel Heller-Roazen. Stanford: Stanford University Press.

———. 2011. *The Kingdom and the Glory: For a Theological Genealogy of Economy and Government*. Translated by Lorenzo Chiesa (with Matteo Mandarini). Stanford: Stanford University Press.

Deleuze, Gilles. 1987. *Dialogues*. Translated by Claire Parnet. New York: Columbia University Press.

Derrida, Jacques. 1995. *The Gift of Death*. Translated by David Wills. Chicago: University of Chicago Press.

———. 2009. *The Beast and the Sovereign*. Translated by Geoffrey Bennington and Peggy Kamuf. Chicago: University of Chicago Press.

Donne, John. 2004. 'Holy Sonnet X: Death, Be Not Proud'. In *The Norton Anthology of Poetry* (shorter fifth edition), edited by Margaret Ferguson, Mary Jo Salter and Jon Stallworthy, 207. New York: W.W. Norton & Co.

Juffer, Jane Ann. 2013. *Intimacy across Borders: Race, Religion, and Migration in the U.S. Midwest*. Philadelphia: Temple University Press.

Mudimbe, V-Y. 1988. *The Invention of Africa: Gnosis, Philosophy, and the Order of Knowledge*. Bloomington: Indiana University Press.

——. 1991. *Parables and Fables: Exegesis, Textuality, and Politics in Central Africa*. Madison: University of Wisconsin Press.

——. 1997. *Tales of Faith: Religion as Political Performance in Central Africa*. London: Athlone Press.

Patočka, Jan. 1996. *Heretical Essays in the Philosophy of History*. Translated by Ezrazim Kohák. Chicago: Open Court.

Schmitt, Carl. 2005. *Political Theology: Four Chapters on the Concept of Sovereignty*. Chicago: University of Chicago Press.

Shirley, James. 1968. 'Death the Leveller'. In *Poems of Protest, Old and New: A Selection of Poetry*, edited by Arnold Kenseth, 30. New York: Macmillan.

Wordsworth, William. 1916. 'Lines Composed a Few Miles above Tintern Abbey'. In *The Spirit of Man*, edited by Robert Bridges. London: Longmans, Green & Co.

Žižek, Slavoj. 2000. *Fragile Absolute: Or, Why Is the Christian Legacy Worth Fighting For?* London: Verso.

CHAPTER 3

Violence of Details and Details of Violence in Novels by V-Y Mudimbe

Justin K. Bisanswa

V-Y Mudimbe's first novel, *Entre les eaux*, opens as follows, abruptly:

> Every time my eyes rest upon the dormitory's packed earth wall and that they land on my crucifix of fortune, hidden amongst the branches, I have the urge to grimace. A new habit? Or is it a new feeling possessing me? The desire is automatic: Regularly followed by the painful rise of something foul presently inhabiting my throat: The horror of physical decay (1973: 3).

The simple, self-conscious language induces a displeasing effect, mixing contradictions and disparities by equating opposite values. How can it not be seen that the process of analogical homologation, which Mudimbe wants to demonstrate, increasingly introduces into this very process a principle that also destroys it? In this context, oxymoron and contrast act as a sort of hologram of an operator presiding over the entirety of the novel: the textual presence of the 'Logos', operator of all types of mediation, establishes a distance in the novel from itself. As a result, the illusion created by mediation is weakened. What remains intact of *Négritude* and of the verbal means it established? The *Négritude* analogy portrays a united world, assembled magically, where the totality of things can be seen as a giant 'Whole', organising and distributing its contents. Mudimbe's analogy, on the contrary, evokes an incoherent world, dispersed and unstable. With a touch of cruel irony, using the very means that upheld the regime of *Négritude*, Mudimbe renders the image of a world that is not only chaotic, but also lacks a backdrop, wherein fictional mediation only reaches the surface of things. This world is one of signs in an advanced state of petrification.

Does Mudimbe's modernity reside only in this predatory circle where language closes in on itself, sealed with the entirety of literature and poetry in a sort of 'perpetual rat trap'? It is tempting to answer affirmatively, considering the mix of genres and disciplines to which Mudimbe's novels owe part of their power and seduction. Their landscape resembles a library after an earthquake, where books from diverse disciplines in human and social sciences, dictionaries and encyclopedias, are strewn in disorder all over the floor. In reading Mudimbe, one discovers a man of books, of brochures and reading rooms, taking note, here and there, of a certain quote, a maxim, of a particular figure, of a sublime or ridiculous remark, of a verse or two of a Bible chapter, in order to sew them into the fabric of whatever work is placed on his table for mental dissection. He is a man of books, evident in the way in which the epic and the didactic, the solemn and the melodramatic, the sacred and the profane, the sublime and the low, the lyrical and the novelesque, enter by a sort of collision in his fiction. These texts are a sort of miniature model of the vast table of genres offered to readers and that symbolise, in the fictional realm, diverse figures of hybridisation.

A laboratory of language, the Mudimbean novel converts into text the modern human's experience of violence. The novel is therefore a new terrain of literary dismemberment: against the exotic literature of *Négritude*, against the militant literature that followed it, against mimetic literature, but for a literature of life, which reflects on the world and constructs and deconstructs itself. Think of his heros' or heroines' overpowering lucidity: they comment on their own frailty, all the while unable to escape it, thus becoming victims by consent. Think of the winding narration, its suspenseful and enigmatic reflections. Deconstruction, therefore, of the pieces or of the individual strings of a genre. In *Entre les eaux* (1973), Pierre Landu, a Roman Catholic priest who joins rebel combatants and leaves the Church, which did not meet his expectations, and enrols in politics, in the same government he was fighting during the rebellion, finally gets married, abandons his pregnant wife and joins a Cistercian monastery. All of this shows how the elasticity of time and space in the tragic hero's successive metamorphoses responds to the time and space of a physical and mental wandering around a few fundamental reference points. The practice of the Gospel remains a target of numerous provocations, but they seem to take form on an opposition, as sarcastic as it is scattered, towards the intrusion of politics. As if the fall of the Church and the fall of the political regime were precipitated by a simple parable. As if the novel, by tracing in its pages the signature of a violent revolt that, as part of literature, would thereby resolve itself through political and religious propaganda.

The desire to subvert is omnipresent in Mudimbe's works, whether it takes the form of parody or excess. Subversion of morals, of taste, of modesty, of politics. But the Mudimbean method critiques, first and foremost, social institutions that instil and maintain values of order. In fact, no social institution escapes the fury of Mudimbe's heroes, whether it be mechanisms of repression or ideological mechanisms of the state. First is the family, a cell, in the novels, of all sorts of tortures. The Church is the other institution taken to task. It is unnecessary to list the many critiques of the Roman Church's hierarchy, as well as those addressed to figures of the law. It is also useless to bring up the overwhelming sarcasm targeting priests. All forms of gullibility and of symbolic scaffolding used by human beings, like quivering crutches, can be placed in one hat. School, or more generally, education, the moment where so many ideas are instilled, is not exempt.

The literary institution is also not left unscathed. The entirety of Mudimbe's novels can be seen as the parallel development of two negative allegories, where each contests the other: the allegory of literature, displayed by its inventive and rhetorical excesses, and the allegory of literary communication, exhibited in its hidden conclusions. Genres, rhetorical codes, reading pacts, all find themselves mocked, subjects of irony, which is often displayed by highlighting, albeit discretely, their often arbitrary functioning. More generally, the incarnation of the author and the reader, meaning of their reciprocal sacralisation, is at play. From there, numerous interventions by a scribe dismantling his own tricks. But these interventions also reside within the text, displaying their need to be fed and the desire to procreate. It is a way to insist on the torments of the imaginary and to revoke the act of writing. It is also a way of demonstrating, through the absurd, the myth of the author's two bodies, the spiritual body and the carnal body, the spirit and the material, the brain and the skin. Furthermore, it is a way, by way of consequence, of exposing (in both senses of the term) the reader because the reader is implicated in the work as an independent actor in the scene and the framework for the reading experience is broken.

Reflexivity is the word for Mudimbe's enigma, the trademark of both his singular grandeur and his limitations. Concerning the literary institution, the author of *Entre les eaux* has a pre-critical vision that, while displaying great rigour, examines only the extremities of the phenomenon. On one side are writing models, important texts. On the other side are descriptive practices and obsessions. His conception balances a hyperconceptual vision and a hypermaterialist one. As if it was that of a writer, still young, who is well read and who strongly believes that literature is only made in books and on writing tables. With *Shaba deux* (1989) comes maturity: a less destructive vision, meaning also a more integrated one, where literature, made of texts and signs, of codes and of forms, is increasingly and skilfully ordered in relation to a network of exchanges and formalities within a social microsystem.

Mudimbe's writing, with its rhetorical means, corresponds to a paradigm shift in rhetorical regimes in which metonymy and allegory replace the reigning metaphor. This shift is in response to a new world view. The collective presence of two common traits – increasing formal irony and shaking up the metaphor's reign – seems to indicate, in any case, that Mudimbe's novels, as singular as they are, are not similar to an aerolite fallen from who knows what obscure sky. They are, rather, the expression, unarguably the most convulsive, of an earthquake striking the novel's landscape in the 1970s. Its shock waves are still felt and continue to expand.

However, if Mudimbe's novels have the ambition of totalising the real, they do so by detailing. His novels seek to grasp large ensembles, whose tight textual architecture is elaborated with fear of the most harmless variety. Of course, these strategies allow the author to authenticate content, to highlight its context and circumstances. But their systemic use displays their necessity and positions them as a major stake in the project. Mudimbe thereby gives the novel the function of accessing a concrete reality. Thus, the tendency in his works is to recount or describe what is singular, accessory, to detail speech and to multiply it through diverse strategies. Sometimes, details are deployed in strict order within a vast description and obtain the value of a methodical inventory. Other times, they are delivered in a disjointed manner, following the wanderings of a gaze or miming the effervescence of life. Then again, the detail finds itself isolated and highlighted by the narration. And in other cases, it becomes the object of a descriptive expansion. Each use has its own function within a large range of possibilities.

Because the detail is immanent, contingent, contradictory, traits of all 'effect of reality' crystallise in the detail. But if the detail attests to the violence of the 'real' better than anything else, it is, at the same time, sliding into insignificance. Each reading is an opportunity to grasp this duality.

Once it is multiplied and weighs the representation down with minor indications, the detail, by its violence, has the effect of fatigue and impatience. It is like the text's admitted redundancy. The reader wants to finish quickly. But it takes little to retain a strong meaning. Take a moment to stop and break things down: Pierre Landu's crucifix of fortune, the large reproduction of the Cène d'Andrea del Castagno, the mosquitoes and the air conditioning gone awry in Ahmed Mara's hotel room, the minister's asleep while the president of the national commission of defence holds a meeting on the country's security, instead of dealing with threats brought upon by the rebellion. These attributes have an important power of evocation. They are linked both to individuals and to uses exterior to them: The pieces define themselves in interaction with one another. At the beginning of *L'écart* (1979), the description of Nara's fatigue, of the heat, of his patient wait, of lies told by the hotel owner, all depict the inseparability of human beings in a social context, making the former – people – emblems of the latter. From insignificance, we have moved on to violence through oversignificance.

In its very contingency, the detail belongs to the grand order of necessity, meaning it enters into a system of determination that is the principle credo of the enterprise of truthfulness. Also, even when it seems like a futile notation, the detail is directly engaged in a vast system of causal explanations and of finalisation of all circumstances of an action. Concerning its status as a secondary phenomenon, it is always reusable as an element of the famous 'influence of the environment', as boasted by the positivist approach. The detail contributes, more or less, to the general atmosphere affecting individuals, orienting them, defining their paths without their knowing it. Mudimbe excels at creating these falsely innocent climates, where all components casually flow back towards the character at the centre of the intrigue.

The effects of detailing do not stop here. At this point, a whole order of representation is disturbed. The usual hierarchy of what is essential and what is accessory, the general and the particular, is invalidated. Here, what is secondary obtains a new value and dignity. It becomes a place of obligatory passage towards what is fundamental. *Entre les eaux* begins with a scene of introspection and of picturesque and anecdotal recollection, expressed through the violence of rhetorical questions. *L'écart* begins with a long description of the decaying state of the hotel where Nara is staying:

So, Nara? Still at the hotel?
    – Ah, yeah, still in my hole . . . An excavation site: An unfinished stairway ramp . . . eczema marked walls . . . concrete slabs that used to be beige . . . now faded . . . and cracking . . . You have to see it to believe it . . . [. . .] The ceiling is a mouldy scab . . . It sweats from all the rain . . .

My saving grace is my own excess . . . a small table, a chair, a hard bed . . .
And piles of books everywhere. They lead me astray and offer me shelter,
too (1979: 20).

One can even evoke the much vaster opening of *Le bel immonde* (1976) that is
Ya's wait in a nightclub, overwhelmed by music. There is something provocative
about the way in which a scene is set up, in the sense that the reader has the right
to believe that the story is led astray by futile episodes. Literary critics have been
shocked by these detours, including some of the cited examples. The problem is not
seeing that new criteria are required to judge the importance of textual elements.
In my examples, it is often what follows in the text that fosters a re-evaluation of
details that, on first impression, seem unimportant.

Regardless of how, we become spectators to the act of highlighting registers
of the self that, before now, were either neglected or marginalised. For instance,
everything belonging to the inside: to daily life, to the body and to decor. Evoking
these areas of meaning implies the detail. It expresses things like a menu. The
perception of the world from day to day, through journals, diaries, notebooks,
confessions, is a short-sighted perception. Mudimbe's realism therefore revels in
these moments and in the immediacy that seems, to him, as close as possible to
real life itself. Moving from the concrete object to feelings retained, without going
much further, it establishes itself in a very immediate phenomenology, fascinated
by the presence of things and beings.

One could ask if, ideologically speaking, there is a strong relationship between
'detailism' and feminisation in Mudimbe's novels. It must be recognised that his
works make space for women and femininity like none other. The phenomenon
is expressed in the access of feminine characters to first-tier roles, as if to take
into consideration what makes their universe singular. Over time, an intense and
inspiring emergence of figures ranging from d'Antoinette to Misse Poubelle, from
Ya to Aminata and Isabelle, or furthermore, from Marie-Gertrude to Véronique.
Many of these heroines are extraordinarily glorious characters. This can mean
that they exceed their 'sphere of competence' or also that they use this competence
to accomplish something with particular brilliance. It is in this light that we see
more than one female character reigning over the world of objects and, thus, over
details in the text and imposing their mark on them. *Le bel immonde* (1976) marks
the first time in the history of the African novel that a story's theme is female

homosexuality. *Shaba deux* (1989) shows the conflicts and rivalries between female characters, beyond difference in dress or in rituals from the religious orders to which they belong. There is, in *Le bel immonde*, a descriptive eroticism that, pertaining to bodies or to decors, is marked by a feminine presence. The novel also features a number of small high-society customs. Thus, what is decorative and what is sensory in the novel has power over the text, in concomitance with the increasingly important female characters. *Le bel immonde* ends as it begins: The heroine waits in a nightclub, a testimony to the strength of this female character whom we believed to be weak.

In the preface of *Une fille d'Ève*, Honoré de Balzac offers this great phrase: 'Our civilisation is immense with details' (1839: 5). He thereby notes an overturned society, no longer organised by a simple order with a clear hierarchy. 'In the past,' he adds, 'everything was simplified by monarchical institutions' (6). Mobile, this new society becomes more socially diversified, generating, amongst those attempting to describe it, a proliferation of details. For Mudimbe, the social actor is achieved through behaviours, gestures, physical traits and objects defining his or her singularity. The narrative takes over in a rich eruption of meaning. Mudimbe welcomes into the text many details, giving a sort of literary value to the objects of life. The story stages inquiries into the diverse realities of the world.

In this perspective, favouring the factual, the most tangible or material appears as the guarantor of what is true or lived. It is this palpable reality that is described and detailed. Of course, acts, thoughts and feelings also garner attention and are described through narrative. Does the object make the detail less harmless? Obviously, objects play a strategic role in stories. Other objects are pretexts for attributing symbolic or decorative value. Ordinarily, however, as it appears within a mess of description, the objectified detail finds itself in a much more hesitant situation. On the one hand, it is taken seriously and it does not take much before the text allows it to transcend into secondary signification, making the detail revelatory. But, on the other hand, it never rids itself of its primary contingency. While reading, the detail is perceived for what it is: banal, trivial and lacking a decisive importance. It is saying that, with the detail, the text is either lightened or becomes sticky. Its only chance of valorisation is to be welcomed into an actor's perceptive movement and to benefit from this person's aura. Mudimbe plays with the subjectivity of things, highlighting what perception has that is relative and sometimes misleading. But, in each case, an interpretive interest is present and visibly participates in an operation of deciphering and of knowledge.

Since 1996, Zaïre, once called the Congo Free State, Belgian Congo, Republic of the Congo and renamed Democratic Republic of the Congo (DRC) with the advent of what we were eager to cynically call liberation, has been under the occupation of the Rwandan, Ugandan and Burundian armies. How, then, can you make the horror of this war of occupation felt by those who have never known the war? It consists, firstly, again and always, of our difference, of our non-belonging; that is, also, of our social alienation and our poorly understood relationship to unconsciousness. How is it possible to render the war's horror, a horror that does not vanish, an abstract horror that weighs down on people and things, a horror that seems to be on the outside, on people's faces, but also inside, inside things, breaking lives, obstructing the future? Calm, violent and stable, almost discrete, it colours the dreams of entire populations, like the most primal thought. It is both the path their conscience follows and the meaning of the world. What is there in common between the war punctuating Mudimbe's novels and the country's present situation, overrun by armies (neighbouring countries' armies, to be precise) who pull so easily on the trigger and where statistics ranging from six to ten million deaths have become 'collateral damage', meaning an unimportant news item, and therefore banal like any other?

I deemed this preamble necessary so that an ill-intentioned reader does not use my text as a pretext to confuse the war appearing quietly in Mudimbe's novels with the horrible reality of present-day DRC. No. There is no common measure. Wars, violence and literature: a survey of wars that bloody the African Great Lakes region, as 'imagined' by Mudimbe. Jean-Paul Sartre made a remark about this type of critic:

> The contemporary critic cannot be bothered by such inane prudence: His pleasure lies in extrapolating. After each new work he takes stock as though that work marked the end of history and literature. *Balance-Sheet of the Occupation*, *Balance-Sheet of the Year 1945*, *Balance-Sheet of Contemporary Theater*: He adores balance sheets (1975: 38).

In all four of Mudimbe's novels, war works the story and is worked into the story, often with a great deal of stubbornness and force. It is around the war that the direct action of its passage near to us seems to shine. It is around the war and through the war that we are obliged to reflect on its silence. Pierre Landu, in *Entre les eaux*, decides to quit the convent and join the guerrillas of the Maoist rebels, fighting against the central government. The story of the minister's idyll and of the young university student who combine to form the intrigue of *Le bel immonde* has, as a backdrop, the war between the democratic revolutionary movement and the government of Kinshasa around 1964. *L'écart* examines a group of young leftists that Nara associates with, who are against the central government of Krishville. *Shaba deux* is set within the two Shaba wars that occurred in 1977 and 1978. Each time, government troops reverse the situation and re-establish order, or, as Landu says, 'the usual and blessed lack of order' (1973: 17).

However, as we will see in the examples that follow, Mudimbe's novels have, by their very intention of narrating the war, an epic dimension. If one decides to follow what Mudimbe says in his autobiography, *Les corps glorieux des mots et des êtres* (1994), he is referring to the rebellion he saw in Kwilu while he was there teaching Latin. And Mudimbe did live through, as did everyone inhabiting Lubumbashi at the time, the two wars of Shaba, brought on by police from Katanga against Mobutu Sese Seko's central government. But, precisely, the two facts – the imaginary fact and the historic coincidence – find themselves mixed together, actualised one after the other, provoking in the novels complicated narrative networks that demand a plural interpretation through the few historical references found in the texts, enlarging them to the point of giving them an epic dimension.

The barbaric violence of the Marxist rebels in *Entre les eaux* or in *Le bel immonde*, the pillaging for which they are responsible, coincides with the government soldiers' brutality when these soldiers take control of areas previously in the hands of the rebels. But the political rebellion is paired with Pierre Landu's religious rebellion against the Roman Catholic Church. The narrator speaks in the present of what he lived in the past. The rebellions that bloodied the Congo in 1964 are mixed with the political situation of the 1970s in *Le bel immonde* and the years 1977–80 in *Shaba deux*. The defocalised contours are micro-stories, whether they are practised through paraleipsis, prolepsis or analepsis. Regardless, the paraleipsis is the defocalising element par excellence. And it has a double value: on the one hand, the paraleipsis breaks narrative flow because it has neither, as defined by Roland Barthes (1977: 29), an antecedent nor an explicit consequence. On the other hand, the paraleipsis establishes a dose of poetry in the text, without which the novel would be either very minimalist in expression or very dry.

Written in such a way that enunciation is brought to the forefront and deploys all of its networks, it is normal that every core of a sequence breaks into many other cores, to the point of altering the force of the presumed or supposed core that is at the centre. The witchcraft of Kaayowa (Pierre's wife) is mentioned in *Entre les eaux*, anthropophagy in *Le bel immonde*, the way in which Marie-Gertrude was tortured in *Shaba deux*. All of this projects us into a mythological universe, in an atmosphere similar to that of the *Iliad*, by the emphasis on its initial violence. The rebels in *Entre les eaux* explode dynamite in a dormitory where government soldiers are sleeping. Through this universe, a desire seeps into the text of atemporality and of a historic blurriness that can serve to broaden the spectrum to all resistances past and present. This mythical place is, in one sense, the DRC, corresponding as such to the very project Mudimbe undertook of narrating the situation of African countries, the contact with Western civilisation, colonisation, Christianity, at the beginning of history, outside of history, 'outside of chronology', in the words of Michel Foucault (1997: 158).

Mudimbe's novels are thus presented as parables. The combination of times – past, present and future – which I will mention shortly, has an empty reference, commenting on nothing but its own address, its own lack of precision. This parody is reminiscent of biblical openings and refers to an ancient period, helping to situate with greater historical accuracy place names that appear in the novels. Temporality – for instance, the imperfect, present and the simple past – reinforces the imprecision surrounding the date of an event, trivialises an utterance and establishes the permanence of a war, where its intensity is underscored by the enunciation of major traits in the present of the indicative. This tense favours and isolates facts belonging to the past and installs them in the present. They thereby correspond to more precise historical references than the novels display, such as the rebellion of 1964; President Joseph Kasavubu's speech; ministerial changes by Mobutu's regime; prostitution; political assassinations; the two Shaba wars; the repatriation of people from Western countries, even of priests, the moment that war breaks out in an African country; the relation between politics and witchcraft or occult practices; tribalism; spying; Rome; museums – evocations referring to an old world, but also to a new one, both by their historicity and by practices linked to them, such as witchcraft, buying one's baptism and the material privileges of priests.

These subjects appear as areas of conflict: war connotations are strong and also establish a sexualised opposition. In *Shaba deux*, the arrival of two European nuns at an Emmaus convent causes a ruckus in the primarily European convent. The presence of one black woman, Marie-Gertrude, evokes curiosity. Also, the permanence of conflict can be read in the heart of the enunciation, which becomes a reflection of the drama played out in the convent, as Marie-Gertrude remarks, while scrutinising 'the large reproduction of the Cène d'Andrea del Castagno' (1989: 30). She observes a tension on the faces of Jesus, John and Judas, regardless of the general impression of communion.

While examining the texts at such a microscopic level, that of the letter, I will take advantage of the opportunity to underscore the predominance in the novels of the sounds K, G, S and Z. All of them are whistling sounds, sometimes inaudible, and contribute to creating an atmosphere of war by the sequence of consonance. Impulse or desire is suggested by the letter K. Is this letter not used to designate the phallus in the four novels? In the Congo, rape against women is used as a weapon. Through the grinding of occlusive sounds and the whistling Zs, there are reminders in the texts of the rigours of war, the permanence of the body, the gush of the phallus. Because it is also about that. The soul's delight is nothing more than Kinshasa's symbolic castration, reduced to a state of servitude and of subjection, with the pragmatic flee of the nourishing mother, of mother nature towards the sea (a river or rain water), the vital sea and fertile strength, other images of desire. The guerrillas in the forest, the forest where the minister solicits the ancestors' strength, in opposition to Kinshasa, 'city of Whites', and home to men who have got rid of their traditions, most of whom conjugate masculine virility with the outbreak of violence and the radiance of tradition with the cold rigour of 'Whites'.

Out of this emerge two principal motifs in Mudimbe's novels: the discourse of desire and the obscenity of the Other.

The discourse of desire

If, in Mudimbe's novels, we can easily and literally identify what forces are present, which are mostly evoked by a relationship of domination versus submission that reinforces the conflicting character of the texts, their potential for aggressiveness becomes greater. In this context, the notion of resistance obtains a double meaning. In *Le bel immonde*, Ya spies on the minister with whom she lives, in order to transmit information about government decisions and projects to rebels of her tribe. Even when violently struck by state security agents when they suspect her betrayal, the notion of resistance conceals the function and the secret isotope is never recognised. Similarly, the minister himself remains silent after sacrificing Ya's friend to the ancestors. There is a parallel made between resistance and speech, as though to combat the resistance with speech, or to combat the resistance of speech. This brings us to the remark that the resistance of speech is equivalent to the resistance of bodies. This is why enunciation plays in a present that continually moves from one present to another, establishing the time and space of an instant that is multiple, outside of time, as long as time is a function of language.

Slavery, in this perspective, appears as a reflection of the damnation of bodies and creates the first antitheses: 'white versus black', 'coloniser versus colonised', 'dominant versus dominated', 'religious versus laymen'. These antitheses appear in the novels as a sort of outline of an exploitative relationship, where the fascination of power exercises an attraction that reinforces the dependency of bodies. In *Shaba deux* (1989), the physical character of this domination is insisted upon in words such as 'cover', 'corpse', 'body', 'naked', 'uncover'. These words are found in phrases such as, 'Everything was covered in corpses, in mutilated bodies', where the term 'covered' refers to a metonymic covering of the city with bodies. 'Covering' is associated with a sexual figuration, suggested by the word 'spellbound'. Or, furthermore:

> Sand beaches . . . covered with bodies and death. The impression of grief. On a deserted beach, tracks . . . I follow them. Sand. The monstrous sea . . . I call out. With force. My voice's echo. I scream. In vain. There are sometimes minuscule drops of blood in the holes left by a step (Mudimbe 1979: 143).

The 'cover', an expression of sexual vigour, is always associated with the power of death. Everything in these novels revolves around the impulsive dualism consisting of desire and of killing. Eros and Thanatos, the origin and the antithesis on which the text is founded, whether pertaining to the abstract opposition between life and death or the opposition between white and black, colonisers and colonised, witch and bewitched, dominant and dominated. Impulse is spread out in the text, becoming the expression of a desire turned open, transformed and a work on language in and by the evocation of love. We can conclude here, along with Barthes, that in language, 'it is the phallus that is speaking' (1982: 192). According to the ideology of domination, fault involves falling into the hands of the enemy, being amongst the defeated: *Vae victis* is, in fact, the moral law giving connotation to this ideology. It is the ideology of power, where power dynamics are implied on a moral level. For instance:

> dominant versus dominated
> good versus bad.

Such a connotation only valorises, after the fact, the two *states* of power. It does not reduce them to values. The principal virtue of *power* is to exist and the axiological perversion consists precisely in turning existence into value, not only confusing the being with what could be, but also replacing one with the other and thereby creating an ideology based on non-values.

The forest, suggested by the metaphor of the '*maquis*' (scrubland, but also underground fighting) and the river, referring here to the guardian of tradition (for instance, recognising the powers of witches), to human warmth, to the youth of bodies, carry a growing sexuality. Their positivity can be read through actions such as the gift of 'lightning', capable of heating the earth, and the 'mirror' of knowledge. Its symbolism is double: climatic and sexual. The leaders of Kinshasa will always look to understand the origin of the hardship inflicted upon them. But the city (Kinshasa) refers here only to rigour and frailty, the evocation of a cold sexuality blossoming in the stories. It has an erotic decor, suggested by the 'red sun', where Nara and his group of young leftists go each night to get drunk, the nightclub where Ya waits for clients, every night, eyes half closed. And revenge, for the government soldiers, consists of setting the forest on fire, while the young leftists express their desire to have a 'lighter' on hand that could set everything alight. The permanent wall built by the antithesis of fire versus water (a large rain falls while the government soldiers are squashing the rebellion in *Entre les eaux*) reminds us of Jacques Lacan's words in *Séminaire XVI*: 'There is no sexual rapport' (1969: 226).

Death (colonisation, war, witchcraft, dictatorship) appears as an impulsive motor that transforms tears into blood. In the following example, the opposition of Kinshasa versus '*maquis*' (scrubland) is represented by the antonyms 'order versus disorder'. There is constantly a question of human blood, consumed by leaders to build their strength. Actualising 'blood' and 'tears' that, for most 'modern' texts, hold an erotic character, introduces us into a poetic of the element, endowed with the same symbolism as that of water (river, rain). A large part of the process, as inscribed in the text, is linked to sex (Guyotat 1972: 55). 'Blood' and 'tears' make up the transgression of another antithesis: 'eroticism versus mystique' (Bataille 1945: 150). The passage is easy from one to the other, as is already suggested through the substitution of rebels by fetishes. Similarly, the erotic figure of the dominant or strong person replaces the mystical image of ancient clan leaders. The effects of these transgressions make up my following point.

The obscenity of Eros

In Barthes's words: 'The story is no longer only a strong system (ancient narrative system), but it is also, and contradictorily, a simple space, a field of permanence and of permutation' (1982: 57). Here, there is a graphic rupture marked by the second isotope that places emphasis, in each novel, on the humiliation of defeat and surrender, regardless of their vigour and resistance. This occurs in the same climate of violence and sadistic hatred where sexual instinct, conveyed by the 'savage' text, and a discourse of abjection transform into an urge to death.

Also founded upon a game of antitheses, the present isotope opposes notions of justice and injustice, of clarity and the tarnished, of storm and light, of happiness and pain, of prosperity and decay. For instance: a dialogue in a nightclub where a young lawyer opposes the purity of tradition to prostitution stemming from colonial occupation. This humiliation puts an end to the idea of an idyllic relation, through a dirty and triumphant penetration: the troops circle the entire city before taking it by firing cannons. Victory, suggested by the promenade, on foot, across the city (let us note, in passing, its symbolic character), is proof of a dual position: placing the 'conqueror' in the heart of the city, but also in a crucial point of the 'ville-femme', the feminine space ... the duality of conquest and of political ascension, where military and economic gain is confounded with sexual victory. Meanwhile, a fierce resistance is organised, its rage is revealed by the distance between the means granted and the attained objectives.

Speech is part of a small, limited frame, the intimate realm of a family's grief, or of a dark room, semi-obscure, almost empty, where we see nothing but a large rat,[1] a frame thus stripped of all military connotation. In this context, speech successively attaches us to an ideological resistance incarnated by a tribe, a group of intellectuals and by the announcement of a war of resistance, the scarcity of economic means suggested by the mention of 'darts in hand, against the canons, with the help of proletarian slogans' (Mudimbe 1976: 120–21). The resistance's determination can be read through a remarkably elliptical and sober use of speech. Articulated around the pivotal segment 'his piece of cake' (121), this discourse accentuates the disproportion between the precariousness of means and the ambitiousness of their goal: ending social injustice by starting a new government.

In this context, the conqueror's cruelty towards the rebels or the sentiment of revenge against the populations of Kantanga (in *Shaba deux*), through what is considered 'pacification', is merely an expression of hatred towards an identified enemy. The image, in fact, usually inspires only repulsion and disgust. But this fact is placed at a distance accentuated by the sadistic acts of the government military, the image of blood that is only a replica of blood already spilled in the stories and that feeds those in search of power. The image of these individuals covered in their victims' blood is re-presented to us, re-presented in the etymological sense of the term. Also represented is the eroticism implied by the first message, where sexual urge is transformed into sadism, impulse and death. In this perspective, Marie-Gertrude's meditation between contemplation and action, the lightness of nuns who studied at the university of Lubumbashi, the 'tissue' that Ya pulls from her handbag after the sexual act in the minister's office: these examples function as signs while reading. Regarding the first isotope, the 'tissue' and Ya's attire – 'the cost of a white dress blouse with long sleeves that you wore, bought specially for your rendezvous, chosen because it was in his taste, in natural silk and buttoned in the front, all the way . . . so that he can open it easily if he so desires' (Mudimbe 1976: 95) – is, in fact, the replica of descriptive traits previously evoked, in which the sexual notion of 'covering' was intimately linked to the impulse of death.

Constructed to reflect its own image, this isotope appears as a place of permanencies, on the one hand and, on the other, as the product of a reversal whereby the country pulls misfortune from its own fortune and becomes unrecognisable, humiliated by the population's exploitation, misery and developmental delay. We are introduced into a field of lust (the red sun, the nightclub, 'residence of the appalling spirit' (Kristeva 1980: 36) and so on) that, with a latent eroticism, pushes us towards the abjectness of death (59). The dictator and his chaos, war the permanence of horror and anxiety . . . this atmosphere of disorder and crisis is translated by a sort of laziness in the sentences, identifiable in constructions such as:

The army will hold the population ransom. The arrests are without discrepancy. Old animosity and jealousies are resolved by denunciations. The collaborators are impossible to count. All of Katanga's enemies are enemies of the Republic. The prisons will be, it seems, already full. As not to be burdened with useless mouths, the soldiers practiced using bladed weapons on prisoners. Sister Marie-Cécile adds that she lost all authority at school. Teachers, like students, are pinned against each other. And the army kidnaps 'Katangais' who are Katangais only in the minds of their accusers. It is the reign of informers and of fake witnesses (Mudimbe 1989: 118).

Repeating the terms 'body', 'mirror', 'blood', 'tears', 'resistance', 'forest', 'fire', river' and 'fetish' not only illustrates a thematic position, but also engenders a monotony reflecting the duration of these dark years of murderous war. The textual truth is here closer than the historic truth: the failure of all of these rebellions and of the government's provincial reconquests, helped by Western military forces, Pierre Landu's return to a Cistercian monastery, last corrupted figuration of the father. Failure to rhyme what is true with what is likely. Thus torn between Africa and the West, between dream and reality, Mudimbe's texts place these notions back to back and shatter them.

The narrators' extra-diegetic position contributes to a cold description, made up of punctual notations that reinforce the texts' sobriety. However, interlacing narrative and symbolic networks situate us in the atemporality I highlighted earlier, leaving the reader with only the space of horror, of fright and anxiety in the first degree and of a poetic reconstruction on a second level of reading. War and its variants define a new space, that of '*écri-tu-re*'. This breakdown of the French word for writing was proposed by Marcelin Pleynet and reveals wonderfully a contract of desire with the other, the '*hypocrite reader*', our *fellow human*, our *brother* or just *us*. There is a poetry in these rhythmic and sound games (alliterative dissonance and resonance prolong the clashes of combat) that already turn war in Mudimbe's novels into a sort of gap, between life and of death, between Eros and Thanatos, between a nourishing and dreadful earth where, in the same stream, runs the flow of these atrocities and excesses made of blood, sperm and tears.

Conclusion: Daring to think the detail for oneself

We can now bring up the question of whether or not the apparent spontaneity of these militias or armed groups in the DRC and elsewhere, their claims and manifestations have been thought by themselves, the people from the concerned countries, far from historic allegiances and beliefs, far from prejudice and guides of all sorts. What autonomy of thought existed and brought about these movements? Borrowing from Immanuel Kant, the people of the Great Lakes, were they acting on their own understanding and free will, without influence from the 'conduct of the other'? Did they 'determine their orientation'? The revolution should favour an end to prejudice, the guardianship of another, the access to enlightenment (*Aufklärung*), taking charge of one's destiny and conducting one's path, according to the very path that we just traced. How can we admit that it is possible for these movements not to be explained by prejudice, meaning beliefs where the people who enact them are not the authors or masters of these ideas or of their own judgement? They gave their assent, they agreed, they said 'yes' – that is believing – but they said 'yes' before truly thinking for themselves.

Are these individuals ready to admit that their thoughts – their beliefs, their personal opinions – are, and can only be, a borrowed and worn outfit? It is difficult to separate from ourselves what we think is a part of us. Our personal opinions are thoughts to which we hold, they are beliefs that constitute our thinking and even our being, but are we capable of identifying on what our confidence is founded? Is it not just the times? Knowledge is not made of opinions. Are not most of our thoughts preconceived ideas, ideas that nobody made, as in Paul Valéry (1968), thoughts that are within us that we believe to be our own, although we did not really form them by a free and complete examination of their truth. Nothing is closer to a cliché than a cherished personal opinion; nothing is less free. Our strongest beliefs are generally clichés or, simply, the echo of our era. We take for our own what is only ready-made thought.

Only people who are free and capable of thinking for themselves can live in a republican and non-despotic state, meaning a state where they are citizens, instead of being subjects of a despot or slaves of a master. And this liberation, because it makes human beings capable of using their judgement, their reason, does not threaten or put into peril the state and religion, whilst men of religion object that the liberation of humanity would bring the destruction of internal morality. The revolution is therefore the education of humankind. The first moment of thought for she who wants to think for herself is the moment she critiques her own thinking. Critiquing is judging – crisis, in Greek, is judgement (Kant 1960). It is, in one sense, a negative moment of crisis. It is important then to note that refusal or contesting should not be confused with the critique. It is not sufficient to be opposed to others to be free. Thinking against another is not thinking for oneself. We have lost more than one to this paradox, who refused, while having many reasons to believe. It is dangerous to passively echo common beliefs or to take the opposite stance. And a dialectic opposing the 'for' and the 'against' of a question is false. It is important not to confound freedom of speech (confounded with speaking or 'parlerie') with freedom of expression, understanding that speech is risk. The freedom to say 'no' is often an illusion and the opinion we value is first and foremost a prejudice.

It would be useful, therefore, to understand of what consists true religion, religiosity. Adimante, Plato's brother, in Book II of *The Republic* (1992), proposes a radical critique of the religious education that men underwent. Is it worth it, to be a good man, asks Socrates, if morality consists in acting in a manner that will be compensated not only in this life, but after death, in that we escape the pains of hells, as we have been told since we were children? Those moralist stories symbolise the way in which we teach children what we call 'moral'. This expression, always understood today in a pejorative way, means in these conditions an ensemble of rules necessary for people's coexistence in a given society. These rules are themselves, of course, useful, we think, but without value in themselves. We do not respect them for themselves, but because we are scared of punishment or waiting for compensation. For those who, on the contrary, justice is a supreme good in itself and for itself, a value, committing an injustice is a greater evil than to have it perpetrated against oneself. It is not simply bad for those to whom one is unjust. In the same manner, this individual knows that it is worse to run away from punishment than to be punished.

Social pressure imposes what we call 'values' on humanity, beliefs that are not anchored in people any more than being struck by fear or by love of pleasures and honours. Through these values, human beings recognise their truth. The stories we tell about the spirit's destiny after death have therefore been invented to strike the imagination of people who have become crazed by the fear of death and they assure a social cohesion that could be threatened if people thought they would be rid of punishment after death. The ministry of cults and religion is a department of the ministry of the interior. We need a vice squad. Under these different forms that are diverse religions, the belief in God and in the spirit's immortality therefore seems to govern people only by fear and lust – the carrot and the stick, 'discipline and punish', as Foucault (1997) observed. If this is the case, if humanity is transformed by all things sensitive, meaning like an animal, spirituality is only a story. Just as, in the name of God and the sacred, people have committed the worst crimes and atrocities. Thus, the story of Christianity, 'when it is embraced with a single glance, like a painting, the exclamation can be justified: *Tantum religio potuit suadere malorum* [Lucretius, *De Natura Rerum*]! So many crimes have been counselled by religion . . .' (Kant 1965: 131). Kant continues by opposing what history has done with Christianity to the original idea that animated Christianity in the spirit of its foundation. This is the critical truth of materialism: fables about the hereafter having an effect only on those who fear death. Epicurus (2009) shows that death has in it nothing that can make this phantasmagoria disappear.

For Lucretius and Epicurus, the principle of this critique of morals and of religion contains a great idea of what is moral: the idea of a justice that would be desired for itself and not for the advantages it entails, a practice of what is good in itself and not simply in the framework of bargaining that is sometimes the business of humankind. It is this justice that Adimante wants to force Socrates to describe to him because Adimante knows that this justice is the only true good and that Socrates practised it all his life. In another dialogue, *Euthyphron* (Plato 1979), Socrates asks if one should be pious because the gods want us to be or if piety has an absolute value independent from the wishes of the gods, such that it is this absolute value that determines the will of the gods or the will of pious men. Must one live justly and honestly to please the gods or is justice worthy enough in itself to merit its practice? Is justice, for us, a real good or only a currency to exchange? If it is only a question of business and bargaining, then it suffices to maintain appearances, to pretend to be just or to try not to be caught. A religious practice and a cult serving God to obtain rewards are fundamentally immoral; fetishism or superstition, belief by which we imagine being capable of weakening the Almighty, are thus the summit of immorality because it is hypocritical to call such low motives religiousness and morality.

True faith, on the contrary, is first and foremost faith in virtue and in justice. It is a faith in humankind, a faith in oneself, understood in the courage of the most humble person to do his or her duty. This faith is religious. The individual who reflects cannot miss seeing that the world's lessons do not conform to his or her heart's desires. On the heels of changes brought about in that part of the world, there is a necessity of social cohesion, of integration of minority cultures, ethnicities, languages, religions and so on, in order to get rid of the idea of second-rate citizens. Thus, the universal, humanity in itself, cannot be reduced to a group of people, regardless of their numbers. Their judgement does not engage posterity that must, in turn, make its own decisions. This is why no decision made can be seen as definitive. The rights of human beings are something greater than those of the citizen and those of the citizen are not rights so long as they do not allow the fulfilment of the rights of human beings, of the humanity of humankind. Once we start considering the rights of the citizen as the only rights, it is the end of the state of law. What is therefore necessary is 'daring to know', daring to seek knowledge for oneself and to think the detail for oneself, instead of relying on beliefs, opinions and illusions.

Notes

All translations, unless otherwise indicated, are the author's.

1. The *lexème* 'rat' appears frequently in *L'écart*.

References

Balzac, Honoré de. 1839. *Une fille d'Ève*. Brussels: Cans et Co.

Barthes, Roland. 1977. *Poétique du récit*. Paris: Seuil.

———. 1982. *L'obvie et l'obtus*. Paris: Seuil.

Bataille, George. 1945. *Sur Nietzsche: Volonté de chance*. Paris: Gallimard.

Épicure. 2009. *Lettre à Ménécée*. Translated by Pierre-Marie Morel. Paris: Flammarion.

Foucault, Michel. 1997. *Surveiller et punir: Naissance de la prison*. Paris: Gallimard.

Guyotat, Pierre. 1972. *Littérature interdite*. Paris: Gallimard.

Kant, Immanuel. 1960. *Critique du jugement*. Paris: Vrin.

———. 1965. *La religion dans les limites de la simple raison, II, 2, AK, VI*. Translated by J. Gibelin. Paris: Vrin.

Kristeva, Julia. 1980. *Pouvoirs de l'horreur: Essai sur l'abjection*. Paris: Seuil.

Lacan, Jacques. 1969. *Séminaire XVI*. Paris: Seuil.

Lucrèce. 1993. *La nature des choses: De natura rerum*. Translated by José Kany-Turpin. Paris: Aubier.

Mudimbe, V-Y. 1973. *Entre les eaux: Dieu, un prêtre, la révolution*. Paris: Présence Africaine.

———1976. *Le bel immonde: Récit*. Paris: Présence Africaine.

———. 1979. *L'écart*. Paris: Présence Africaine.

———. 1989. *Shaba deux: Les carnets de Mère Marie-Gertrude*. Paris: Présence Africaine.

———. 1994. *Les corps glorieux des mots et des êtres: Esquisse d'un jardin africain à la bénédictine*. Paris: Présence Africaine and Montreal: Humanitas.

Plato. 1979. *Euthyphron*. Paris: Pédagogie moderne.

———. 1992. *La république: Livres 1 à 10*. Translated by Émile Chambry. Paris: Gallimard.

Sartre, Jean-Paul. 1975 [1948]. *Situations, II: Qu'est-ce que la littérature?* Paris: Gallimard.

Valéry, Paul. 1968. *Œuvres*. Paris: Gallimard.

CHAPTER 4

Representations of Violence in V-Y Mudimbe's Novels

Olga Hél-Bongo

In the context of a reflection on violence in the Great Lakes region and on the writings of V-Y Mudimbe, this chapter focuses on modes of representation of violence in his novels. *Entre les eaux*, *Le bel immonde*, *L'écart* and *Shaba deux* release a violence that is thematic, epistemological and formal. This representation of violence affects the singular and collective life of the African subject. History and the present of writing, the fictional practice and theory of fiction, singular and collective life all come together to produce a work that is reflexive and 'modern', as defined by Pierre Reverdy or Charles Baudelaire. For Reverdy, '*L'éthique, c'est l'esthétique du dedans*' (ethics are the aesthetics of the interior) (1989: 154).[1] Baudelaire, commenting the work of painter friend Constantin Guys, asserts that beauty is always double (1961: 1152). The beauty of a work is the possibility, at the artist's disposal, of celebrating the convergence of what is historical and what is contingent, of an era and of a being, of what is eternal and what is transient. In *Entre les eaux*, Pierre Landu, African priest and intellectual, asks: 'Is it my era or my space that is killing me?' (1973: 4), interrogating a key anxiety; he is constructing a self-analysis of his condition.

I examine the reasons for the anxiety of Mudimbe's characters, based on the distinction between morality and ethics (Badiou 1993). Morality has a religious connotation. It implies the idea of control imposed from the outside. It is concerned with what is good and bad and operates by creating obligations. It refers to an ensemble of rules pertaining to actions and to values functioning as norms within a society. Morality implies the notion of right and of justice. Ethics, however, is quotidian. It contains the element of self-control inside the individual and is concerned with the negative and positive aspects of things; it makes us reflect and gives us a sense of responsibility. Mudimbe's novels offer the ethics practised by Pierre Landu, Marie-Gertrude, Ahmed Nara or Ya, characters who self-analyse by questioning the violence of their social environment, thereby calling into question religious morality, seen as norms imposed on the Other in a colonial context. The mix of reflexivity and aesthetics in the characters' questioning engenders a modern prose on the self and on the world. This chapter argues that the enunciation of violence is expressed through rhetoric or, in Justin Bisanswa's terms, by a triple experience of singularity that characterises modernity:

> *Expérience d'un sujet aux prises avec un langage. Expérience d'un discours aux prises avec une Histoire. Expérience d'une autonomie conjuguée avec un affrontement aux événements du présent. Cette triple expérience s'éprouve dans une conscience aiguë de l'historicité du roman et au regard d'une histoire spécifique de l'écriture romanesque*
> (Experience of a subject struggling with language. Experience of a discourse struggling with a History. Experience of an autonomy conjugated with the confrontation of present events. This triple experience is present in the sharp consciousness of the novel's historicity and with regard to a specific story of fictional writing) (2012: 8).

The ethical preoccupation of Mudimbe's protagonists wants to render the passage from implicitly to explicitly readable by raising questions about religious hypocrisy in Africa, questions about the violence of power, the lies of colonialism, the schism of the colonised intellectual and political assassinations. Oxymoron and antithesis, central figures in Mudimbe's novels, combine to make an aesthetic of duplicity of enunciation that is constantly at work. The heroes, in part because they question themselves, reflect and condemn themselves; irony, miraculous weapon (Césaire 1970) for placing violence at a distance, while showing itself for what it is – a tool for critical thought. The protagonists use irony to express and denounce different types of violence: historical (colonisation), collective (the Shaba wars, scenes of massacre and of political assassination), ideological and individual (the malaise of the colonised black intellectual), sexual and gender (being a woman) and symbolic, the worst form of violence, according to Pierre Bourdieu (1992), in its capacity to perpetuate power dynamics by hiding them from those they dominate. Here, we are reminded of the practice of insinuation by the priests and nuns in the convents in *Entre les eaux* and *Shaba deux*.

It seems legitimate to ask about the role of the novel in Mudimbe's thought on modes of representation of violence and the critique of ideology. The strength of

Mudimbe's novels seems to be in a shift in meaning, often preceded by a 'blocking'. Pierre Landu, Ahmed Nara and Marie-Gertrude are faced with the inadequacy of scientific discourse in the face of life. The distance and alienation spark an interior crisis and provoke their deaths. The Mudimbean novel therefore is turned around itself by these tormented characters, perplexed but also ironic, who interrogate their surroundings with a pretend naivety.

Ethics and aesthetics of violence

In *Entre les eaux*, Pierre Landu is the incarnation of what Max Weber called the '*désenchantement du monde*' (disenchantment of the world) (1959: 61–107). Pierre's trajectory as an intellectual and a man of politics reveals a reiterated attempt to master the course of events by a rationalisation of ideologies that he questions and evaluates by a constant self-criticism (Kasende 2000).

In the beginning of the novel, Pierre reveals his personal motives for becoming involved in Marxism: 'It's true, Marx was kind of in style' (Mudimbe 1973: 13). But his European brothers dissuade him from this path:

> *Sur Marx, Lénine, la Révolution et tous les autres mythes néfastes, ils se contentaient d'avoir des idées définitives qu'ils inculquaient aux élèves des écoles*
> (On Marx, Lenin, the Revolution and all the other harmful myths, they [my Flemish compatriots] were content to have definitive ideas that they ingrained in school students) (Mudimbe 1973: 13).

Speech used by the priests works towards increasing its own influence. It wants to colonise the thoughts of young African students in schools, without concerning itself with peace or social justice in Africa. Pierre revolts against a church that chooses to be involved in certain political actions, which are profitable for itself, but does not become involved in others.

> *À présent, se dit Pierre, je suis convaincu: la haine de la hiérarchie catholique pour tous les mouvements nationalistes relève partiellement d'une volonté nette de sauvegarder à tout prix des avantages injustifiés hérités de l'époque coloniale*
> ('Presently,' says Pierre, 'I am convinced: the Catholic hierarchy's hatred for all the nationalist movements stems partially from the clear desire to

save, at all costs, the unjustified advantages inherited from colonial times') (Mudimbe 1973: 38).

Pierre takes a stance against the church's institutionalised violence and against a symbolic violence that often passes through language: '*Comment accepter ces belles phrases violentes qui cachent trop bien leur poids de cadavres?*' (How to accept these beautiful, violent sentences that hide all too well their weight of dead bodies?) (Mudimbe 1973: 12). Pierre opts for a violent justice (10), seen as a necessary evil. That is the chief of the camp's opinion, for whom,

> *une lutte de libération se condamne dès qu'elle accepte des nuances entre le bon et le mauvais, dès qu'elle remet en cause, ne fût-ce qu'une fois, le bien-fondé de ses objectifs*
> (a struggle for liberation condemns itself the moment it accepts nuances between the good and the bad, the moment it questions, be it only one time, the solid foundation of its objectives) (Mudimbe 1973: 49).

The revolution is ethical in the sense that it does not compromise itself.

Pierre does not escape from a more in-depth interrogation into his epistemological condition, linked to his trajectory as a priest. He questions '*les phrases de la vie*': '*Ne les ai-je pas longtemps appréciées, aimées sur un plan purement esthétique et un peu conformiste?*' (Hadn't I appreciated them for a long time, liked them on a purely aesthetic level and a bit by conformism?) (Mudimbe 1973: 14). Pierre goes back and forth between ethical desires and aesthetic outpourings. Added to this conditioning is the question of the origins he feels he is betraying by espousing the alienating religious values of the West. When Father Howard wants to place him on the right track, far from Marxism, by reminding him that he is a priest, Pierre answers: '*Un prêtre noir*' (A black priest) (18). Pierre's words are projectiles causing Father Howard great anxiety. This malaise is returned to him like a boomerang when the chief of the camp tells Pierre that the Jesuits are his true masters. And that his drama is being both a black priest and a colonised intellectual (53).

Pierre often practises a Socratic irony as he wants to articulate truths and lies about his ambivalent experience as a priest/revolutionary, traitor/martyr, *Pietro* Christian/Landu African (Harrow 1990: 172–73). His personal itinerary exposes the story of an African religious culture dominated by ideologies that are strangers to him. The way to get away from the malaise of the colonised is wonderfully expressed in *L'écart*. The contradiction does not only touch discourse and Pierre's ideas, but also his actions. One day, he sees a soldier at the camp covered in blood. As a priest, he wants to save him, but the soldier spits in his face. Miss Poubelle (an authoritative feminine character with a deliberately entertaining name) asks Pierre to kill him, even though Pierre sees that the soldier is already dead. Pierre reflects on the absurd violence of the scene. However, he executes the soldier and gives himself the courage to do so by citing words from the Bible. Rerouting a religious quotation is used in the novel to critique the hypocrisy of religious language in a context of war. The violence appears here doubled in this ludicrous enunciation of violence.

The thematic violence in *Entre les eaux* does not only aim to critique the religious institution and the contradiction between language and action. It also targets Pierre, scrutinising himself, having interiorised mechanic gestures of masochist inspiration. First he complains about mosquito bites (*les nkusu*) attacking his body, then he accepts them:

> *Depuis quelque temps, les petits coups d'épingle m'apportent un plaisir indicible*
> (For some time now, the little bites bring me unspeakable pleasure)
> *Réveillé quelques heures plus tard, je me replonge dans ce que je considérais comme les signes de ma participation aux stigmates divins*
> (Waking a few hours later, I reimmerse myself in what I consider the signs of my participation in the divine stigmata) (Mudimbe 1973: 5).

The lexical irony ('divine stigmata') is intertwined to display the novel's mix of ethics and aesthetics. It consists of interpreting the mosquito bites (a trivial element) as a divine sign (a sacred element); meaning, it involves joining, in one figure, the antitheses: the low and high, suffering and pleasure, mixing pleasure and the impulse of death. Should we interpret this violence against oneself as a heresy against two alienating life practices or as an auto-censor of one's own indoctrination? Doubt remains.

The painting of violence

Le bel immonde, published in 1976, is a particularly distinct work in Mudimbe's trajectory, not only for the theme of marginality it holds in terms of lesbianism, homosexuality and power, according to Drocella Mwisha Rwanika (2003: 264–81), but also for the picturesque gaze proposed in order to decrypt the pieces of a social universe built on violence. The novel's violence involves the body and is sexual, but is also found in symbolic and power domination. *L'immonde* – the appalling, the foul, conjures religious notions of impurity and raises ethical and aesthetic questions, while paying homage to the war in love and the beauty in what is wrong. The appalling generates a textual violence that hides itself in the banality of discourse, in the everyday gesture, such as in the silence of Ya, who dreams, meditates and uses her critical thinking. The violence appears firstly in the imposing vulgarity of the opening scene. Ya searches for her prince to leave the vulgarity of her cumbersome and vain clients. These clients are described pejoratively: the 'debauchery of cigarette smoke', the 'overwhelming music' and the 'stench of alcohol':

> *Elle attend. Comme chaque soir. Les yeux mi-clos, elle sourit, la main droite caressant paresseusement son châle de soie. Elle espère toujours, cherche son seigneur, visiblement exaltée et lassée à la fois par cette musique envahissante qui l'englue dans une débauche de fumée de cigarettes et de relents d'alcool*
> (She is waiting. Like every night. Eyes half-closed, she smiles, her right hand lazily caressing her silk shawl. She always hopes, looks for her saviour, visibly exalted and tired by the overwhelming music that holds her in the debauchery of cigarette smoke and the stench of alcohol) (Mudimbe 1976: 17).

The languor established through her half-closed eyes, in her smile, in the slowness of her gestures, evokes her sensuality, behind which hides an ironic smile that constitutes the portrait's shadow. The painting of the detail that retains our attention indicates a general awareness of consciousness, such as the fact she is a victim of her illusions. Because Ya knows that she is in the act of dreaming, as is proved by the metatextual status of the song in *Le bel immonde*:

> *[Ya] aurait aimé danser; s'accrocher à Stefan George, se convaincre du mystére de son propre cœur de manière à pouvoir s'inscrire avec bonheur dans la mort des mots bien entretenus par la vie d'un air:*
> > *Ne les prends point au glaive, au trône!*
> > *De tout grade, les dignitaires ont tous l'œil*
> > *Vulgaire et charnel*
> > *Le même œil de bête à l'affût . . .*

([Ya] would have liked to be dancing; to be clinging to Stefan George, to be convinced of the mystery of her own heart so that she could enter joyfully into the death of words, so well preserved by the life of a melody:

Don't judge them by their swords or thrones!
All notables, of any rank, still have an eye
Coarse and carnal
The same raw look of a leering beast . . .) (Mudimbe 1976: 17).

The metatextual lexical field of the novel's characters displays, as Bisanswa (2000) highlights, the confidence of Pierre Landu, Ahmed Nara and Ya in words, susceptible to conjugating prose and the world. The text's silent violence often has the value of a warning: danger is imminent. The textual violence appears in the choice of words, the narrative structure and the picturesque representation of violence. The narration resembles an expressionist painting, where the work is, in a sense, cut into pieces: '*Les lumières tombaient en lanières multicolores. L'orchestre saignaient un slow. Des syncopes claires, charnues, jaillissent en cascade*' (Thus lights fell in multicoloured strips. The orchestra bled out a slow song. Clear and abundant musical syncopations gushed like a waterfall) (Mudimbe 1976: 71). The violence of language configures, in the detail, a totality in which the separate pieces give the characters their own aesthetic de-figuration:

C'est en passant devant la porte vitrée *qui conduisait à la cuisine qu'il se réveilla tout à fait et se rappela sa conversation avec le maître. Il s'arrêta un instant. Oui, c'est cela. Le* lampadaire *à côté duquel ils étaient* transformait *curieusement le visage du maître* [. . .]. *Son* strabisme *accusé* lui donnait une expression effrayante
(It was while passing in front of *the glass door* leading to the kitchen that he woke up suddenly and remembered his conversation with the master. He stopped an instant. Yes, that's it. The *lamp* beside him was curiously *transforming* the master's face [. . .]. His accusatory *squint gave him a frightening expression*) (Mudimbe 1976: 77, emphasis added).

The violence increases through the motif of the grip, tightening and crushing individuals. How many times are the characters in *Le bel immonde* squeezed until they basically pass out while dancing? The same phenomenon occurs in *L'écart*, when Nara complains about the pressure of Salim's hand (Mudimbe 1979: 22).

The grip, the clutch and the embrace are monstrous: they suggest the appalling character of an undesired proximity to the Other. The motif of crushing threatens the expressionist representation, bringing representation back to a plain surface, cubist, of the utterance and of its apparent banality.

The banality of the clichéd inaugural scene of *Le bel immonde*, where Ya waits for her client at a nightclub, is reminiscent of Edward Hopper's imagery in his painting *Nighthawks*. As in Hopper's painting, where a woman is sitting in a bar, waiting, a man staring at her, Ya's monotonous daily life follows the rhythm of repetitive scenes revolving around the same songs, the same men, in the same nightclub. But the banality is only in appearance. The same seems to be a utopia, a fact of the characters' discourse (which is most often an interior monologue). The characters become aware, regardless of their level of education, that subtle differences are hidden within the same. The novel denounces with apparent neutrality the violence of abuses done to a physical body (individual and social), exploited by the domination of power, by the popular belief in witchcraft, by greed and by fear. In *Le bel immonde*, literary criticism usually focuses solely on themes of adultery, treason, lesbianism, homosexuality, witchcraft, cannibalism. To this violence of the utterance, we must add an enunciation of violence. The mixing of parameters generates a modern work that is complex, worked by the hand of an artist.

Economic and sexual violence

Violence in *L'écart* begins with the awareness that culture is an ideological and symbolic prison leading to two impasses: alienation of the self and falsification of scientific sources on African culture. The idea of the lie of ethnological sources on Kouba culture blocks Nara in his doctoral thesis. The novel, however, highlights a new dimension of violence: economic and sexual. In Nara's eyes, his (girl)friend Isabelle symbolises Europe, economic power, the place of prejudice and stereotypes of Africans. More of an enemy than a lover, she reflects Nara's economic and sexual dependence, fruits of his humiliation. Beside Isabelle, Nara feels like a 'phallus' (Mudimbe 1979: 34) or a 'a clingy dog' (53). With Aminata, Nara seeks human and maternal warmth.

The relationship of infantilisation linking Nara to his two partners of different cultures, Isabelle and Aminata, reproduces an Oedipal-like scheme (Mouralis 1988: 125–28). With his status as sexual object, submissive and dependent, against that of the narrator-scribe, Nara liberates his voice and those of other characters in the novel: '*l'Afrique vierge et sans archives reconnues par [les] sciences [occidentales] est un terrain idéal pour tous les trafics*' (Virgin Africa and without archives recognised by Western sciences is an ideal terrain for all sorts of matters) (1979: 66). The affective and epistemological dependence Nara has on the West and on the mythical Africa of Western ethnographers, on Aminata, his lover reminiscent of a mother, and on Isabelle, the European, all stem from the same source – colonisation and stereotypes on the African subject: eternal child, eternal object.

For Nara, the deconstruction of these stereotypes passes through an interior revolution that takes place in language. The protagonist's symbolic weapon is the pen, ready to pour out a lot of ink: '*Je peux écrire aussi avec mon sang*' (I can also write with my blood) (Mudimbe 1979: 153). *L'écart*'s violent writing is the site of this cut, in the same way that Mudimbe's writing is the site of perpetual ruptures. The sentences are cut, unfinished. The language 'in hysteria' makes Nara write words of madness: '*Je déraille, c'est certain*' (I'm completely off my rocker, that's for sure) (149) and '*Un délire m'accueille*' (A frenzy welcomes me) (151).

Intersubjective violence

The violence of intersubjective relations, in the context of a war, is at stake in *Shaba deux* (Mudimbe 1989). Like Nara in *L'écart*, Marie-Gertrude has a journal. The events related in her 'notebooks' take place the night before the beginning of the Shaba wars in the Congo. Marie-Gertrude learns to detach herself little by little from *a* truth to get closer to *her* truth. She searches for a path in the enunciation of an individual and private faith, adapted to her daily life and surroundings. She must, to do so, place at a distance representations of faith incarnated by the Mother Superior and by Father Gasemans. Their faith conveys the precepts of an 'encultured' Christianity. Its major trait, or mission, is to transplant European representations of religion into Africa. Marie-Gertrude searches to define a belief that is in tune with her own daily life, meaning with the realism and violence of the war. We can observe a parallel between the protagonist's experiments and what Mudimbe affirms in his essay *L'odeur du Père*: '*l'ordre du Christianisme dans ses thèmes comme dans ses parcours historiques ne coïncide pas nécessairement avec celui des axiomes de la Foi*' (The order of Christianity in its themes, like in its historical path, does not necessarily coincide with the path of the axioms of Faith') (1982: 69).

Nara and Marie-Gertrude are the first and primary witnesses of their interior torments, but, contrary to Nara, Marie-Gertrude surpasses them in her actions.

Torn, firstly, between contemplation and action, she breaks the barrier of the paradox between biblical writings and her own daily life and manages to integrate them with reciprocity. While the brothers and sisters of the convent see Mary as the ideal figure of contemplation and Martha as a symbol of practice, Marie-Gertrude hesitates between reality and action. What path to follow, knowing that Mary is imposed on her by authority and that Martha responds more to her interior voice? As a nurse, Marie-Gertrude takes care of the injured, practises abortions, stays with young girls who are dying. How to contemplate the violence, when common sense favours action and the search for solutions?

> *Face à la croix, à d'autres symboles, je projette mon marché intérieur [. . .] L'action, seule, me rend adulte. Le Père Marc me rend raison. 'Marthe est celle qui est présente . . . Elle est seulement là. Prête à servir . . . Savoir être là, comme elle. L'eau qui fertilise, le souffle qui anime, la main qui nourrit. Elle entoure, couvre et soutient'*
> (Facing the cross, and other symbols, I project my interior progression [. . .] Only action makes me an adult. Father Marc correctly saw it in me: 'Martha is she who is present . . . She is alone there. Ready to serve . . . Know being here, like her. Water that fertilises, an animating gust of wind, the nourishing hand. She covers, surrounds and supports') (Mudimbe 1989: 38).

Marie-Gertrude exchanges her status of Mother Superior for only 'mother', which is ideal. In the eyes of others, Marie-Gertrude is a nun more than she is a woman. However, her feeling of revolt touches her gendered and sexual identity. Marie-Gertrude defines, in sum, universality and cultural diversity based on her own singular experience. The universal consists of being a woman, assuming her desire and her humanity. The cultural diversity is the right to affirm that there exists for her both an order of nature and a religious discourse. A dialogue between Marie-Gertrude and a young woman who just had an abortion illustrates this idea:

> *J'ai mal fait . . . Mes parents ne savent rien . . . Vous me condamnez, n'est-ce pas? Je lui tapotai l'épaule. Parce que je suis religieuse, elle s'attendait à un sermon*
> (I acted badly . . . My parents know nothing . . . You condemn me, right? I tapped on her shoulder. Because I am a nun, she expected a sermon) (Mudimbe 1989: 20).

In *Shaba deux*, the act of surpassing the conflict between religious discourse and nature, Africa and Europe, also appears through the voice of Father Marc. His voice comments on Marie-Gertrude's situation and signals that a truth imposed by another is not a truth (Mudimbe 1989: 40). He insinuates, through the fable, or parable, that religion should not serve as a pretext to justify our existence. The Father's meditation is the expression of a quest, an effort. It aspires towards an elevation, without necessarily pretending to achieve it. Mudimbe seems, in this excerpt from *Shaba deux*, to be commenting on his own trajectory. Is he not speaking to himself, borrowing the implicit path of a confession? Think again about the two priests' insinuations, as Mudimbe relates them in his autobiography, to reflect on the question. These priests, under the pretext of confessing that they no longer wish to be priests, seem to be verifying Mudimbe's religious convictions (1994: 22). We can extrapolate from these meditations that it is difficult to create a discourse on the Other and that it is difficult to rid oneself of one's own beliefs and prejudices, or to live with impunity in the schism. Ahmed Nara and Marie-Gertrude sacrifice their lives, the latter dying in conditions of extreme violence.

Conclusion

The singularity of Mudimbe's work resides notably in writing where the enunciation of violence, even more than what is said, is of primary importance. The enunciation of violence in the novels is not a homogenous entity. It assumes multiple forms: thematic, symbolic, epistemological, sexual, generic (and gendered). With Mudimbe came the '*ère de soupçon*' (era of suspicion), to quote Nathalie Sarraute's expression (1987), in the sense that the author contributes to the renewal of the foundations of the novel. Thanks to Mudimbe, the francophone novel turned towards itself, learned to cultivate its form and is profoundly characterised by self-reflexivity. The reference to the world is progressively transformed into a reference to the self – meaning, to literature. Self-reflexivity in Mudimbe's novels shows a way to be and to behave in the world. Mudimbe uses irony and several types of violence (verbal, religious, political, economic, sexual) with strength and audacity. The power of his writing lies in the way he paints violence, either with spectacular effects, or hiding it implicitly within discourse. He therefore uses strategies and figures such as insinuation, parables and metaphors, all commenting on the events being written.

In fact, the intrusion of the essay in the novel displays a literature that wishes to inscribe itself, albeit paradoxically, in a social practice. The novels have the ambition of reformulating the world and contributing to its understanding. Thus, with an implacable irony, Mudimbe calls upon a reflection on the irreducibility of Otherness. And we see how the metatext opens the text towards an outside, far from reference to the novel itself, appearing as a form of resistance towards the closedness of the literary realm. Mudimbe's novel, like any *objet d'art*, is part of a social context whose vision and discomfort it reveals. Fundamentally characterised by heterogeneity, *Entre les eaux*, *L'écart*, *Shaba deux* and *Le bel immonde* all adopt tunes, rhythms and accents, depending on context, mixing fiction with meditation and dream. Thus, Mudimbe's novels propose an image of the human condition in which life, governed by fate, finds in social degeneration and generic hybridity an exact, but gloomy metaphor of modernity. The expected social and cultural repercussions are an awareness of human diversity and a great attention in order not to forget that the self cannot be without the Other. The francophone novel always tells relations between people and cultures. In the realm of diversity, the writer aspires to find a singular speech.

Mudimbe also analyses, in his theory of the novel, the source of misunderstandings and of stereotypes in the 'colonial library'. All of this suggests that Mudimbe's novels express a political and social history as much as a literary one. But his fictions construct and deconstruct this history laterally. The story is that of colonisation. In spite of the enunciative ruptures and detours of thought, Mudimbe never ceases his relentless examination of the search for truth. The desire to express the world is articulated by a discursive strategy, the dominant strategy of the dialectic of the subject, bringing forth paradoxes of social and human sciences that captivate Mudimbe. The question of the Other (the Other sex, class, culture, the distant Other or the intimate Other, the Other in ourselves) remains the ultimate question in Mudimbe's novels.

Note

1. All translations, unless otherwise noted, are the author's own.

References

Badiou, Alain. 1993. *L'éthique*. Paris: Hatier.

Baudelaire, Charles. 1961. *Œuvres complètes*. Paris: Gallimard.

Bisanswa, Justin. 2000. *Conflit de mémoires: V.Y. Mudimbe et la traversée des signes*. Frankfurt: Iko-Verlag für Interkulturelle Kommunikation.

———. 2012. 'Présentation: Scénographies romanesques africaines de la modernité'. *Présence francophone* 78: 5–14.

Bourdieu, Pierre. 1992. *Les règles de l'art: Genèse et structure du champ littéraire*. Paris: Seuil.

Césaire, Aimé. 1970. *Les armes miraculeuses*. Paris: Gallimard.

Harrow, Kenneth W. 1990. 'V.Y. Mudimbe's *Entre les eaux*: The Literature of the Oxymoron'. In *Literature of Africa and the African Continuum*, edited by Jonathan A. Peters and Mildred P. Mortimer, 163–75. Washington, DC: Three Continents and African Literature Association.

Kasende, Jean Christophe. 2000. 'L'ironie comme modalité de réévaluation des discours hégémoniques dans *Entre les eaux* de V.Y. Mudimbe'. *Études littéraires* 33(1): 169–85.

Mouralis, Bernard. 1988. *V.Y. Mudimbe ou le discours, l'écart et l'écriture*. Paris: Présence Africaine.

Mudimbe, V-Y. 1973. *Entre les eaux: Dieu, un prêtre, la révolution; roman*. Paris: Présence Africaine.

———. 1976. *Le bel immonde: Récit*. Paris: Présence Africaine.

———. 1979. *L'écart*. Paris: Présence Africaine.

———. 1982. *L'odeur du Père*. Paris: Présence Africaine.

———. 1989. *Shaba deux: Les carnets de Mère Marie-Gertrude*. Paris: Présence Africaine.

———. 1994. *Les corps glorieux des mots et des êtres: Esquisse d'un jardin africain à la bénédictine*. Paris: Présence Africaine and Montreal: Humanitas.

Reverdy, Pierre. 1989. *Le livre de mon bord: Notes 1930–1936*. Paris: Mercure de France.

Rwanika, Drocella Mwisha. 2003. 'V.Y. Mudimbe: Écrivain de l'écart ou de la norme?' In *L'Afrique au miroir des littératures, des sciences de l'homme et de la société: Mélanges offerts à V.Y. Mudimbe*, edited by Mukala Kadima-Nzuji and Sélom Komlan Gbanou, 264–81. Paris: L'Harmattan and Bruxelles: Archives et Musée de la littérature.

Sarraute, Nathalie. 1987 [1956]. *L'ère du soupçon: Essais sur le roman*. Paris: Gallimard.

Weber, Max. 1959. *Le savant et le politique*. Paris: Plon.

CHAPTER 5

Making Visible and Eradicating Congo's History of Violence
Maiming the Female/National Body

Ngwarsungu Chiwengo

They cut one ear from someone and left him another. They forced a woman to have sexual relations with her son. If she refuses, they kill her . . . They had a breast cut off a woman and left her another . . . They obliged a boy to have sex with his mother, if not they kill him.

> — Edmond Boelaert, Honoré Vinck and Charles Lonkama,
> '*Arrivée des blancs sur les bords des rivières équatoriales*'

They went after my daughter, and I knew they would rape her. But she resisted and said she would rather die than have relations with them. They cut off her left breast and put it in her hand. They said, 'Are you still resisting us?' She said she would rather die than be with them. They cut off her genital labia and showed them to her. She said, 'Please kill me.' They took a knife and put it to her neck and then made a long vertical incision down her chest and split her body open. She was crying but finally she died. She died with her breast in her hand.

> — Human Rights Watch, *The War within the War*

It was disconcerting, as I wrote this essay for the colloquium on 'Violence in/and the Great Lakes: The Thought of V-Y Mudimbe and Beyond', that my childhood in Congo began with the Indonesian United Nations peacekeepers; in my late adulthood, they (the United Nations Organization Stabilization Mission in the Democratic Republic of the Congo or MONUSCO) still cruise the roads of Goma, Bukavu and Lubumbashi, silently observing the March 23 Movement (M23) perpetuate their terror in Kiwandja.[1] The early childhood adult tales of the deaths of Pastor Sendwe and Pastor Mwamba haunt my present, yet we speak again of the Mai-Mai leader, Gédéon Kyungu Mutanga, who terrorises north and central Katanga and is known to wear a necklace of human sex organs around his neck as a sign, I presume, of virility and power. In the 1960s, the United Nations marked its presence with 'USA oil not for sale'; today, it is with the United Nations' tarps used for a variety of purposes – such as providing mourning friends and families with refuge from the elements. The woman chopped into pieces in upper Katanga, the refugees from Moba, the women buried alive in Mwenga, the massacred children, men and women in the Kivus remind me again of the *zingzongs* (specialised security units' killers), the *hibous* (security units' killers referred to as owls), the massacre of the students at the University of Lubumbashi, the disembowelled pregnant women on their way to the hospital in Lubumbashi, the raped grandmothers with fistulas in both north and central Katanga and the raped babies, boys, girls, grandmothers, women and men in the Kivus.

The cycle of violence in post-independence Democratic Republic of the Congo (DRC) is, ironically, not limited to our era, but has its genesis in the Congo Free State, as the similarities between the two epigraphs at the beginning of this chapter (from 1904 and 2006) demonstrate. Violence is the quintessence of the Congo; it is the site of 'horror,' according to Joseph Conrad's Kurtz (1981), and one inextricably intertwined with the history of colonialism, as is demonstrated by '*Congo Mbolo Matadi*' (Congo Penis Matadi) – a pun on '*Congo Bula-Matari*' by women in southern Africa in the 1960s. These women understood very well the phallic relationship between violence, rape and power in colonial Congo where, Julie and Herman Schwendinger claim: 'The *Force Publique* of the Congo, a native colonial army, adopted the ethos of their imperial Belgian masters; they too raped and plundered Congolese people' (1981: 14). My grandfather's tears when he told stories of people being whipped (*balimu pika fimbo*) were an eloquent testimony to the violence and pain of an era long gone. Has the Congo not been dubbed 'the capital of rape' and has not violence been so normalised that the phrase 'crimes against humanity' – coined in the Congo a century ago by George Washington Williams – fails to capture any meaningful response to the violence? As Lindsay Hilsum reminds us:

> Williams wrote an open letter from Kisangani to King Leopold of Belgium, protesting at the forced labour, torture and massacres visited on the native workers . . . Such practices began under the colonial regime, and continued during the reign of Mobutu Sese Seko. Now they are happening under the auspices of the new power in the land (1997: 9).

Violence is, indeed, a trademark of the DRC. Since 1996, however, the massacres, mutilations and the rapes of both women and men that resulted from foreign-initiated invasions, have been observed with indifference by an international community less concerned with the stories of the wounded than with those of the machete wielders. It is, therefore, with gratitude that I was able to attend the Thinking Africa colloquium and to share my thoughts on the nature, significance and implications of violence for the Congolese nation and its citizens. Most of all, I was grateful to make the wounds of Congolese people tell their stories, so that we can feel their pain because, as Josué Mufula Jive writes in *Enfant de guerre*: '*Lorsque une plaie n'est pas sur votre proper corps, on ne peut pas estimer valablement la douleur qu'elle cause*' (When a wound is not on your own body, it is impossible to accurately gauge the pain it generates) (2006: 39).

V-Y Mudimbe and violence

V-Y Mudimbe, around whom our conversation on violence revolves, is very familiar with the nature of violence, having experienced the brutality of Mobutu's Congo when he was incarcerated, along with National University of Zaïre professors Mufuta, Kinyongo and Bola, for protesting the low wages of the faculty. He also experienced first hand the Hutu/Tutsi violent conflicts. It is therefore unsurprising that political violence and war are major themes in his fiction and autobiography – *Les corps glorieux des mots et des êtres* (1994) and *Cheminements* (2006), which chronicles his intellectual and daily activities during a stay in Berlin while he ponders the life of Conrad and his *Heart of Darkness* (1981), which coined the metaphor of the Congo as site of horror and violence. In the same space where the Berlin conference was once held, Mudimbe reflects on the arbitrary geographical divisions of the African continent, which have led to the loss of millions of innocent human lives and notes the horrifying nature of Adam Hochschild and Thomas Pakenham's accounts of violence in the Congo. Intrigued by the absence of violence in Isidore Ndaywel è Nziem's *Histoire générale du Congo*, Mudimbe muses on how an intellectual and historian could erase such monumental events from the collective memory, while also reminding us – in 'Save the African Continent,' a review of an article by Achille Mbembe – how he himself had participated, through his four novels and essays, in the *déballage* (exposure) of the failings of post-independence rulers, such as Mobutu, who imitated their colonial predecessors. Indeed, Mudimbe has made visible the ethnic conflicts and the maimed bodies of women on which the battles for power are inscribed in his fiction. Does this history of trauma, he wonders in *Cheminements*, originate from colonial brutality and arbitrary boundaries and is it necessary to return to our historical roots in order to exorcise the demons of that violence? Is it possible, he asks, to manage the present more adequately through the imagination? We have had enough of masochism, he contends, and so it is time 'to balance our critiques with concrete and programmatic projects' (1992: 62).

Through his fiction, Mudimbe most certainly imagines a better future for the Congo and reflects on the status and role of women and the violence they have endured in Congolese society. *Le bel immonde* (1976) and *Shaba deux* (1989) depict the incompetence of post-independence leaders, Congolese conflicts and the centrality of the female body on which male/national domination is inscribed. These two novels respectively portray the conflicts of the 1960s and 1970s when women were raped en masse in Kisangani during the Mai-Mai insurgency. While *Le bel immonde* delineates the political corruption and organisation of political power in the 1960s from the perspective of individual consciousness, *Shaba deux* – as Kasereka Kavwahirehi points out in *V.Y. Mudimbe et la ré-invention de l'Afrique* (2006) – focuses on the 1978 Front for the National Liberation of the Congo (FNLC) invasion of Kolwezi. It is the lack of governmental organisation that, according to Mudimbe, has sent the country adrift:

> *Des structures héritées de la colonie tournent à vide, disloquées, incohérentes. Il n'existe point un accord social, un contrat originel à partir duquel, dans la cite africaine, le mot d'Aristote pourrait avoir un sens: c'est la Cite qui doit enseigner les valeurs au citoyens*
> (Inherited colonial structures turned empty, dislocated, incoherent. There is no social agreement, an original contract from which, in the African city, Aristotle's words can have meaning: It is the city that should teach values to citizens) (1994: 54).

It is power, he contends, that creates monsters who deem themselves above the law, rape and mutilate women to assert their dominance and who contaminate the nation by failing to consider the citizen as a person who can be gazed at and comprehended as 'self'.

In *Le bel immonde* and *Shaba deux*, Mudimbe examines the devastating consequences of the concept of alterity, which entails a subjective gaze and the submission of another to one's own gaze, as he contends in *Réflexions sur la vie quotidienne* (1972). He also explores the devastating effects of phallic power manifest through race and religion. *Le bel immonde* delineates the domestic and cultural oppression of the minister's spouse and his oppressive relationship with his lover Ya, whom he subjugates through violence perpetuated on the body of her friend for daring to talk about Ya's entrapment and need of freedom. During the friend's ritual sacrifice, he consumes and subsumes her and, following this cannibalistic act, it is his gaze that causes Ya, now ashamed and in despair, to lose her voice and to direct her own gaze at the floor. Ya subsequently loses her voice again during her interactions with the rebels who brutalise and objectify her. Similarly, and despite her attempt to escape domestic entrapment, Marie- Gertrude in *Shaba deux*, experiences the same confinement, patriarchal marginalisation and racial Othering within the convent. Wishing to help her people during the war, she becomes the object of military violence when she is found mutilated after an interrogation. As he endangered his own life during the Mobutu era by portraying the Congolese wars inflicted on female bodies, Mudimbe affirms his responsibility and commitment to national and individual freedom and respect for female subjectivities. He denounces the violence of these wars and also the patriarchal subjugation and oppression of women, which he highlights, ponders and rejects. His literary works and essays articulate his desire to de-alienate the African woman and to free her from violence and African traditional practices. Most importantly, his fictional works compel us to think beyond the literary in order to interrogate current war practices that perpetuate the conquest and subjugation of women and assert hatred through the mutilations of their bodies.

Ambiguities in Congo war discourses

While Mudimbe is the focal point of this colloquium, it is the nature of violence in/and the Great Lakes region that we seek to explore. Though the violence in the DRC has been widely represented in the media, it has failed to provoke general empathy and a will to action. Although the violence has consisted of both internal rebellions and foreign invasions, the media has until very recently characterised it as Congolese self-inflicted. Even though the Congolese have maintained, since the beginning of the DRC conflicts, that they were not simply civil wars but invasions, the international community has consistently pointed to the Congolese government, ethnicity and Congolese xenophobia as root causes of the problem. As Hilsum (1997) claims, these stories, produced by the media to fit 'the Procrustean bed', have often been full of omissions and disinformation. The

Congo and its population have, moreover, been discursively assaulted both from within and outside of the Congo; internally, by a government that has denied both foreign human rights atrocities and its own involvement in perpetrating these, and externally by the 'genocide story' that has consistently superseded all other Congolese stories. Tellingly, Paul Richards states:

> War itself is a type of text – a violent attempt to 'tell a story' or to 'cut in on the conversation' of others from whose company the belligerents feel excluded. Understanding war as text and discourse is not an intellectual affectation, but a vital necessity, because only when 'war talk' is fully comprehended is it possible for conciliators to outline more pacific options in softer tones (1996: xxiv).

If war is a discourse that needs interpretation and comprehension, the conversation on the DRC is stifled both inside and outside the Congo because tactics to traumatise, disorient and demoralise the Congolese nation are continuously devised to cover the looting, the massacres and the depopulation of territories and to promote the economic, political and ethical interests of certain multinational corporations and/ or nation-states. Nowhere else is this violence more forcefully inscribed than on the body of the (Congolese) female who is also representative of the Congo nation. As Achille Mbembe contends:

> Male domination derives in large measure from the power and the spectacle of the phallus – not so much from the threat to life during war as from the individual male's ability to demonstrate his virility at the expense of a woman and to obtain its validation from the subjugated woman herself (2001: 23).

It thus behoves intellectuals and academics to cut in on the conversation with critical analyses, even as the events are unfolding, in order to counteract representations of the conflict that are informed by foreign national politics and interests.

But can the DRC actually speak or appropriate language when its voice, along with its population, has been so marginalised and constructed as the 'primordial Other', distinct from its rational and organised neighbours; its men depicted as immature and irresponsible delinquents who wallow in promiscuous sexuality, dance and music? Can the Congo's wounds tell their stories as long as the country remains associated with atavism, the practice of cannibalism and a 'return to the jungle' (as was indeed suggested, albeit figuratively, by Ted Koppel's *Still the Heart of Darkness*)? Can this land of extreme darkness, cannibalism and immorality, a country inhabited by people who apparently lack all subjectivity, ever elicit sufficient empathy in order for it to intervene, perhaps even manipulate, in the interpretation and reading of its own narrative? Certainly, the ethnological gaze that defines the Congolese as Other, the ecological gorilla narratives that accompany Western stories of Congolese trauma, combined with the power of the single Rwandan genocide narrative that still dominates the Congolese voice and its violence, suggest otherwise. Even though there exist Congolese first-person narratives embedded in Western newspaper articles and human rights narratives, these voices seldom, if ever, determine the emplotment, word choices and images that accompany their stories.

The current nationalist Congolese ideology, which promotes *la liberation de la modernité* (liberation through modernity), and the absence of Independence Day parades, seeking to otherwise foster national unity among the nation through all provinces' empathy with eastern Congolese compatriots, have, however, transformed national discourse and centred the Congolese in international conversations. For several years, the national political discourse was ambiguous because, while there was a distinctly wronged victim, there was at best an amorphous perpetrator of violence, at times defended and even spoken for. Even as the discourse on violence, rape and trauma has become more nationalistic (through, for instance, the naming of the perpetrator), the enemy remains nameless within international discourses – as was evident in the 2013 declarations that President Obama made from Tanzania when he called upon Congo's nebulous 'neighbours' to stop funding the rebel groups, as well as the most recent United Nations Security Council debate on the Congo and its recommendations.

Our conversation at this Thinking Africa colloquium has also contributed to this marginalisation of the Congolese tragedy – particularly the eastern Congo – for the actors within these conflicts, their desiderata and the geographical space in which the Congolese people experience violence, have remained nebulous. This spatial ambiguity was intensified by the phrase 'Great Lakes' that we used to refer to eastern Congo. Indeed, 'Great Lakes region' suggests an entity spatially external to the Congo. Great Lakes, in my opinion, conflates Congolese conflicts, violence and rapes with all other regional acts of horror that are connected, or disconnected, to the Congolese reality. Perhaps it also explains why, in many contributions to this volume, violence is often theorised in a manner that is neutral, non-engaged and universalising.

In an unpublished paper, 'Bestialisation, Dehumanisation and Counter-Interstitial Voices: (Mis)-Representations of Congo (DRC) Conflicts and Rape', I argue that the term *Grands Lacs* (Great Lakes) was first used during Belgian colonisation, more specifically, at a time when Ruanda-Urundi was a protectorate of Belgium. According to Francoise de Moor and Jean-Pierre Jacquemin (2000: 46–47), it is Rwanda and Burundi, referred to as the two countries of the Great Lakes to represent the Congo (guess why?) that are confused, in the term Great Lakes, with Congo through the surreptitious Rwandan images utilised by the Belgian rulers. Conversely, recent use of the phrase *les pays des Grands Lacs* (the Great Lakes countries) severs eastern Congo from its nation – a severance nowhere more apparent than in statements such as those made by Timothy Smock in his testimony before the Congressional Human Rights Caucus when he claimed: 'The Great Lakes Region in general and Zaire in particular experienced a great dramatic turn of events starting in September 1996' (Smock 1996). In this manner, eastern Congo (localised within the Great Lakes region) becomes, through the conjunction 'and', meaning an addition, an entity entirely distinct from Zaire. *The New World Encyclopedia* corroborates this by defining the Great Lakes region as a term referring to the 'area lying between northern Lake Tanganyika, western Lake Victoria, and lakes Kivu, Edward and Albert. This comprises Burundi, Rwanda, northeastern Democratic Republic of Congo, Uganda, and northwestern Kenya and Tanzania'.[2] Intriguingly, all the countries, except Congo and Kenya, are nominally referred to in the above enumeration of countries that comprise the Great Lakes region. Tellingly, Wikipedia's representation of the populations of the Great Lakes region in 2011 let slip the ideological will to conceptualise eastern Congo as a Rwandan territory and to affirm the arbitrariness of its borders (although the border arbitrariness of Belgium, encompassing two different ethnicities, was not underscored) by emphasising the affinity of its population with that of Rwanda. Indeed, according to this entry, eastern Congo has Kinyarwanda-speaking people; its territory used to be under the influence of the Rwandan monarchy and it has local slave populations – 'the Bashi, Bafulero, and Batetela [*sic*]' – that were integrated by the Tutsi.

Interestingly, before the 1996 crises, the Kivus were not considered entities of the Great Lakes countries, even though at the time there was much talk of the Economic Community of the Great Lakes Countries (ECGLC), but they were consigned to a Great Lake 'sub-region', an administrative area within the Congo. Numerous Internet articles discuss the rapes in Congo under the rubric of the 'Great Lakes'. There appears to be a conflation of the rapes that occur in the Congo with those in Rwanda, a blurring of space in articles such as 'Eleven DR Congo Soldiers Facing "Mobile Gender Court" on Mass Rape' (GLV Correspondent 2011) and 'The Impact of HIV on the Rape Crisis in the African Great Lakes Region' (Hentz 2005). Yet, in 2011, when Father Steven Ochieng reported a massacre in north-western Kenya, the area in question was specifically referred to as 'north-western Kenya' and *not* the Great Lakes region.[3] By the same token, we do not refer to the 'Great Lakes genocide', but rather to the 'Rwandan genocide', nor are Kenyan and Tanzanian conflicts or activities referred to in such vague terms. It seems as if eastern Congo has become, like Bukavu at the time of the dismantling of the Rwandan Hutu refugee camps, merely the site where the Rwandan crisis continues to unfold; a foil to the Rwandan genocide, sometimes even conflated with Rwanda. Indeed, articles such as Global Security's 'Congo Civil War' and certain documentaries – such as *The Greatest Silence* (2008) – that deal with the topic of Congolese massacres and rape ultimately obliterate its trauma and violence by foregrounding the neighbouring country's worse tragedy, while reducing the Congo invasion and subsequent conflicts to 'mere' civil wars.[4] When they are not referred to as civil wars, the dead of Rwanda and eastern Congo are conflated. For example, Dana Montague and Frida Berrigan (2001) give a total of four million victims that have died in both Rwanda and eastern Congo, but this combined figure was reached by collapsing the more than three million Congolese who had died at the time with the 800 000 Rwandans. This conflation of countries is nowhere more apparent than in the same article's use of the nebulous third person when speaking of the deaths, the lack of health services and ethnic conflicts. I will therefore avoid using 'Great Lakes' to refer to the unfolding Congolese tragedy, even though both the DRC and the international community have adopted this terminology that leaves the Kivus severed, occupied by Rwanda or indirectly controlled through the M23 rebels.

Violence in eastern Congo

While Mudimbe's fiction demonstrates the mobilisation of power and the domination inscribed on female bodies, the continual violence and heinous rapes in eastern Congo these past years remain perplexing and troubling. Despite their obvious economic and political contexts, the rapes have been naturalised as a culturally specific, Congolese characteristic and, additionally, have become political currency, much like yesterday's red rubber or today's coltan, gold and diamonds. The DRC has been dubbed the 'capital of rape' and the horror and violence inflicted on the bodies of women in the eastern Congo have been commodified, converted into the currency of political discourses aimed at expressing the inexpressible pain and trauma of the country. This is so, despite the fact that, as Nancy Hunt (2009) argues, the amputated hands and feet on public display during King Léopold's era (1885–1908) and the 1904 rapes of Congolese women – which at the time could not be heard through European mediated representations – can clearly be heard today through the women's depositions before King Léopold's Commission of Enquiry. Still, the mediated voices of contemporary Congolese raped women, men, girls, boys and babies fail to be heeded in both national and international representational spaces. Rape and fistulas have become slogans for humanitarian and political action against national trauma, aggression and the destruction of the social fabric of Congolese society. Yet, if we are to create a better future in which Congolese human and, specifically, women's rights are to be respected, national recognition through an in-depth public discussion of rape will be an indispensable part of a larger process of re-envisioning Congolese female ontology that will have to start by reimagining Congolese educational, political, religious and gender discourses. If violence and rapes are to cease, the Congolese people must also embrace and assert their subjectivity, value and centrality as human beings and as a people.

Congolese female ontology appears to be non-existent, in as much as she was first defined, reshaped and modelled as complementary to her spouse during the colonial era, later liberated through both Patrice Lumumba and Mobutu's political agendas and given parity by United Nations' charters. Childlike, she is to be guided, spoken for and elevated to modernity by the international community. As a result, her suffering and pain are therefore often met with indifference or apathy and normalised by a culture in which men have no respect for women. This woman, for whom we are called upon to have empathy, is a body on which 'tribe', alterity, and inferiority are inscribed. As in the case of the cake in the shape of a naked black woman created by the artist Makode Aj Linde, which Swedish culture minister, Lena Adelsohn Liljeroth, cut into – which was supposed to elicit empathy in order to bring the African woman into modernity, but which engendered international protest against Swedish racism – the Congolese woman's cries and pain remain feeble and inaudible because of her Otherness – projected on to the cake by the 'tribal' markings, the racialised history inscribed on the black icing of the cake body and her 'primitivism', signalled by her sagging breasts.[5] Indeed, as I have demonstrated elsewhere (Chiwengo 2008), Congolese women's rapes become visible only when more than 200 000 women are raped; and, discouragingly, even though these rapes have resulted in diminishing the violence in eastern Congo and generating an outpouring of numerous and significant humanitarian contributions, the rapes continue and the economic empowerment of most women remain relatively low today.

So why does the plight of Congolese women not engender much more empathy and why does the international action aimed at protecting the population appear hesitant and, at times, misguided? I believe it is largely because numerous titles of newspaper articles on the DRC conflicts and violence allude to Conrad's *Heart of Darkness*, with the result that the violence is normalised as a natural condition of the country and its people. Certainly, the numerous references to violence and mutilated Congolese bodies in the fiction of, for example, Langston Hughes, Wole Soyinka and Chimamanda Ngozi Adichie, corroborate the idea that the DRC has become a metaphor of violence and horror as such.

The literature on the rape of Congolese women and the violence they are subjected to reveals, moreover, that they are almost monolithically defined as uneducated and culturally submissive. Human rights and newspaper reports generally foreground their cultural and legal subordination. Wikipedia, one of the most accessible sites for general Internet readers, in the entry 'Women in the Democratic Republic of the Congo', states:

> Women have not attained full equality with men, with their struggle continuing to this day. Although the Mobutu regime paid lip service to the important role of women in society, and although women enjoy some legal rights (e.g. the right to own property and the right to participate in the economic and political sectors), custom and legal constraints still limit their opportunities.[6]

The numerous woes reinforcing Congolese women's inferiority, embedded in the indigenous social system, include female genital mutilation, women's status during colonisation, family codes of law that restrict their freedom while submitting them to their spouses and political under-representation. It would most certainly be preposterous to assume that culture and the codes of family laws do not subordinate Congolese women. But this is not a uniquely Congolese characteristic in as much as women are globally oppressed. Nonetheless, it behoves researchers and other writers on the DRC to provide a more heterogeneous representation of women – rural, urban, educated, uneducated, professional, stay-at-home mothers and so on – in order to trace the development of women's ontology historically, rather than to essentialise their womanhood. Certainly, the Wikipedia article quoted above notes that women dominate the market trade and that women in certain ethnic groups, notably the Lemba, have better lives. Yet the majority of newspapers' and non-governmental organisations' descriptions of Congolese women focus on the labour exploitation of women, who carry heavy burdens on their backs, while harnessed like mules. These women are, concomitantly, depicted as courageous and resilient, as 'just learning to be self-sufficient' when they are assisted with start-up money for a trade or a sewing machine – as in the case of the woman described in an entry of the International Rescue Committee's blog, as having become 'financially independent for the first time in their lives'.[7] Yet, when one listens attentively to the interstitial kiSwahili utterances of women in Eric Metzgar's *Reporter* (2009) and the Pulitzer Center's video, *World Focus: Rape as a Weapon of War in Congo*, it is clear that some of these women worked and were indeed productive prior to the rapes.[8] As the women in the film and the video respectively contend, 'they farmed' and their husbands sold goods. In *World Focus*, Georgine Kaseke claims: 'I was well off before. I had goats, I had gardens, and I was selling ten bags of *bilikalika*.' Georgina's spouse, Andre Shakakere, confirms they were well off before. Contrary to the dissemination of international images of powerless Congolese women lacking economic direction, this and other videos and films clearly illustrate the pre-conflict productivity of the Congolese and how they have become powerless because of the war and its attendant sexual violence.

Such negative explanations of the condition of Congolese women before and after the Congo conflicts also reinforce the assumed barbarity of Congolese men, while eliding the participation of other rebel groups and the peacekeepers in the rape and exploitation of women. Young girls and women were most certainly vulnerable to military advances because of poverty, but this does not exculpate the invading armies. Yet, the pornography and paedophilia of peacekeepers have been forgotten and when Ugandan soldiers were in the news for their sexual exploits, the starvation of the women and their eagerness to leave with the soldiers were often the focus of the articles.

Even though all rebel groups and peacekeepers have raped women during these conflicts, Congolese soldiers, the Mai-Mais and the Interahamwes have been the major culprits. Interestingly, in Lisa Jackson's *The Greatest Silence*, the Congolese soldiers are featured numerous times in the filmic narrative – even though all parties including Tutsis, Mai-Mais, Congolese and Hutus have committed the sexual atrocities – and are depicted as barbaric and irresponsible men who have failed to protect their women. Currently, the *génocidaire* Interahamwe and the Congolese army appear to be responsible for the majority of heinous crimes. Yet, the Congolese army, despite its propensity to rape, as Dénis Mukwege argues, has never been regulated since the postcolonial era, has been corrupted by the numerous militia amalgamations of past conflicts and been destabilised by the integration of foreign elements (in Braeckman 2012: 93-96).

No matter who perpetuates the atrocities on Congolese women, the perpetrators need to be held accountable for their crimes. But this accountability, despite the existence of zero-tolerance laws, has not been forthcoming. The peacekeepers' punishments, promised to be enacted in their respective countries, have to date not taken place; Congolese perpetuators easily escape their prisons and others, such as Laurent Nkunda Batware and Bosco Ntaganda, were rewarded with house arrests and protection in neighbouring Rwanda and The Hague. Would the gang-raped women – shot in the vagina and stabbed; sticks, rifles and glass thrust into their vaginas; mutilated and petrol poured into their vaginas – be met with indifference, denied an international tribunal and justice, had they been American, British or French? In addition to this indifference, how can human trafficking elicit empathy while Congolese sex slaves are considered the norm? Are the raped three-year-olds, grandmothers, teenagers and babies not people or human? Are the mothers forced to have sex with their sons, fathers with their daughters, brothers with their sisters and fathers forced to hold their daughters' legs while soldiers rape them not subjects worthy of justice? Would these atrocities go unpunished if the Congolese were considered ethical people with subjectivities akin to those who create, repair and invent?

Concrete action

It is this apathy and the combined feelings of violation and helplessness that have fuelled Congokazi: Congo Woman Association's desire to make Congolese female voices heard and to bring an indigenous voice to the war discourse. But this intellectual female Congolese voice has proved difficult to negotiate and to insert into the international public space, where Congolese women are always spoken for or their voices embedded within the voice-over of governmental, diasporic males and Western females. This is a voice often marginalised and willed to silence as is evident in videos such as Friends of the Congo's *Crisis in the Congo: Uncovering the Truth* (2011), where women's voices remain peripheral. Indeed, a woman in Kivu complained to Congokazi two years ago: 'Our stories of rape have been appropriated by men. We cannot even tell our stories.' Yet, this female voice has to be launched into the international public space so that Congolese women can become visible, so that their gaze and their horrendous experiences can reconfigure the images and reality of war.

In November 2009, the displacement of Congolese people and the mass rapes of 200 000 women denied them their humanity. Women were objectified through rape, the Congolese nation itself was humiliated and the value of our national identity and selfhood diminished. Because Congolese women were denied the right to justice and liberty, we women within the United States diaspora organised a march in Washington, DC to affirm our subjectivities, our need for justice and our humanity. The continual massacres of the Congolese population and the rapes of women also took us to New York City in an attempt to humanise the numbers and give visibility to the suffering of Congolese women.

Our first objective was to humanise Congolese women and men; the former, because they have only a few voices on the international scene that, while addressing the horrors these women have been experiencing, generally do not address the economic and political causes of the violence; the latter because he is often depicted as a sadistic and irrational sexual predator, incapable of creating a society. While women's pain and terror are often, to some extent, visible in the public space, perpetrators hide behind the invisibility afforded them by their amalgamated identity: 'merciless, immoral and disgruntled Mai-Mai', 'Congolese rebels' and 'soldiers involved in civil war'. But the rapes of Congolese women were/are never random, violent occurrences; rather, they are sadistic and abnormal acts that, through the cutting off of lips and ears, through the mutilations of female sexual organs, attempt to silence and destroy, also, the social/national body – as was suggested by the statement of a soldier in *The Greatest Silence* (2008). As these soldiers departed, they left behind them not only traces of their violence – scars, cuts and corpses – to tell the phallic story of their dominance and conquest, but also sorrow, broken souls and broken communities. As one woman stated at the 2011 Congokazi Bukavu convention: 'Our village suffers from collective trauma. If you were raped, your neighbor's wife, daughter, child, mother, or grandmother was raped. Your neighbor was killed, cut, or mutilated.'

More often than not, the wars waged in the name of democracy and the violence in the DRC are depicted as the immediate consequence of the Rwandan genocide. For this reason, it is imperative for women to enter the conversation so that we can contribute to the creation of a third space, where additional perspectives, the experiences of evil and transgressions can be heard and discussed. One such additional perspective to have emerged from the war narrative carved on the flesh of Congolese women is that the conflicts have been driven by a war economy, which turned these conflicts into profitable means for the perpetrators' acquisition of resources, visibility and power.

Raped women are not alone in feeling powerless, worthless and culpable because the rapes of Congolese women demoralised both women and men in as much as rape has been used as a strategy to both destroy the social fabric and humiliate Congolese for having 'failed' to protect their women. As Mukwege stated so passionately at the United Nations:

> How can one be proud of belonging to a nation without defences, fighting itself, completely pillaged and powerless in the face of 500,000 of its girls raped during 16 years; 6,000,000 of its sons and daughters killed during 16 years without any lasting solution in sight? No, I do not have the honour nor the privilege to be here today. My heart is heavy (Mukwege 2012).

Despite the indiscriminate nature of the rapes, it is now incontestable – given the various stories from the field, the testimonies of soldiers in *The Greatest Silence*, Human Rights Watch's *The War within the War* and Mukwege's declaration – that the most heinous rapes have been committed by foreign soldiers. These rapes are not random war crimes; they are economically induced acts of unspeakable violence committed with the intent to destabilise and disorganise Congolese society so that rebels, neighbouring countries and multinational corporations can have access to niobium, tantalum, gold and land. How else does one explain the continual depopulation of certain territories under rebel control and the instructions, issued over the years, for the army to cease advancing? How else does one explain that these lands are then often repopulated by cows and new populations? How else does one explain the fact that the location of the mines of Rubaya in Masisis and Bisie (western North Kivu) are the choice areas for M23 control? It is the economy that drives the war – as abandoned spouses in Mwenga discovered when their spouses rushed off to the goldmines in Maniema.

Writings on the bodies

In the majority of media reports that confirm the deaths of over six million Congolese, famine and disease, not violent massacres, are foregrounded as the causes of these deaths. Statistical studies have also been conducted to 'demonstrate' that the number of dead is far lower than five million. This will to trivialise, by reducing, the number of casualties in Congo conflicts speaks of a Western denial of Congolese subjectivity and the reality of democide – or, forms of political murder not covered by the term genocide – inscribed on the corpses of women who had been raped with branches thrust into their vaginas; deaths caused by individuals who intentionally mark their superiority through the rape, murder, starvation and objectification of Congolese men and women. What is written on the bodies of the internally and externally displaced refugees is democide, for these non-combatants, according to R.J. Rummel's (1998) definition of the term, are subjected to forced displacements, deprived of food and medication, raped (as an end to demoralise and sterilise) and then either intentionally killed or terrorised, depopulated and forced into submission. Since Congolese women, throughout the pre-colonial and colonial era, dominated the economic market, incapacitating them or diminishing their ability to work, sterilising them by thrusting branches into and mutilating their vaginas, is nothing but a will to eliminate a population by diminishing their ability to procreate and prosper. Through these displacements, rapes and violence, the scarcity of food, as exemplified in Metzgar's *Reporter* (2009), is inextricably associated with the creation of conditions conducive to disease and death.

Also written on the bodies of the raped women, who nurture and fend for their children, is the stunted growth of those children and the lack of future opportunities as a result of having been deprived of their childhoods and of schooling. Traumatised by the violent ordeals they have experienced, many children need inaccessible psychiatric care. Raped girls, who realise they will never be 'women', suffer from post-traumatic stress disorder, exacerbated by the fact that for women in the DRC womanhood and identity are defined by maternity and marriage. Dishonoured by the rapes and the sexual abuses they have been subjected to, Congolese women and girls are, as Mukwege puts it, 'in dishonour'. He adds: 'I constantly with my own eyes see the elder women, the young girls, the mothers and even the babies dishonored. Still today, many are subjected to sexual slavery; others are used as a weapon of war. Their organs are exposed to the most abhorrent ill-treatment' (Mukwege 2012).

Young girls who have been raped will grow up with the stigma of having been raped. They suffer from fear of being touched and some of being totally alienated from the world. How does one deal psychologically with the trauma of having seen one's father raped, killed or maimed by soldiers? And how does one transcend one's experience as a child soldier who has murdered and killed people? Jive's account of his own experience of being a child soldier highlights the psychological trauma of child soldiers and their subsequent alienation from the world around them: *'repousses; tout celui qui avait eu vent de notre statut antérieur nous évitait. On nous considerait comme des ennemis, des mauvais'* (rebuffed; all those who had ever heard about our previous status avoided us. We were considered enemies, bad people) (Jive 2006: 35). While Jive was able to reintegrate into society and to complete high school, many ex-child soldiers, once they lose the financial support of non-governmental organisations, return to the army or simply become street children.

On the thigh of the raped girl's corpse and the little castrated boy's arm, flung on a pile of adult corpses, is carved 'International Corporate Greed'. The girl and boy may never be buried, but they need not worry because it was all for the sake of technological progress, the improvement of foreign national economies and the creation of a Congolese upper class. Coltan is good. It develops those nations that have become exploiters of minerals that do not exist in their own lands. The international corporations, which, according to *Still the Heart of Darkness* (2003), no longer go to Kisangani to purchase their minerals but to Rwanda, indirectly participated in the rapes and killing of young girls and boys – in exactly the same way that the colonists who gazed into the vagina of a Congolese woman, who had had cement thrust into her as punishment for failing to produce the required amount of bricks, participated in her violation. The colonists were not necessarily always the active perpetrators, but they were then, as they remain today, the passive benefactors of the dehumanising pain.

On the body of every baby is inscribed the logic of 'selective ethnicity', which prohibits conversation and productive analysis of the war. The DRC has eleven provinces and borders on nine other countries; it is multicultural and has numerous minority groups in power, but despite this pluralism, one minority in the eastern Congo has succeeded in hijacking the suffering and humiliation of the entire nation because each invasion is framed in genocidal terms. While the Banyamurenge have the privilege to uphold their humanity – as the 2009 National Congress for the Defence of the People (CNDP) agreement with the government showed – Congolese women and men are objects easily disposed of. In *Reporter* (2009), Laurent Nkunda Batware contends that he is a soldier of God and that their struggle is aimed at upholding democracy and protecting the Congolese Tutsis from potential genocide. Ironically, Lieve Joris, a journalist who tracked Tutsi rebels 'supported by the Tutsi Rwanda regime' (2008: xv) during their Congo invasion, describes the contempt of the Tutsis towards Congolese and how they are considered '*igicucu* (blockheads), *m'jinga* (ignoramus), *nyamaswa* (barbarian): the Rwandans had plenty of abusive terms for Congolese and used them at every opportunity' (166). Despite this demeaning attitude, it is, according to Joris, the myth of Tutsi suffering that prevails and the voices of Congolese that are silenced.

On the corpses of the women, grandmothers, fathers and babies is inscribed 'Congolese Relentless Hunger for Power and Lack of Nationalism'. The enemy came, but he did not come alone. He came with our brother, son, husband and father in order to loot, destroy and spill blood in the name of false democracy, resource exploitation and power. Of the greed of these power-seekers – dubbed by the Rwandans 'BMWs' (Beer, Music and Women) – Joris writes: 'They regularly visited Kigali, where they had themselves feted in luxury hotels and told their Rwandan masters what other insurgents were up to. "The current president of the rebel movement is in Joseph Kabila's pocket," they whispered. "Make me president and I'll be your man in Kinshasa"' (2008: 225).

Finally, the raped women's body symbolically represents the land to be conquered and imploded – as suggested by Joris (2008) and Boris Diop (2002). This land-grabbing to build a Hima/Tutsi empire, encompassing Tutsi and ethnic groups close to Tutsis, has been dismissed as mere speculation, yet a global view of DRC suggests the violence should be examined in depth – particularly the Katanga area with its Kata Katanga (secessionist Mai- Mai rebel group) phenomenon, insecurity and rumours of the creation of a multicultural Katanga. Because minerals attract conflict and sow division, this will to access and control mineral resources informs the DRC's national wars. Is the violence we witnessed in Katanga over the last few months simply a means of asserting the legitimacy of the state or is it ultimately aimed at imploding the country, wearing down its people the better to access its minerals?

Conclusion

The war continues to be waged and women to be raped. Resilient, the Congolese have sought both political and military solutions to end the violence and to democratise the country, but have been hindered from achieving their dream of determining their own future. During these years of adversity and war, women have paid an excessive price. Millions of dollars have been poured into eastern Congo to assist the raped women and the displaced Congolese; numerous peace accords have been signed and perhaps, one day, Congo will be freed of conflicts. Yet, after the guns are silenced, the raped women, children and men will carry their war scars for years to come. Violence and rape may subside, but rape, as in all countries, will continue to haunt us. There is therefore an urgent need to turn the United Nations' terms of gender parity into cultural, as opposed to political and professional, norms. This will require, as a first step, changing our current primary, secondary and college textbooks and curricula, which still reinforce male privilege and patriarchal dominance. These texts must, moreover, enable Congolese to learn about their history and place in the world to better develop Congolese nationalism, but equally importantly, enable them to see their citizens as people and not as Others who are to be oppressed. I believe this process has begun. In addition to these changes, Congolese female scholars need to rethink the concept of an 'authentic African female identity' that has been so essentialised, as Mudimbe asserts in *Les corps glorieux des mots et des êtres* (1994), that women cannot recognise themselves beneath male, colonial and postcolonial constructions. Women will need, moreover, to gain ownership of their bodies by questioning received religious and cultural assumptions of being created to 'assist men' and to 'be sexually available at all times'.

Elimination of violence entails understanding the centrality of one's ontology, understanding one's value and one's relationship with another and *natus*, defined by Mudimbe in *Cheminements*, as a group of people having a common origin, having an awareness of an identity and the will to maintain it and having a sense of *natio*, a country (2006: 87). It is not, however, about solely seeking one's selfhood and value through materialism, lest we become, as Placide Tempels (1959) prophesied, *Lupitelos* – driven by the lust of money. It is about seeing the Other as an extension of the self because only then can the Other become him- or herself. And only then can one be freed from hegemonic egotism and others, such as women and our neighbours, be recognised as people entitled to respect and consideration as people with whom one lives and shares a world. Violence calls us, hence, to praxis and not merely to reflection. Personhood is possible only through communal engagement and development within a framework of communal values and aspirations.

Notes

All translations in this chapter are the author's.

1. Until 2010, MONUSCO was known as the United Nations Mission in the Democratic Republic of Congo or MONUC.
2. https://www.newworldencyclopedia.org/entry/African_Great_Lakes.
3. http://www.indcatholicnews.com/news.php?viewStory=18311.
4. See http://www.globalsecurity.org/military/world/war/congo.htm.
5. See http://www.huffingtonpost.com/2012/04/17/lena-adelsohn-liljeroth-cake_n_1431544.html.
6. See http://en.wikipedia.org/wiki/Women_in_the_Democratic_Republic_of_the_Congo.
7. See http://www.rescue.org/blog/photo-share-sewing-and-surviving-congo.
8. See https://www.youtube.com/watch?v=MaOl98KVAqM.

References

Boelaert, Edmond, Honoré Vinck and Charles Lonkama. 1995. '*Arrivée des blancs sur les bords des rivières équatoriales*'. *Annales Aequatoria* 17: 7–415.

Braeckman, Colette. 2012. *L'homme qui répare les femmes: Violences sexuelles au Congo – Le combat du docteur Mukwege*. Leuven: Grip/André Versailles.

Chiwengo, Ngwarsungu. 2008. 'When Wounds and Corpses Fail to Speak: Narratives of Violence and Rape in Congo (DRC)'. *Comparative Studies of South Asia, Africa and the Middle East* 28(1): 78–92.

———. Unpublished paper. 'Bestialisation, Dehumanisation and Counter-Interstitial Voices: (Mis)-Representation of Congo (DRC) Conflicts and Rape'.

Conrad, Joseph. 1981. *The Heart of Darkness*. New York: Bantam Books.

De Moor, Francoise and Jean-Pierre Jacquemin. 2000. *Notre Congo/Onze Congo*. Bruxelles: CEC (Coopération par l'Éducation et la Culture).

Diop, Boris. 2002. '*Entretien avec Boubakar Boris Diop, Ecrivain Senegalais Marque par le Genocidaire Rwandais*'. Interviewed by Lilyan Fongang-Kesteloot. In *Figures et Paradoxes de l'Histoire au Burundi et au Rwanda Vol. 2.* Paris: Archives et Musée de la littérature/ CELIBECO.

Friends of the Congo. 2011. *Crisis in the Congo: Uncovering the Truth*, available at https:// www.youtube.com/watch?v=vLV9szEu9Ag.

GLV Correspondent. 2011. 'Eleven DR Congo Soldiers Facing "Mobile Gender Court" on Mass Rape', 11 February, available at http://greatlakesvoice.com/11-fardc-soldiers-facing- 'gender-mobile-court'-on-mass-rape/.

The Greatest Silence: Rape in the Congo. 2008. DVD. Dir. Jackson, Lisa. Dist. Women for Women.

Hentz, Jennifer M. 2005. 'The Impact of HIV on the Rape Crisis in the African Great Lakes Region', *African Files*, 6 May, available at http://www.africafiles.org/article.asp?ID =8703&ThisURL=./humanrights.asp&URLName=Human+Rights.

Hilsum, Lindsay. 1997. 'In the Land of the Lion King'. *Times Literary Supplement*, 23 May: 9.

Human Rights Watch. 2002. *The War within the War. Sexual Violence against Women and Girls*. New York: Human Rights Watch, available at http://www.hrw.org/sites/default/files/ reports/congo0602.pdf.

Hunt, Nancy R. 2009. 'An Acoustic Register, Tenacious Images, and Congolese Scenes of Rape and Repetition'. *Cultural Anthropology* 23(3): 220–53.

Jive, Mufula Josué. 2006. *Enfant de guerre: Les souvenirs d'un ex-kadogo*. Kinshasa: Médiaspaul.

Joris, Lieve. 2008. *The Rebels' Hour*. New York: Grove Press.

Kavwahirehi, Kasereka. 2006. *V.Y. Mudimbe et la ré-invention de l'Afrique: Poétique et politique de la décolonisation des sciences humaines*. Amsterdam: Rodopi.

Mbembe, Achille. 2001. *On the Postcolony*. Berkeley: University of California Press.

Montague, Dana and Frida Berrigan. 2001. 'The Business of War in the Democratic Republic of Congo', available at http://www.thirdworldtraveler.com/Africa/Business_War_Congo.html.

Mudimbe, V-Y. 1972. *Réflexions sur la vie quotidienne*. Kinshasa: Editions du Mont Noir.

———. 1976. *Le bel immonde: Récit*. Paris: Présence Africaine.

———. 1989. *Shaba deux: Les carnets de Mère Marie-Gertrude*. Paris: Présence Africaine.

———. 1992. 'Save the African Continent'. *Public Culture* 5(1): 61–62.

———. 1994. *Les corps glorieux des mots et des êtres: Esquisse d'un jardin africain à la bénédictine*. Paris: Présence Africaine and Montreal: Humanitas.

———. 2006. *Cheminements: Carnets de Berlin (avril–juin 1999)*. Montreal: Humanitas.

Mukwege, Dénis. 2012. 'Presentation to the United Nations 25/09/2012 by Dr. Dénis Mukwege', available at http://www.panzihospital.org/archives/1027.

Reporter. 2009. DVD. Dir. Metzgar, Eric. Pro. Mikaela Beardsley and Steven Cantor. Merigold Moving Pictures.

Richards, Paul. 1996. *Fighting for the Rain Forest: War, Youth and Resources in Sierra Leone*. Oxford: International African Institute.

Rummel, R.J. 1998. 'Democide Versus Genocide: Which Is What?', available at http://www.hawaii.edu/powerkills/GENOCIDE.HTM.

Schwendinger, Julie and Herman Schwendinger. 1981. 'Rape, Sexual Inequality and Levels of Violence'. *Crime and Social Justice* 16: 3–31.

Smock, David. 1996. 'Exploring Conflict in the Great Lakes Region: Testimony of David Smock before the Congressional Human Rights Caucus', United States Institute of Peace, 4 December, available at http://www.usip.org/publications/exploring-conflict-great-lakes-region.

Still the Heart of Darkness: The Killing in the Congo, Part 1; *War in the Congo – An Overview*. 2003. DVD. Prod. Ted Koppel. ABC News. Films for the Humanities and Sciences.

Tempels, Placide. 1959. *Bantu Philosophy*. Paris: Présence Africaine.

CHAPTER 6

A Phenomenology of Violence

Laura Kerr

There has always been violence. There will always be violence. Although possibly true, these statements fail to grapple with the sheer number of people brutalised, terrorised and killed in the Great Lakes region. According to one source, around 38 000 people die each month in the eastern Congo due to war-related causes (Lemarchand 2009). If the killings in Rwanda and Burundi are included, approximately 5.5 million people have died in this region from war-related causes since 1994. The inevitability of violence also does not excuse the long history of muted response from the international community to the crimes against humanity and human rights abuses committed in the Great Lakes region. Popular judgements of the violence as 'incomprehensible', 'unimaginable', 'unspeakable' and 'evil' temper efforts to intervene or to recognise our moral responsibility for the victims. Along with such judgements are attitudes such as: *The situation is complex. How do we help what we cannot comprehend? Anyway, how can anyone begin to 'fix' such atrocities?* Less commonly, people mention shame for the violence of colonisation that complicates any heroic effort to rescue people in the region. How could any response be straightforwardly and selflessly humanitarian given the well-chronicled colonial exploitation of the Congo, or the potential for future exploitation and profit from the abundant natural resources? Wouldn't any gesture naturally be met with scepticism? Especially given the failure to respond to the Rwandan genocide of 1994, this shame is very real, complicated and not easily swept away.

I would like to argue that the failure to protect victims of violence is not related solely to the history of the Great Lakes region, or to racism or colonialism, but reveals aspects of the deep psychology of Western modernity. The people of the Great Lakes region are learning first-hand how victimisation is often handled in modern, shame-avoiding, capitalist democracies. The shame of violence, as well as the feelings of vulnerability and self-loathing that shame characteristically calls forth, are often dissociated from the modern individual's awareness. Furthermore, the denial of shame not only keeps people from feeling their own suffering, but also acknowledging the suffering of others.

Following the Rwandan genocide, General Paul Kagame spoke of the failure of the international community to emotionally witness the impact of genocide on the Rwandan people:

> Sometimes I think this is contempt for us. I used to quarrel with these Europeans who used to come, giving us sodas, telling us, 'You should not do this, you should do this, you don't do this, do this.' I said, 'Don't you have feelings?' These feelings have affected people (in Gourevitch 1998: 337).

The contempt Kagame identified may well be real and could be the result of the demand for an emotional response. In the United States, denial of victimhood seems to be part of the phenomenology of violence. Indeed, the failure to protect the most vulnerable, or to even acknowledge their suffering, appears to be a central aspect of the individual's unspoken education for becoming 'modern'.

In this chapter, I provide a depth psychology perspective of the violence perpetrated in the Great Lakes region, as well as of the passive violence committed by the West when it fails to sufficiently intervene and protect victims and potential victims. The phenomenology of violence presented here draws from my experiences as a trauma-focused psychotherapist and from lectures given by Professor V-Y Mudimbe in an advanced graduate seminar at Stanford University titled 'Phenomenology of Madness' (Mudimbe et al. 1997). I have had the great pleasure and honour of working with Professor Mudimbe on this and other projects throughout my career (see, for example, Mudimbe, Iwele and Kerr 2007). Yet, it was the ideas he shared in these lectures and the guidance he gave me in the development of my own research agenda that initiated my belief that psychological ruptures and the denial of emotions such as shame are central to the phenomenology of both madness and violence (Kerr 2000, 2010). Through the reflections on violence as implicit in the formation of Western thought, Mudimbe's work has been foundational to my search for psychologies that foster people's humanity. As I grapple with how the West contributes to violence in the Great Lakes region, I am also searching for ways to return humanity to the area. As a student of Mudimbe's, I inherited a respect and regard for humanity and for all life that I am compelled to pay forward.

The centrality of shame for violence

As a specialist in the treatment of psychological trauma, I have worked with both men and women in the United States who have long histories of violence, sometimes reaching back to their first days of life. Furthermore, many of my clients are minorities and often disenfranchised by the capitalist system. As well as childhood abuse, they have suffered the violence of racism, classism and/or sexism. Each of their histories includes several of the following phenomena: homelessness, domestic violence, sexual assault, incarceration, prostitution, attempted murder, armed robbery and/or involvement in gangs. Throughout their lives, they have struggled with drug addictions. All have been victims of violence, even the perpetrators.

Few people ever hear about my clients' histories of violence, unless they somehow make headlines. Then they momentarily grab attention, but are quickly forgotten again, as if violence is the order of things for people who live on the fringes of society. My clients – their actions and their lives – are often also greeted with words such as 'incomprehensible', 'unimaginable', 'unspeakable' and 'evil'. When I examine the West's response to the violence in the Great Lakes region, I see rough similarities to the way my clients are left to struggle with violence and the effects of violence. In many regards, although not as severely, these Americans are treated in ways similar to how people subjected to violence in the Great Lakes region are being treated by the West: their injuries often go unaddressed or are even ignored and they are often left responsible for their housing, food, education, health care and, perhaps most importantly, safety.

According to the American historical novelist Russell Banks (2008), race is the 'ur-narrative' that drives my country's neglect of its most vulnerable members. Yet, as a white woman who grew up in a profoundly sexist (and racist) time in the history of the United States South and who has experienced violence as well as marginalisation due to my own struggles with victimhood, I tend to broaden the context beyond race. I see a psychological split that is fundamental to the deep psychology of the United States. This split or rupture originates in violence and is also the foundation on which the roles of perpetrator and victim are played out. Banks wrote about this split and how central it is to the United States' psychological landscape:

> We are in a sense a schizophrenic people. I don't mean that we have a split
> identity. We're at war with ourselves. And this explains, I think, why we

so often march off to war against others – as horrific as foreign wars are, they are much easier for us at home than it would be to face the internal battles of being at war within ourselves. Anything to avoid the war within ourselves that is still actively forging our identity, a war whose outcome hasn't been decided yet; and until it is, we won't really know who we are (2008: 27).

When I hear that some people believe that one of the greatest obstacles to healing the wounds of genocides and conflict-related atrocities in the Great Lakes region is the fact that perpetrators and victims are expected to continue living as neighbours, I imagine an unspoken assumption that either the people in the Great Lakes region have not yet developed enough to manage their aggressions, or that they lack the necessary mobility and physical distance to escape the psychological consequences of violence. Nowhere have I heard it questioned that managing violence is fundamentally what becoming 'modern' is about – not because people are inherently violent, but because modernity seems to be a form of 'civilisation' that thrives through the propagation of defences against fully acknowledging and remediating the consequences of violence. One example of how this occurs is through the split identity that Banks describes as characteristic of the United States.

Some of the conditions at the root of the conflict in the Great Lakes region occur in other places around the world, too – problems such as reduced access to farmable land, the breakdown of traditional social networks and large numbers of young people without direction or opportunities for meaningful and profitable work. Such conditions can ignite criminality and disregard for another's humanity, especially when an individual feels cheated by life, while at the same time being exposed to the political and social advantages of extreme wealth. Furthermore, since the end of the Cold War – which has resulted in a flood of smaller, relatively inexpensive weapons into the marketplace – the stage for conflicts is less often the isolated battlefield or aerial assault than it is within communities, where rebels and soldiers prey on civilians, brutally raping women as well as abducting children for the purpose of filling their armed ranks.

Rather than revolutionary armies dedicated to a noble and legitimate cause, rebel groups in the Great Lakes region have been described as functioning more like criminal gangs, who swell their numbers by recruiting young boys and girls when these children are most vulnerable to the pressures of group identity for their sense of ethics and morality (Lemarchand 2009). These children may be threatened with losing their own lives and/or those of their family members if they attempt to escape the rebel groups who 'recruited' them, or if they were to resist perpetrating acts of violence, which often includes killing innocent people.

The reliance on child soldiers in conflicts in the Great Lakes region is particularly troublesome. Child soldiers learn to meet their needs for attachment and safety through the dominance and exploitation they must mimic as dependants on armed and violent groups. As social beings, our basic human need for attachment and safety, preferably met by family bonds and communal ties, is both biologically and socially predetermined (Wallin 2007). Children have limited internal resources for resisting attachment needs, which makes them particularly susceptible to behaving horrifically if doing so will contribute to their sense of belonging and safety. Furthermore, power and dominance become ready substitutes for healthy bonding, particularly when they represent the shared aspirations of the group. For many child soldiers, a shared love of power and the avoidance of feelings of vulnerability and shame become a unifying bond, one that psychoanalyst Sandor Ferenczi has described as 'identifying with the aggressor' – a common psychological method for meeting dependency needs when a caretaker is abusive. This is how many armed commanders of rebel groups have been described in their treatment of child 'recruits' (Ferenczi 1988; *The Children's War* 2010).

I have worked with perpetrators of violence, including people who have attempted to commit murder. Before they could identify with their own histories of victimisation, it was not uncommon for them to reminisce about the exhilaration they had felt in having power over their victims. But they also do not know how to become non-aggressive individuals. They felt cut off from humanity, impotent and obsessive in their approach to 'normal' life. Hatred and an us-versus-them mentality often resurfaced when they got close to a deeply denied shame that seemed to haunt all of them. According to psychiatrist James Gilligan, who spent his career working with convicted murderers in the United States, an avoidance of shame motivated the killings committed by every one of the murderers he interviewed for his book *Violence* (1997). For them, violence became a defence against feeling the shame associated with past experiences of having been a victim, which usually involved severe childhood abuse.

Here it may be important to distinguish between shame and guilt because they function differently, but are often confused. Typically, what we call 'guilt' refers to those feeling-states associated with remorse for having failed to uphold one's own ethics concerning right and wrong. Guilt is a response to the relationship between oneself and one's personal notions of what it means to live a good life and to be a good person. As such, it is often associated with our treatment of others, such as the experience of 'survivor guilt' that often plagues people who have survived atrocities, while others close to them perished. Such people sense that, as 'a good person', they should have done more to save victims, including sacrificing their own lives.

In contrast, 'shame' is a common emotional response to feeling devalued, even degraded, by others. At its core, shame is the fear of disconnection. As such, it has evolved to support prosocial behaviour and acting in ways that secure membership in a group and, through that, one's survival. Shame also functions to (re)inforce social hierarchies. The demonstration of shame typically signifies submission to a more powerful person, group, aggressor or even the status quo (Kerr 2008). It thus indirectly builds social bonds. Shame signals to others that one is aware of having failed to respond as expected and that one is aware of existing power differences. The humiliation, sadness, fear and anger that shame causes reduce the likelihood that a person will in the future repeat the actions that led to feelings of shame. The expression of shame signifies that one is no longer a threat while, at the same time, contributing to the aggressor's increased sense of power. But for the person feeling shame, this powerful emotion can also ignite feelings of envy, jealousy and even pride as a defence against feeling inferior to another.

Shame takes on a more defensive role when it occurs in response to chronic abuse. Rather than an emotional motivation to honour group norms or avoid power struggles, the emotional impact of shame is avoided, if not completely dissociated, from awareness. Especially when abuse is chronic – in cases of severe childhood abuse, for instance – a child's awareness will likely split off from feelings of shame and the overwhelming sense of fear he or she experienced while victimised. By splitting from awareness the shame, fear and anger that arise during abuse, the child is able to remain attached to the caregiver, thus continuing to meet dependency needs during those times when the abuse is not occurring. However, when feelings of shame are later elicited – including when the child becomes an adult – these feelings can also trigger unconscious reminders of the abuse, including feelings of degradation and fear. One consequence of this is that shame loses its potential as a prosocial emotional state and instead produces *anti-social* behaviour. Aggression now becomes a powerful defence against the threatening experience of once again feeling like a victim and of being degraded.

The psychological dynamics that emerge between an abused child and the offending caregiver are complex. Submission is also gained by intermittently rewarding the child for compliance and good behaviour. Furthermore, they are phenomenologically similar to what is experienced during any state of captivity in which both abuse and care are received from a person or persons within a larger context of terror. The psychological effects of captivity have been explored in the context of domestic violence, prisoners of war, cults and other social groups in which demoralisation and subjugation are accomplished in part through the exploitation of dependency needs (Herman 1997) and where an individual's submission is maintained by intermittent rewards for compliance and good behaviour. Colonisation, too, seems to gain power through the same psychological mechanisms.

The intergenerational transmission of violence

In the case of colonialism and the struggle for freedom, the intergenerational transmission of traumatic experiences – especially through psychological defences such as splitting and the avoidance of shame – continue to organise the psychological defences and belief systems of later generations and contribute to bonds between survivors. And in the Great Lakes region, the crimes of colonisation are legendary for their brutality (Hochschild 1998). During colonisation of the region, dependency on the colonisers was enforced through horrific abuses of power that seem to have fostered psychological splitting in the psyches of the peoples of the Congo and influenced their conduct and interactions. This was exacerbated by the colonial Belgians' exploitation of differences between Hutus and Tutsis in the Belgians' attempts to reproduce Western social hierarchies in the region as part of a regime of indirect rule.

Many Tutsis and Hutus likely internalised a psychological rupture between aggressor and victim in which the debased group – in the original scenario, the Hutus – were degraded to the lowest rung of the social ladder. Rather than witnessing their culpability, perpetrators of colonisation would blame Hutu victims (along with Tutsis and other ethnic groups) for the violence committed against them, enlisting both science and religion (Mudimbe 1988; Hochschild 1998) to rationalise their atrocities and split from awareness the inhumane and shameful nature of their actions. However, the Tutsis sometimes were allowed to benefit from their identification with the aggressor (or, actually, the aggressor's identification *with them* through the Hamitic hypothesis), which initially led to greater opportunities for Tutsis within the Western capitalist system. Yet, from a depth psychology perspective, both Hutus and Tutsis learned to identify with the aggressor and feared the experience of being victimised. In other words, both groups internalised the psychological split between aggressor and victim through their subjugation to the conditions of colonisation.

This rupture between the psychological states of aggressor and victim seems to continually play out in the dynamics of violence in the Great Lakes region. Any one group can assume the role of aggressor as long as another group is available to assume, or be forced to assume, the role of victim. As René Lemarchand observes:

> Ethnicity has a capacity to be manipulated for the pursuit of preeminently immoral goals, to profoundly alter collective perceptions of the 'other.' It can be distorted using images whose purpose it is to draw rigid boundaries between good and evil, civic virtue and moral depravity, freedom and oppression, and foreigners and autochthons (2009: 50).

From a depth psychology perspective, ethnicity becomes a tactic for escaping an unstable and emotionally threatening internal rupture by projecting the unwanted aspects of the self, including shame, onto opposing ethnic groups. And this, of course, was exactly how many of the colonisers of the region reacted to indigenous Africans – as shameful, if not lacking humanity, and thus deserving of the most atrocious treatment.

Phenomenologically speaking, to be a victim of violence or any traumatic experience is to experience a rupture. Since the work of French psychiatrist Pierre Janet in the nineteenth century, it has been known that traumatic events overwhelm not only our minds, but also our bodies and that in the process much of what was experienced during the trauma is split from conscious awareness. Recent studies of traumatic stress (for example, Ogden, Minton and Pain 2006) have identified the biological mechanisms through which this fragmentation occurs. Thinking about a threat while it is happening slows down survival responses, thus energy is diverted away from the frontal lobes, which is the part of the brain responsible for higher-order cognitive processes, including creating coherent narratives of events. With the frontal lobes shut down, there is no way of integrating overwhelming sensory information into a meaningful and linear narrative of the trauma. Instead, emotional reactions are split off from sensory memories, muscle memories, perceptions and thoughts registered at the time of the traumatic event. Consequently, survival comes at a price: fragmented memories in search of integration haunt many trauma survivors long after the danger has passed.

If the society that the traumatised individual inhabits does not foster integration and healing from traumatic events, the largely unconscious, split-off images, emotions and thoughts associated with past traumas are more likely to be projected onto others, who are then identified as the source of inexplicable suffering. For persons with severe histories of abuse and victimisation who themselves later engage in violence, the split-off experiences of subjugation frequently get projected and are then acted out in brutal and dehumanising ways that intensely shame the victim (De Mause 2002). What is so profound about this process is the co-ordination of the human body's experience of trauma with the social group's response to trauma. The significance and depth of this connection, and how it relates to social exclusion and victimisation, was a major point of Mudimbe's lectures on the phenomenology of madness. In that regard, he made an important observation that also applies to violence: 'When we speak of madness [or violence] in our culture, we tend to understand it as a dysfunction. Yet that dysfunction can be understood as constituting a system in its own right, a system of resistance, a system of reaction to an untenable situation' (Mudimbe et al. 1997).

With reference to Michel Foucault's *The Order of Things* (1970), Mudimbe portrays madness as generated within a system of thought that inscribes the bodies of the subjects of madness, as well as the social body that projects madness onto some of its members:

> How do we perceive, how do we understand, how do we analyze this phenomenon that we tend to perceive as dysfunctionality, as abnormality, even as madness? I propose a grid from the work of Michel Foucault, *The Order of Things*, in which he suggests that all our disciplines today, and the history of our disciplines, can be understood thanks to a table of three pairs of concepts: function and norm, conflicts and rules, signification and system (Mudimbe et al. 1997).

Mudimbe also stresses that language is the most influential of the disciplines governing how we become subjects as well as objects of discursive practices. Madness and violence are both partially produced through language and formulate texts in their own right. Their subjects are victims of language's capacity for abstraction from the particular and unique experiences of the individual – a practice that Jean-Paul Sartre associated with *bad faith* and that Foucault explored in terms of *biopower* (Sartre 1965; Rabinow 1984). Mudimbe also locates this tension between the particular and the abstract in the work of Ferdinand de Saussure:

We might be today living a last moment, a new one, which is dominated by language, by the symbolism and the power of language; more exactly, by the tension introduced in our minds at the beginning of this century by the Swiss linguist, Ferdinand de Saussure, who first elaborated this new paradigm which dominates us. On the one hand, language exists as an abstraction, including concepts and institutionalized discourses, and on the other hand, a concrete actualization of that abstraction, which is speech. This is the tension between *langue* and *parole*, in French (Mudimbe et al. 1997).

Yet, as Mudimbe so incisively observes, to be objectified through knowledge and to be the subject of abstraction carries with it its own violence:

There is something like a moment of dissolution, which passes from the object to the knowing subject. You prepare your technique, you advance, you possess, you digest, you understand, and you get knowledge. And, indeed, from there we can understand the concept of sadism, that is, the pleasure of possessing. Possessing a human body, possessing a knowledge (Mudimbe et al. 1997).

However, with regards to both madness and violence, the rupture of thought from the body may be the seminal rupture through which both massive killings and indifference to the suffering of others commence. This rupture between mind and body coincides with the origins of modernity, especially the work of René Descartes and his Cartesian method.

The violence of the Cartesian method
The Cartesian method, as described by Mudimbe, is foundational for prioritising thought and language over lived experience:

We see, all of us, the sun rising in the morning and going down at the end of the day. We see it, we observe it as objective, yet in our classrooms and in our papers, we say that it is not true. We teach our children not to believe what they see because it is not true. We introduce a heliocentric model explaining that it is the earth that goes around the sun. This is a good way of preparing a radical disbelief. Who to trust? Am I speaking to you right now? Am I dreaming? Am I here? I can doubt everything and I should doubt everything but the only thing that I cannot doubt is that I am doubting, that I am thinking. This is the Cartesian *cogito*, the foundation for our way of thinking (Mudimbe et al. 1997).

Over the centuries, the value of the Cartesian method has been inflated (and vilified) with regard to its status as an intellectual achievement. But I would like to argue that Descartes's method is really an *emotional* 'achievement'. For, as much as Descartes can be considered a central architect of the European Enlightenment, so too must psychological defences against alienation and the effects of violence be seen as the root of the Cartesian method and, consequently, the foundation for Western modernity. Rather than formulating a radical distinction between soma and psyche or a defence against tradition and superstition, Descartes was simply attempting to stop his own unbearable suffering.

Descartes was only 25 years old and a soldier when he first formulated the Cartesian method. Although it would take seventeen years before he penned his philosophy, it was a younger, more vulnerable Descartes – caught in the ambivalence characteristic of youth and struggling with life as a soldier – who saw reflective wisdom as a way to distance himself from feeling overwhelmed by his imagination, emotions and senses. Initially, the method was his bridge back to sanity (Davoine and Gaudillière 2004). However, rather than becoming a novel practice for keeping madness at bay, Descartes's method would become an epistemic foundation for Western modernity – itself a maddening world that would become increasingly violent, in part because of the paradigm introduced by this method.

As a young man, Descartes was a freelance fighter for the Duke of Bavaria during the Thirty Years' War. When he first discovered the method – really, a grasping at straws – he was on reprieve from battle due to a hiatus of aggressions during the deadness of winter. As an intellectual, he had been feeling alienated from his fellow fighters. He had a zest for life and freedom, but he was also extraordinarily brilliant and was beginning to see philosophy and science as his true calling.

In this unsettled state, both physically alone and psychically alienated, Descartes reached the edge of madness. On the night of 10 November 1619, he had two consecutive nightmares:

In the first, ghosts stir up whirlwinds and infernal spirits bent on his downfall. In the second, there is a horrendous noise followed by sparks of fire dancing around his room. A pain he felt upon wakening made him fear that some evil demon was at work, trying to seduce him (Davoine and Gaudillière 2004: 93).

Such dreams are not unusual for soldiers who regularly witness death and explosions. They speak to the power of our imaginations to both hold overwhelming imagery as well as make sense of what we are too frightened to confront in our lived realities. The *imaginal* – that psychic process where dreams, perceptions, memories and fantasies can confront one another without the limits of the real – is also the space for making meaningful what would otherwise remain incomprehensible. And although we moderns (thanks, in part, to Descartes) perceive the imaginal as largely a projected, disembodied space (much like the Internet), for pre-modern populations, especially, perhaps, the indigenous populations of pre-colonial Africa, the imaginal had always been fostered and lived through myths and rituals shared by the collective.

With the term 'myth' I am not referring to manufactured stories or lies meant to propagate political agendas or ideologies as present aggressors in the Great Lakes region have been accused of doing (Lemarchand 2009). Rather, I am referring to the stories passed down through generations, which signify the ethos of the culture and expectations of its members. Such myths are part of the communal practices and traditions that not only create cohesion between members of the group, but also model the different roles each individual will assume over their lifespan – child, maiden, warrior, parent, crone, elder and so on. These myths and rituals contribute to processes of social and individual integration and, traditionally, have been central to the manner in which indigenous cultures reintegrated following traumatic events, while also limiting the likelihood of extreme power differences emerging from within the group (Fabrega 2002; Levine 1997; Pelton 1989).

Mythological figures such as Legba of West Africa, Loki of Norse mythology, the Trickster of the American Winnebago Indian tales, Krishna in India, Hermes for the ancient Greeks are all symbolic of social worlds where violence played or continues to play an active role in creation and becoming. In worlds ordered by myths and the cycle of life, where violence is both the threat of destruction and the source of creation, violence is a life-destroying force, yes, but it is also one of the greatest motivations for personal and social regeneration. The point here is not to morally condone destructive acts or cruelty, but to recognise the possibility of violence, or otherwise traumatising events, in most lives and thus the necessity of creating societies that take seriously both violence's destructive impact *and* the need for re-establishing cultural and individual integration following violence and other traumatic events. Violence is a more formidable foe when you are prepared to witness and feel its effects.

When something traumatic happens to a person, and what occurred remains unsynthesised with the rest of the life story, the unarticulated bits of memory haunt the survivor, much the way a phantom limb recalls the disastrous injury that led to loss. Trauma births its own world, one that exists beside the regular, expressed order of things, where life stories are normalised, validated, even valorised. In trauma's otherworldly realm – the imaginal landscapes of our minds – travel the fragmented narratives of what transpired, but also of what failed to transpire: escape from harm, facing down threat, regaining a sense of safety. Here we find the birthplace of grief, but also of creativity, the origins of trauma stories, and also of their erasure, all vying for connection with what can no longer be – or become – now that trauma has claimed its space. Modernity seems to perpetuate dissociated imaginal states, which, rather than contributing to change and integration, become states of escape and fantasy. In modernity, these dissociative states replace the more malleable and transient imaginal worlds that myth-based societies accessed as avenues for reintegrating body awareness with split-off memories of trauma and for reintegrating traumatised people back into the collective.

What made Descartes's Cartesian method so radical, as well as dangerous, is that for the first time a method was offered for legitimately dissociating from those imaginal contents of the psyche that emerge as a result of violence, but without reconnecting with the human body or the 'body' of the collective. One could now effectively dissociate from awareness many of violence's psychological and physical traces – or so one was led to believe – without repairing the inevitable ruptures that are the natural outcome of overwhelming fear and incomprehension. This is the legacy of Western modernity. It is a psychological colonisation. The Cartesian method replaces practices that might move psychological and social ruptures towards integration with an acceptance of rupture as the natural order of things.

We inherited from Descartes and Western modernity a tourniquet between mind and body that limits our capacity to acknowledge our own suffering and that of others. Centuries of practising radical doubt has left Cartesian, Western individuals susceptible to denying their own embodied existences, as well as their humanity and the humanity of others. Thoughts and language without meaningful connections to emotions and the body are always at risk of being empty speech. This 'nowhere land' between body and mind – an experience that lacks the obligation to witness another's humanity – is the crucible in which colonialism was forged, genocides continue to be perpetrated and so-called 'ethnic' conflicts gain traction.

The following remark by Mudimbe relates to the West's maintenance of the split between embodied or so-called *pre-reflective awareness* and the potential for thought as radical doubt. In his lectures on the phenomenology of madness, Mudimbe stressed that the distinction between reflective and pre-reflective awareness not only impacts on us as individuals, but also organises the practices, rules and norms that govern social possibilities. He witnessed how society is organised much like the embodied experience of selfhood. Together self and society inscribe and reproduce one another:

> We might live in or inhabit our cultures, exactly the way we inhabit our personal bodies. And this is a reflection, a meditation on norms, or knowing rules, of knowing – to put it more explicitly, a meditation on a tension existing between the two types of knowledge distinguished by Heidegger in his *Discourse on Thinking* (1966); that is, on the one hand, a calculating thinking – the way we relate to nature, to things, to beings, to others – we calculate in order to understand, in order to domesticate; on the other hand, a meditating way of thinking which is a waiting – here I am just waiting, meditating and trying to understand . . . Abnormality comes from that tension when we don't go by, we don't act according to the background that we call pre-reflexive (Mudimbe et al. 1997).

The point Mudimbe makes about domestication is important to highlight. The implicit rules and norms of modernity drive the capacity to use thoughts to alter feelings and to use the intellect to dominate emotions and the body, altering the interaction between pre-reflective and reflective awareness, which in indigenous cultures leads to the creation of meaning within a context of shared values and with an awareness of the 'voice' of the body. The norms governing the production of Cartesian radical doubt resist limitations placed on the individual by the ethos of the culture, as well as by the state of being embodied. Indeed, *guilt* is an expected response to the failure to control the body and the emotions and, according to Foucault, is central to the experience of madness in modernity. Furthermore, the expression of guilt is expected as a precursor to integration with the larger community. The following observations by Jerrold Seigel include quotations from Foucault's *Madness and Civilization* (1988):

> The new doctors 'substituted for the free terror of madness the stifling anguish of responsibility,' instilling in the patient an organised sense of guilt that made him or her 'an object of punishment always vulnerable to himself and to the Other; and from the acknowledgment of his status as object, from the awareness of his guilt, the madman was to return to his awareness of himself as a free and responsible subject, and consequently to reason' (Seigel 1999: ix).

Similarly, the Western legal system also expects guilt as proof of culpability and evidence of reform. Yet, given what is known about the centrality of shame for perpetrating violence and the inability of violent offenders to confront the atrocities they have committed without first dealing with their own experiences of victimhood, modern societies find themselves in a state of paralysis. For, to expect criminals to express guilt for their actions is also to expect them to feel ashamed. However, for the accused, unless they have changed their relationship with the dissociated victim within themselves, on a pre-reflective level they likely feel 'abnormal', as Mudimbe puts it, as if they are once again becoming the victim.

Without first grappling with their own victimhood, aggressors remain split by the pre-reflective rules and norms governing the psychological production of both aggressor and victim, which for aggressors excludes feelings of shame. Furthermore, this resistance to 'performing' shame and relinquishing the role of the aggressor, in part explains the West's failure to meaningfully intervene in the Great Lakes region or to work in ways that could lead to resolution and the reintegration of communities. Modern, Western societies are themselves organised around the perpetuation of the aggressor-victim rupture. Even benevolent solutions can be experienced as emerging from within an aggressor-victim complex that is projected onto all Westerners, which may explain the increasing number of attacks on humanitarian workers in conflict regions throughout the world. Furthermore, it could be questioned whether Western powers can identify viable solutions to violence in the region, given the centrality of the aggressor-victim dynamic in the collective psychology of countries such as the United States.

It is noteworthy that Mudimbe's reflections on how we inhabit our cultures and the way we inhabit our bodies has anticipated current research exploring how the human body actually conforms to the norms and rules governing the social body. For example, in his book *On Deep History and the Brain* (2008), Daniel Lord Smail makes a connection between global capitalism, social hierarchies and the body's reaction to threats. He argues that capitalism exploits the body's basic survival responses by creating the conditions of psychological domination *as well as* providing relief from the feelings of powerlessness that capitalism and social hierarchies engender. According to Smail, capitalism generates stress through its unpredictability and hierarchical power structures, but it also alleviates stress by producing an economy organised around the production and circulation of addictive substances and practices that numb or manipulate emotions.

In the dynamics of violence, the rupture between the reflective and the pre-reflective, and between *langue* and *parole*, is part of the reproduction of power. The perpetrator holds the position of reflective awareness and radical doubt. The violence enacted is, in part, justified through concepts and beliefs that fortify dissociative stances towards the embodied existence of the Other inscribed by language. Such stances, which are created through radical doubt and the prioritising of abstract concepts over lived experience, are not entirely emotionless, but rather inscribed within a limited set of emotional possibilities. As Mudimbe remarks:

> Looking at the other as if the other were just a thing, the way a table is a table, the way a stool is a stool: that's indifference. Hate – hate is this projection of the other, I reject you, I hate you, you don't exist for me; and desire, which is a sadistic orientation – to desire, to possess, to objectify, so that I can enjoy your reduction into the state of a stone or a table (Mudimbe et al. 1997).

Similarly, victims are inscribed and limited with regard to how they may respond with their bodies, as well as with language. Whereas the perpetrator inhabits the space of abstraction, hate, possession, desire and objectification, the victim is confined to speaking from the space of lived experience and must contain the shame for being degraded, as well as the guilt for failing to safeguard their own humanity (and often those of others less 'fortunate' than themselves). The victims also inhabit the rupture between mind and body, which can be witnessed in their attempts to narrate what has happened, for this rupture both fragments and regulates the stories that can be told about violence.

In *The Antelope's Strategy*, a book about living in Rwanda after the genocide, Jean Hatzfeld shares an interview with Joseph-Désiré Bitero who planned and led co-ordinated killings of Tutsis in the district of Nyamata. For Bitero, the idea of 'Tutsis' – itself a concept amplified by colonial Belgians in their attempt to mirror

Western social hierarchy in the Congo – came to represent memories of oppression, marginalisation and their own experience of victimhood:

> We believed that the *inkotanyi* [the Tutsi-led Rwandan Patriotic Army] once installed on the throne, would be especially oppressive – that the Hutus would be pushed back into their fields and robbed of their words. We told ourselves we didn't want to be demeaned anymore, made to wash the Tutsi ministers' air-conditioned cars, for example, the way we used to carry the kings in hammocks. I was raised in fear of the return of Tutsi privileges, of obeisance and unpaid forced labor, and then that fear began its bloodthirsty march (in Hatzfeld 2009: 118).

These fears – and the images, memories and abstractions that fuelled them – erased bonds between neighbours, pastor and clergy, teacher and pupil, doctor and patient, in an attempt to exterminate an entire 'ethnic group' – itself an abstract portrayal of the victims.

Innocent Rwililiza, a Tutsi who survived the genocide and also lives in Nyamata, is talking about the crucial issue of who can speak for the dead. His words address the limits on the capacity of concepts to grapple with the experience of victimhood. Implicitly, he reclaims the uniqueness of every human being denied by acts of genocide and all acts of violence:

> There are facts and feelings we can manage to describe, and others, no; only the dead could report them if they were here, and we must not describe these things in their name. Why? Because they alone here fully experienced the genocide, so to say. It's not possible to speak in place of the departed, because everyone has a personal way of telling that story. Marie-Louise has her own way, Berthe hers, Jean-Baptist his. The dead have theirs, which would be even more different, since they would be telling their story while holding death by the hand (in Hatzfeld 2009: 132).

Furthermore, during the killings – and the actual state of being victimised – there were no thoughts; there was only the body and the drive for survival. The violence of being hunted had literally killed the sense of self. Again, quoting Rwililiza:

> What did we think about during all those days [of genocide]? I have no answer. We were like puppets up there: we only ran, ate, rested, waited.

Our intelligence was in shock. I don't remember now, I have no answer. I can't come up with anything, I don't even want to try anymore. I really can't remember if I thought at all. We were living a new existence. We were desolate, we were just stunned. It's impossible to say why no thoughts came to mind. When you get right down to it . . . we weren't alive enough for that (in Hatzfeld 2009: 65).

Language is one of the most powerful ways through which we know ourselves and communicate our uniqueness to others. Concepts and ideas also contribute to self-expression and, depending on how they are used, can lead to justice. But they also can dehumanise and lead to crimes against the humanity of another. Of course, concepts and abstractions, per se, do not lead to violence. Rather, opportunities to dissociate from lived experience, which are fostered by abstractions, reside on a dangerous and slippery slope to denying the uniqueness and humanity of another.

Conclusion

When I read about violence in the Great Lakes region, I often feel overwhelmed by feelings of despair. It is easy to lose hope, even though, as a psychotherapist, I am part of a discipline sometimes referred to as the 'hope-manufacturing business'. However, because I have witnessed people regain their humanity following a lifetime of violence and degradation, I am fortunate to have reservoirs of hope on which to draw. Yet, I also know that the first step to healing the effects of violence is perhaps the most crucial and that the first step consists in regaining a sense of safety. This safety must exist in the actual environment and, especially, in the social environment. Yet, safety must also be established within the individual's thoughts, emotions and body. For this internal work, curiosity and mindfulness is a central part of the process. There is no space for judgement, shame or guilt – at least, not in the beginning. These emotions resurface later, when the person feels whole again and when he or she is ready also to witness the wholeness of others. Only then can emotions such as shame regain their prosocial role within the collective.

The challenge, of course, is how to create the conditions that foster safety in the social environments of the Great Lakes region, which can then become the foundation for healing and wholeness. In this regard, I question if the West can meaningfully contribute to fostering peace and healing in the region. I fear that without acknowledging the central role aggression plays in Western psyches and societies, violence in this and other regions of the world will continue to bear the weight of Western projections and will too often remain *incomprehensible, unimaginable, unspeakable* and *evil.* Hopefully, the time is near when the people of the Great Lakes region show the West how trauma is resolved and peace regained, thus escaping the dehumanisation that arguably has been colonisation's most lasting legacy.

References

Banks, Russell. 2008. *Dreaming up America*. New York: Seven Stories Press.

The Children's War. DVD. 2010. Directed by Andrew Krakower. Austin: Rare World Features.

Davoine, Françoise and Jean-Max Gaudillière. 2004. *History beyond Trauma*. Translated by Susan Fairfield. New York: Other Press.

De Mause, Lloyd. 2002. *The Emotional Life of Nations*. New York: Karnac.

Fabrega, Horacio. 2002. *Origins of Psychopathology: The Phylogenetic and Cultural Basis of Mental Illness*. New Brunswick: Rutgers University Press.

Ferenczi, Sandor. 1988. 'Confusion of Tongues between Adults and the Child'. *Contemporary Psychoanalysis* 24: 196–206.

Foucault, Michel. 1970. *The Order of Things: An Archaeology of the Human Sciences*. New York: Random House.

———. 1988. *Madness and Civilization: A History of Insanity in the Age of Reason*. Translated by Richard Howard. New York: Vintage Books.

Gilligan, James. 1997. *Violence: Reflections on a National Epidemic*. New York: Vintage Books.

Gourevitch, Philip. 1998. *We Wish to Inform You That Tomorrow We Will Be Killed with Our Families: Stories from Rwanda*. New York: Picador.

Hatzfeld, Jean. 2009. *The Antelope's Strategy: Living in Rwanda after the Genocide*. New York: Farrar, Straus and Giroux.

Heidegger, Martin. 1966. *Discourse on Thinking*. Translated by John Anderson and E. Hans Freund. New York: Harper & Row.

Herman, Judith. 1997. *Trauma and Recovery: The Aftermath of Violence – from Domestic Abuse to Political Terror*. New York: Basic Books.

Hochschild, Adam. 1998. *King Leopold's Ghost: A Story of Greed, Terror, and Heroism in Colonial Africa*. New York: Houghton Mifflin.

Kerr, Laura K. 2000. 'How We Become Mentally Ill'. Ph.D. dissertation. Stanford: Stanford University.

———. 2010. 'Dissociation in Late Modern American Society'. Master's thesis, Pacifica Graduate Institute, Carpinteria.

Lemarchand, René. 2009. *The Dynamics of Violence in Central Africa (National and Ethnic Conflict in the 21st Century)*. Philadelphia: University of Pennsylvania.

Levine, Peter. 1997. *Waking the Tiger: Healing Trauma*. Berkeley: North Atlantic Books.

Mudimbe, V-Y. 1988. *The Invention of Africa: Gnosis, Philosophy, and the Order of Knowledge*. Bloomington: Indiana University Press.

Mudimbe, V-Y, Godé Iwele and Laura Kerr. 2007. *The Normal and Its Orders*. Ottawa: Editions Malaïka.

Mudimbe, V-Y, David Jakubec, Laura K. Kerr, Lucien Barrelet and Danielle Trudeau. 1997. 'Phenomenology of Madness'. Unpublished manuscript. Stanford: Stanford University.

Ogden, Pat, Kekuni Minton and Clare Pain. 2006. *Trauma and the Body: A Sensorimotor Approach to Psychotherapy*. New York: W.W. Norton.

Pelton, Robert D. 1989. *The Trickster in West Africa: A Study of Mythic Irony and Sacred Delight*. Los Angeles: University of California Press.

Rabinow, Paul. 1984. *The Foucault Reader*. New York: Pantheon Books.

Sartre, Jean-Paul. 1965. *Being and Nothingness*. New York: Washington Square Press.

Seigel, Jerrold. 1999. 'Foreword'. In *Madness and Democracy: The Modern Psychiatric Universe*, by Marcel Gauchet and Gladys Swain, vii–xxvi. Translated by Catherine Porter. Princeton: Princeton University Press.

Smail, Daniel Lord. 2008. *On Deep History and the Brain*. Berkeley: University of California Press.

Wallin, David J. 2007. *Attachment in Psychotherapy*. New York: The Guilford Press.

CHAPTER 7

On the Banality of Violence
State, Power and the Everyday in Africa

Zubairu Wai

> Violence would in principle qualify as evil. In this case, etymology is a good path to ethics. In effect, from Latin *violentia* and its semantic field, the meanings of the word violence are organized around the idea of *violare*, to injure, outrage. The word always implies the degradation of an integrity, that of a thing or of a human being. As a matter of fact, *violentia* is a synonym to *iniuria*, affront and injustice in the literal and figurative sense.
>
> — V-Y Mudimbe, 'For Fanon: A Meditation'

In this chapter, I propose a thesis about the banality of violence in Africa.[1] By 'banality of violence' I refer not only to the ubiquity of the routines of violence normalised in the repetition of everyday social and power relations. Nor do I refer simply to the ways hierarchical modes of power are replicated in the everyday sphere of social and power relations. Rather, I refer to the way violence, as a central constitutive element of African social and political life, incarnates the structures of states and society and thus defines and sustains the very nature of everyday social and power relations. This extends from the most grotesque expressions of quotidian terror spearheaded by the state and other political organisms supporting or opposing it to the predictable and utterly banal gestures of everyday interactions, private and public dialogues, institutional and bureaucratic procedures and practices, as well as the ways political, economic and social systems on the continent function and the catastrophic consequences they have on African modes of living and way of life – seen, for example, in the realities of poverty, disease, economic hardships, demographic imbalance and the political, symbolic, systemic and structural forces that create and give expression to them. As a specific form of power, violence, I will argue, is central to the production and maintenance of the myriad of social relations within the states and societies on the African continent and is present in every form of social and power relation; in other words, it is what structures these relations and gives expression to them.

The intermediate space

In the first five, sometimes hardly noticed, pages of *The Invention of Africa* (1988), V-Y Mudimbe introduces a theoretical region that, in its rigour and complexities, challenges the dominant Africanist understanding of African state forms. After briefly reviewing the major positions in the debate on the impulses that drove the imperatives for colonisation of the continent in the nineteenth century, Mudimbe reaches the conclusion that irrespective of what theory or explanation one accepts, the application of colonialism in Africa resulted in the same outcome: a 'colonizing structure responsible for producing marginal societies, cultures and human beings' (1988: 3). Mudimbe refers here to the framework for organising, arranging and transforming African societies into essentially European constructs. This colonising structure, he tells us, consists of three interrelated and complementary aspects. First, is the domination of physical space, which involves the procedures and processes of annexing, distributing, managing and exploiting land in the colonies. The second comprises reforming the minds of the natives through policies of domestication, 'civilisation' and Christianisation. The third involves subsuming and integrating African economies, social and cultural systems and histories into a Western historicity and perspective. This is done through the systematic and progressive destruction and transformation of indigenous political and socio-economic organisations and systems and the institution or imposition of new modes of production, while incorporating the continent and its economies into the global capitalist system through violent appropriative and exploitative processes and institutional arrangements that produce misery and marginality.

Completely embracing the physical, human and spiritual aspects of the colonising experience, this structure also clearly indicated a projected metamorphosis through which African societies would purportedly be regenerated in line with the evolutionist preconceptions of the colonising order and its modernisationist fantasies:

Because of the colonizing structure, a dichotomizing system has emerged, and with it a great number of current paradigmatic oppositions have developed: traditional versus modern; oral versus written and printed;

agrarian and customary communities versus urban and industrialized civilization; subsistence economies versus highly productive economies. In Africa a great deal of attention is generally given to the evolution implied and promised by the passage from the former paradigms to the latter. This presupposed jump from one extremity (underdevelopment) to the other (development) is in fact misleading. By emphasizing the formulation of techniques of economic change, the model tends to neglect a structural mode inherited from colonialism. Between the two extremes there is an intermediate, a diffused space in which social and economic events define the extent of marginality (Mudimbe 1988: 3).

This intermediate space is an amorphous space; it is ambiguous and diffused and although it incarnates multiple contradictory and overlapping tendencies, it illustrates, in very concrete ways, the effects of colonial palimpsestic inscriptions of modernist violence in terms of institutional make-up, spatial and temporal arrangements and practices and identity effects of the colonising order on indigenous African spaces, cultures, societies and beings. It is also a site of violence and designates both an explanation and illustration of the extent of the dangerous precariousness of the continent's colonial past and its present-day marginality:

> Marginality designates the intermediate space between the so-called African tradition and the projected modernity of colonialism. It is apparently an urbanized space in which, as S. Amin noted, 'vestiges of the past, especially the survival of structures that are still living realities (tribal ties, for example) often continue to hide the new structures (ties based on class, or on groups defined by their position in the capitalist system).' This space reveals not so much that new imperatives could achieve a jump into modernity, as the fact that despair gives this intermediate space its precarious pertinence and, simultaneously, its dangerous importance (Mudimbe 1988: 5).

Economically, the nature of this space can be seen, for example, in the extent to which the transformations in the relations, processes and forces of production fashioned by the colonial imposition has led to a systematic disruption of indigenous political, economic and social organisations and the imposition of new economic and social systems:

> If the relatively low productivity of traditional processes of production (formerly adapted to the then-existing markets and range of trade and exchanges) has been disrupted by a new division of labour which depends upon international markets, then transformation has meant a progressive destruction of traditional realms of agriculture and crafts (Mudimbe 1988: 4).

The increasing disintegration of indigenous social organisations and a growing lumpenproletarianisation of urban spaces, seen, for example, in the volumes of rural-urban migrations and the increasing army of poor, angry and unemployed urban youths living in precarious conditions, can be regarded as a result of capitalist transformation of these societies and the destabilisation of their indigenous social and economic organisations and institutions by the largely incoherent establishment of new social and economic arrangements and institutions whose modalities lie elsewhere.

On the cultural and religious plane, while the colonising enterprise, through new institutional set-ups (schools, churches, the press, new audio-visual media and so on), succeeded in diffusing new cultural and social attitudes, both complex and contradictory in terms of their cultural and spiritual values, it also broke what could be regarded as the relative cultural unity and religious integration of most African societies and traditions:

> From that moment on the forms and formulations of the colonial culture and its aims were somehow the means of trivializing the whole traditional mode of life and its spiritual framework. The potential and necessary transformations meant that the mere presence of this new culture was a reason for the rejection of unadapted persons and confused minds (Mudimbe 1988: 3).

Taken together, these interrelated planes that make up the intermediate space constitute an environment or site of violence, misery and despair. It is also the locus of paradoxes where various overlapping and contradictory tendencies exist in tension with each other:

> It reveals the strong tension between a modernity that often is an illusion of development, and a tradition that sometimes reflects a poor image of a mythical past. It also unveils the empirical evidence of this tension by

131

showing concrete examples of developmental failures such as demographic imbalance, extraordinarily high birth rates, progressive disintegration of the classic family structure, illiteracy, severe social and economic disparities, dictatorial regimes functioning under the cathartic name of democracy, the breakdown of religious traditions, the constitution of syncretic churches, etc. (Mudimbe 1988: 5).

These contradictions, which should be taken seriously, invite the need for a critical reassessment of the developmentalist and modernisationist projects in Africa. Any interest in seeking to understand Africa's present-day condition must, Mudimbe insists, first seek to unravel the complexities and multiple dimensions of this intermediate space, which, according to him, remains a major condition of postcolonial governmentality and political, economic, social and cultural realities on the continent. Since the beginning of Africa's colonising experience, the intermediate space has constituted, and remains, a major problem for transformative forces and processes; for 'rather than being a step in the imagined "evolutionary process," it has been the locus of paradoxes that call into question the modalities and implications of modernisation in Africa' (Mudimbe 1988: 5).

The concept of the intermediate space introduces a theoretical region that challenges the dominant ways in which African political and social formations are theorised and understood in mainstream Africanist discourses. As a theoretical (and empirical) region, it demands a rethinking of how political and social formations on the continent are approached. First, it draws attention to the constitutive relationship between the continent's postcolonial present and its colonial past and designates a concrete expression of a colonising structure, which Mudimbe asserts, structures (if not overdetermines) the continent's present-day reality. This point is important and should be emphasised, given especially the persistent tendency among Africanists towards ideological and theoretical approaches predisposed to effacing and rendering invisible the relational and structural logic of the past histories of colonial domination and contemporary imperial power relations, within which African states have historically been constituted and continue to be reconstituted and reimagined. One cannot understand Africa's present-day reality without situating it within larger historical and structural processes that help define those realities.

Second, the concept of the intermediate space theorises African states as 'hybrid' formations fashioned out of the violence of colonial domination. This conception of hybridity can be opposed with Homi Bhabha's interstitial spaces, which represent the ultimate failure of colonial domination since hybridity for him is 'the strategic reversal of the process of domination through disavowal' (1994: 159) and are hence already imbued with regenerative potential, in the sense that they constitute resistance in itself:

> Resistance is not necessarily an oppositional act of political intention, nor is it the simple negation or exclusion of the 'content' of another culture, as a difference once perceived. It is the effect of an ambivalence produced within the rules of recognition of dominating discourses as they articulate the signs of cultural difference and reimplicate them within the deferential relations of colonial power—hierarchy, normalization, marginalization, and so forth (Bhabha 1994: 158).

In contrast, Mudimbe's hybridity is the result of the palimpsestic inscriptions of colonial modernity and its colonising imprints in relation to African spaces, cultures, societies and beings within structures that aim to turn them into essentially European constructs, but which obstruct them in two ways: they are neither quite modern nor authentically traditional; they are neither colonial nor postcolonial, but a haphazard mixing of the several excesses of both systems, so that they reinforce and cadence each other. A palimpsest thus is not a neutral transformative reality devoid of hierarchies. Neither is it the mark of the failure of colonial domination *à la* Bhabha; rather, it is a mark of power and violence, a testament to what has been erased and inscribed upon. Though the colonising is itself contaminated by this encounter, it completely transforms the colonised, leaving faded traces, disjointed memories, sometimes impossible to reconstruct. It thus signifies a violation of what once was or could have been and, as such, signifies the violence of unequal power relations, thus designating a tension between multiple temporalities, rationalities, spatialities and ways of being.

The African case illustrates this well: as an intermediate space, it designates a 'tension between a modernity that often is an illusion of development, and a tradition that sometimes reflects a poor image of a mythical past' (Mudimbe 1988: 5). And this is what, in part, accounts for the tensions, violence and conflictual instability of the continent's postcolonial condition. On the one hand, African states, constituted under concrete conditions of colonial domination, cannot be cut off completely from their historical regions of emergence and remain trapped in the thraldom of the violence of their constitution, which obstructs them in one way. On the other hand, they are cut off from their indigenous roots and thus suspended in the in-between of spatial intermediacy, which obstructs them in another way. As intermediate spaces, African states and societies are thus the locus of multiple contradictory tendencies: seen, as it were, in the existence of plural temporalities, spatialities and realities, simultaneously layered and experienced within a space that is co-produced, but united under the power of a violent order – the colonising structure. The present is layered over a past that is at once visible and invisible, hence the locus of conflicts and tensions.

One recalls here Achille Mbembe's heteroglossic conception of what he calls the 'postcolony', which he suggests is the 'product of several cultures, heritages and traditions of which the features have become entangled over time, to the point where something has emerged that has the look of custom without being reducible to it, and partakes in modernity without being wholly included in it' (2001: 25). This, in its basic structuration, not inscription, speaks to the structural imprints of the intermediate space and draws attention to the multiple tendencies that simultaneously define and limit its reality. Indeed, even questions about 'tradition', 'custom', 'culture' or 'tribe' are not that simple and straightforward. Eric Hobsbawm and Terence Ranger's edited volume, *The Invention of Tradition* (1992), is a telling illustration. Mahmood Mamdani's seminal publication, *Citizen and Subject* (1996), also reminds us about the political nature of such notions, being as they are, at least in the African context, the invention of colonial modernity. As Mamdani tells us, the political modernity instituted by colonialism was partly enunciated through the tribalisation of authority, whereby the customary was systematically produced and distorted by giving an authoritarian bent to 'tradition'. As one of the sites and realms of modern colonial power and authority, this spearheaded the violence of the local state (where much of the violence of the colonial state was concentrated) in a bifurcated state structure. As such, the violence of the everyday, linked to so-called customary institutions, is partially the handiwork of the colonising structure and a violent political legacy.

Third is the demand for understanding this reality of the concept of the intermediate space in its specificity, but in relation to its history of constitution, its socio-historical and power-political regions of emergence and its structural relation with a violent and exploitative global system and how these manifest in concrete political terms in the present. At the heart of this is a methodological predicament. After Mudimbe in *Parables and Fables* (1991), it can be reformulated this way:

can one think about, and comment upon, the specificity of African political and social life without essentialising or pathologising their features, especially given the authority of the colonial library that has over centuries invented and continues to invent Africa as a paradigm of difference? On the other hand, if relationality as a concept can explain the structural realities of past histories of colonial domination and contemporary imperial power relations, within which states in Africa have been historically constituted and are still being reconstituted and reimagined, can one accept their implications without opposing the specificity of the continent's experiences and falling back on comparative methodologies that reduce its conceptual existence to a footnote, or in the shadow (a particular aberrant expression) of the European experience expressed as the universal?

The first question involves the challenge of the pervasive evolutionist thinking central to colonial and postcolonial developmentalist teleologies, which persistently set Africa up against current conceptions of Western modernity (Wai 2012a). Indeed, Africanist scholarship is pervaded by a vulgar universalism that persistently subsumes the historicity of the continent under the totalitarian grip of a Eurocentric, unilinear, evolutionist framework that disregards its specificities. Explicitly or implicitly, this evolutionist framework produces a narrative and a notion of history that holds that African phenomena only really make sense when mirrored on an earlier European history. This notion of history, which Mamdani has called 'history by analogy', 'privileges the European historical experience as the touchstone, and as the historical expression of the universal' (1996: 9ff.). A crucial epistemological stance of Africanism, this conception of history is partially the reason that Africanist scholarship has been unable to come to terms with historically specific African realities and, thus, has not only failed to comprehend (and therefore incorrectly or problematically interpreted) these realities, but has also produced a particular mechanistic conception of history, abstracted from the experience of Europe, conceptualised as the historical expression of the universal that offers a prescription for all to emulate (Mamdani 1996; Wai 2012a, 2012b). As Mamdani (1996) argues, the narrative produced in this way tends to denigrate social and political realities in Africa, thereby reinforcing the image of the continent as a place for the absurd, the aberrant or inadequate, occurring in the shadow of earlier European experiences. In the process, the independent conceptual existence of the continent is denied and its aberrance is named. While its history is reduced to or interpreted as an imperfect recurrence of, or deviation from, earlier patterns or stages in the evolution of European societies, its future, which can only really make sense or can only really be valid if modelled on the trajectories of the evolution of Western societies, is supposed to be already determined.

The problem though, and here I agree with Mbembe (2001), is that these problematic approaches, which legitimate themselves by stressing their capacity for constructing universal grammars informed by historicist and evolutionist teleologies and preconceptions, condemn themselves to making problematic and hare-brained generalisations from the idioms of a provincialism within whose dominant paradigms it is extremely difficult to understand non-Western systems and realities:

> Thus there arises the purely methodological question of knowing whether it is possible to offer an intelligible reading of the forms of social and political imagination in contemporary Africa solely through conceptual structures and fictional representation used precisely to deny African societies any historical depth and to define them as radically *other*, as all that the West is not (Mbembe 2001: 11).

Indeed, as Mudimbe ponders in another context, given that it is a very specific localism with its own ethnocentric biases, can the universal transcend all transhistorical lines and their specific variations without submitting to its own memory and the biases of its *ethnos* (Mudimbe 2013: 187)? The implication of the methodological and epistemological critique is treating African societies like every other society – that is, as systems in their own right, with their own internal structural logics, organisational contingencies and instabilities and possible norms of explanations, but in relation to something else: their historical region of emergence.

The second methodological challenge involves the possibilities of sublating the specific and the relational and reading them dialogically as co-constitutive. What comes to mind again is Mbembe's conception of the 'historicity' of African societies, which he suggests is 'rooted in a multiplicity of times, trajectories, and rationalities, that although particular and sometimes local, cannot be conceptualised outside a world that is, so to speak, globalized' (2001: 9). This alerts us to the fact that the specificity of African life cannot be understood without situating it within larger historical and structural currents and realities of an imperial globality, which from the fifteenth century onwards has necessitated both a will to power and will to truth that have, over the centuries, reproduced African subjectivities, defined the continent's realities and structured its present-day experiences. Though he does not always honour his own methodological and theoretical injunctions – for example, his conception of the 'postcolony', while based on an appropriation of Kafka's 'In the Penal Colony' (1971), is caught up in the thraldoms of the problematic French Africanist scholarship that reads contemporary African political life in terms of criminalisation and disorder (see for example Bayart 1993, 1999; Chabal and Daloz 1999); conceptions that can be interpreted as a reinscription of nineteenth-century racialist conceptions of Africa used to justify *la mission civilisatrice* – Mbembe is right in insisting that

> from the fifteenth century, there is no longer a 'distinctive historicity' of these societies, one not embedded in times and rhythms heavily conditioned by European domination. Therefore, dealing with African societies' 'historicity' requires more than simply giving an account of what occurs on the continent itself at the interface between the working of internal forces and the working of international actors (Mbembe 2001: 9).

Slajov Žižek's statement about the complicity of the workings of global capitalism in the carnage in the Democratic Republic of the Congo (DRC), for example – and this in fact also holds true for Sierra Leone, Liberia and other states in Africa affected by armed conflicts and civil unrest – can help to illustrate this point:

> Beneath the façade of [what is represented as] ethnic warfare, we [. . .] discern the workings of global capitalism [. . .] Each of the [so-called] warlords has business links to a foreign company or corporation exploiting the mostly mining wealth in the region. This arrangement suits both parties: the corporations get mining rights without taxes and other complications, while the warlords get rich. The irony is that many of these minerals are used in high-tech products such as laptops and cell phones – in short: forget about [what is represented as] the savage behavior of the local population, just remove the foreign high-tech companies from the equation and the whole edifice of ethnic warfare fuelled by old passions fall apart [. . .] There certainly is a great deal of darkness in the dense Congolese jungle – but its causes lie elsewhere, in the bright executive offices of our banks and high-tech companies (Žižek 2011: 163–64).

It is therefore problematic to focus mainly on what goes on in the war zones in places such as the DRC without linking them to historical and structural forces – in this case, the functioning of the global capitalist system and the catastrophic consequences it has for places such as the DRC, where its structural violence is displaced and where its effects are more manifestly dire, as seen in the 'active violence of people' (Bourdieu 1997: 233).

The atmosphere of violence

The conception of the intermediate space defines the reality of postcolonial African societies, which, I suggest, exist in an atmosphere of violence. By this, I mean a condition in which, owing in part to the colonising structure and its violent historical, political and structural legacies, an atmosphere exists where every social and political relation – from the most banal gestures, public and private dialogues, interactions and utterances to the institutional and bureaucratic practices and procedures, processes of governing and even everyday interactions in the home, between state and citizens, security forces and protesters, public servants and citizens attempting to access bureaucratic service and so on – easily lends itself to violence, has a potentiality for violence and, in fact, does frequently express itself through violence. Incarnating a space of absolute violence, the structures of everyday social and power relations are sustained by this violence, which puts them permanently on the brink of explosion. This is to say that the states are constantly under the threat of sudden eruption, so that at any given moment, a seemingly peaceful and stable environment can suddenly become dramatic and abruptly erupt in violence.

It was Frantz Fanon (1963) who first alerted us to the existence of this atmosphere of violence. Writing about violence in the colonial context, Fanon designated an *atmosphere of violence* as the general state of anxiety, nervousness and insecurity that intrinsically defines the existential reality of life in a colonial environment. Underneath a thin layer of normality, a state of deep insecurity and potential for violence prevails and can be seen in sporadic outbursts. Although this atmosphere is especially palpable in periods immediately preceding the outbreak of anti-colonial violence when the people respond to the state of siege that colonialism imposes with anti-colonial militant action, it also incorporates the general state of violence that structures power relations in a colonial situation – the violence that defines the mood, structure of feeling, methods of social and political control and the general state of uncertainty and nervousness that characterise colonised societies. Whether in a time immediately preceding anti-colonial outbursts and armed struggle for national liberation or in the general state of being under colonial domination, an atmosphere prevails in which violence ontologically exists under the surface of the thin layer of normality and stability and defines the everyday lived reality of a colonised people. This is, in part, because of the fact that colonialism is a regime of violence and a relation of force that relies on specific instruments of terror and coercion to institute its modalities, legitimate its practices based on its own produced rationality, tar its subjugated populations with visible marks of power (Bhabha 1994: 158) and sustain its hold on captive societies. 'The colonial regime owes its legitimacy to force,' Fanon writes (1963: 84); it is this 'violence which has ruled over the ordering of the colonial world, which has ceaselessly drummed the rhythm for the destruction of native social forms and broken up without reserve the systems of reference of the economy, the customs of dress and external life' (40). This violence is primary and absolute and it defines the entire colonial encounter and edifice in a violent zero-level background: 'The first encounter was marked by violence and their existence together – that is to say the exploitation of the native by the settler – was carried on by dint of a great array of bayonets and cannons' (36). It is this reality that creates and sustains the atmosphere of violence.

The atmosphere of violence can be contrasted with another: *violence in action*, in which the 'active violence' of colonised peoples confronts the terror of colonial domination in open conflict. Bhabha reminds us that it was Fanon who first recognised that the state of emergency, as Walter Benjamin suggests, might be the rule rather than the exception, but it is also always a possible state of emergence, for it invites a response from forces articulating its negation in the form of militant action (Bhabha 1994: 59). *Violence in action* is this counter-violence. It is derivative, triggered by the extremity of colonial alienation and oppression. Driven by the resistance of 'natives' to colonialism, it is violence to end violence, to remove the scourge of colonial humiliation, reverse colonial alienation, affirm the humanity of the colonised subjects and usher in a postcolonial humanism. In violence in action, the atmosphere of violence is no longer disguised in the facade of 'normality' and 'peaceful' violence that colonised societies are steeped in. Rather, the 'the lids blow off' the simmering frustrations and anger and 'the atmosphere becomes dramatic' as the active violence of the 'natives', through a resort to insurgency action, gives utterance to anti-colonial humanist aspirations (Fanon 1963: 71).

These two conditions – an *atmosphere of violence* and *violence in action* – designate moments, not types, of violence. True, Fanon opposes two forms that violence in a colonial situation takes: 'settler' versus 'native' violence and these can be loosely interpreted as corresponding to the two conditions identified above. However, the relationship between the moments of violence, on the one hand, and the types of violence, on the other, is not that straightforward: both types of violence can, in fact, occur in any of these two moments of violence and therefore cannot be said to necessarily designate a corresponding reality. It is important to note, however, that Fanon's concern is not in constructing typologies of violence, but in highlighting the visions and politics mobilised in these moments of violence, as well as figuring out the role or utility of violence in anti-colonial praxis and national liberation struggles: 'Violence alone, violence committed by the people, violence organised and educated by its leaders, makes it possible for the masses to understand social truths and gives the key to them' (Fanon 1963: 147). This choice is absolute and non-negotiable: 'For the native, this violence represents the absolute line of action [. . .] The colonized man finds his freedom in and through violence. This rule of conduct enlightens the agent because it indicates to him the means and the end' (85–86). While privileging violence in action as a counter to the atmosphere of violence constitutive of the colonising order, Fanon is aware of the limits and destructive potentials of violence and warns against a type of violence and brutality that is astonishingly similar to revolutionary violence, but which 'is typically anti-revolutionary, hazardous, and anarchist' and which could bring about the defeat of any revolutionary movement if not recognised and immediately contained and combated (147).

The violence designated by these two moments constitutes a useful way of thinking about violence in postcolonial societies, which have never really been able to transcend the violence of their colonial constitution and the logic of its governmentality. It should be stressed that the 'post' in postcolonial does not refer to an 'end' of colonial violence, but a reproduction and reformulation of the regimes of oppressive power relations, often misunderstood as a temporal category designating an 'end'. The end of formal colonial rule did not also correspond to the end of its regimes of violence and the oppressive power relations it had constructed. Indeed, as Fanon himself reminds us, there is, in the African experience, a violence continuum between the colonial and postcolonial phases: 'The atmosphere of violence, after having coloured the colonial phase, continues to dominate national life' in the postcolonial phase (1963: 76). The main difference, perhaps, has been that with decolonisation, one set of people (Africans) replaced another set (Europeans), but the structures of state, its institutional make-up and logic of power have, because of the colonising structure, largely remained the same, as Mudimbe reminds us. This transition, however, has accented the intimate violence that binds the postcolonial state and its subject populations, in the sense that Africans themselves now preside over the violent structure of the successor of the colonial state, which in turn means that the violence of the system and responses to it are now seen as generative from internal dysfunctions endogenously produced and blamed, in part, on corrupt and dictatorial regimes, while the legacies of colonialism and the catastrophic consequences of the structural realities of the global political economy are written over and absolved from blame.

The atmosphere of violence is grotesque. It temporalises itself as an asphyxiation that suffocates the intermediate space, transforming it into a *habitus* of death, of pain and of 'shuffering and shmiling' as Fela Kuti, the fearless Nigerian musician and Afrobeat pioneer, describes it. It is a space of violence, of injustice, of marginality, of precariousness and, ultimately, of terror and death. It is a rough terrain in the mode of Fela Kuti's 'Roforofo Fight' – the public display of violence seen, for example, in the types of public altercations that erupt between opposing individuals, groups, factions or feuding families out of inconsequential encounters, but which end up uniting both participants and spectators and turning them into unrecognisable beings transformed by violence:

> Roforofo don change them
> Them go look like twins
> You nor go know who be who
> You nor go know your friend from who.

To live in this space, to engage in it, to fight it, or even resist it, is to become it, to be swept in its vortex and become one with it. In this sense, the state of siege that animates the atmosphere of violence can generate or invite militant action, but this invited action is hardly ever capable of transcending its region of emergence since it is structured by the logic of the very violence it is contesting.

Conceptualising violence

Referring to Johan Galtung's (2009) conception of violence, let us proceed by positing a series of conceptual lines to delineate and reconstitute the plurality of violence that incarnates this atmosphere of violence:

1.   manifest versus latent;
2.   visible versus invisible;
3.   subjective versus objective;
4.   physical versus psychological; and
5.   agential versus structural.

The first entries – manifest, visible, subjective, physical and agential – involve the obviously recognisable acts of physical violence performed by and associated with clearly identifiable agents. They designate situations whereby, as Galtung tells us, 'a clear subject-object relation is manifest because it is visible as action. It corresponds to our ideas of what *drama* is, and it is personal because there are persons committing the violence' (2009: 83). Such acts include violent crimes, assaults, wars, genocides, rapes and sexual assaults, acts of terror, torture, political repression, political and civil unrest and so on. It is usually these acts involving the exertion of physical force and their disturbing consequences that dominate popular, mainstream perceptions about violence. This is partly because they are 'personal' and can be captured and expressed verbally and can be attributed to specific subjects committing the violent acts. However, violence is more encompassing than its physical manifestations, for, as already pointed out, it is constitutive of our very political, social, cultural and economic systems; it not only makes them possible, but also sustains and gives expression to them.

The first entries are thus linked to the second entries – latent, invisible, objective, psychological and structural – which are hidden in plain sight in symbolic and systemic arrangements and ideational processes and sustained through structural apparatuses of power and privilege and domination and exploitation, through which terrains of consciousness and ways of being are colonised and controlled. These types of violence are embedded in the structures of society and are responsible for the way our political and economic systems function. They involve 'the more subtle forms of coercion that sustains relations of domination and exploitation' (Žižek 2008: 9) and thus function without directly observable subject-object relations, which makes their complicity in violent outbreaks very difficult to detect. However, it is usually these types of violence that are responsible for the production and sustaining of both global and domestic inequality and domination, privilege and affluence, on the one hand, and marginality and misery, on the other. It is usually these kinds of violence that provide the background and structure that sustain the visible forms of violence performed by identifiable agents. Violence in civil wars, for example, is usually structured by these invisible and latent forces, which are expressed in the political realm of insurgency and counter-insurgency warfare; they represent a passage from one moment of violence – an atmosphere of violence – to another – active violence or violence in action – when conditions in society boil over into active or hot conflict and violent implosion.

The relationship between these conceptual fields, though straightforward and obvious, is often misrecognised, as mainstream discourses on violence typically focus on its physical manifestations, seen in dramatic subject-object relations. But, as Žižek reminds us, violence enacted by social agents is only the most visible form of what for him is a triumvirate of violence: subjective, objective and symbolic (2008: 11). In order to fully understand what gives rise to visible acts of violence performed by identifiable agents, he reminds us, critical attention needs to be paid to the workings of the hidden forces that create the conditions for such violent outbursts. This is because violence never occurs in a vacuum; it is always the result of complex power relations, which have complex socio-historical regions of emergence that not only give it its meaning and dangerous pertinence, but also account for it in an essential way. Like every social reality, violence is structured by power and therefore constitutes a specific manifestation of power.

These two entries can be further disaggregated into the multiple forms they take. The first axis is political. By political violence, I refer to two interrelated things. On the one hand, it designates the idea that all violence is political, in the sense that violence is always the effect and manifestation of power. Conversely, it means that power is intimately connected with violence and thus that which gives expression to it. Jan Patočka's rehabilitation of the Heraclitus dictum about warfare as the central constitutive element of social and political life comes to mind here: 'Polemos is the father of all,' he tells us. It is that which is 'common to all' and that which 'lets everything particular be and manifest itself as what it is' (1996: 43). Since the ancient Greeks and the Romans, he insists, war, a specific expression of violence, has dominated political and social life, for it is what constitutes the polis and, at the same time, 'the primordial insight that makes philosophy possible'. It is the very expression of power and sociality and is situated at the heart of the most 'rational' projects for the promotion of peace and stability; for the same hand that stages orgies is that which also organises everydayness (114). This Patočkan lesson can be applied to violence generally and used to suggest its constitutive character as a major condition of power in every society. What is responsible for wars, terror, brutalities, genocides, mass killings, political repression and so on is, at the same time, what organises everyday lives and sustains our economic, social, political and knowledge systems and makes even the interpretation of violence possible. As such, Žižek is right in insisting on the inseparability of what he has labelled 'subjective' and 'objective' violence, which corresponds to the conceptual lines posited earlier and the way they constitute social and political life:

> Subjective violence is experienced as such against the background of non-violent zero level. It is seen as a perturbation of the 'normal,' peaceful state of things. However, objective violence is precisely the violence inherent to this 'normal' state of things. Objective violence is invisible since it sustains the very zero-level standard against which we perceive something as subjectively violent. Objective violence is thus something like the notorious 'dark matter' of physics, the counterpart to an all-too-visible subjective violence. It may be invisible, but it has to be taken into account if one is to make sense of what otherwise seem to be 'irrational' explosion of subjective violence (Žižek 2008: 2).

This understanding of violence should inform the way violence in postcolonial Africa, which is the very expression of the power associated with states constituted under concrete conditions of colonial domination and which still remain dependent on their ontological region of emergence, is understood and accounted for. Like the Patočkan conception of *polemos* as 'the father of all' and that which is 'common to all', violence is that which structures African societies and informs the very acts of interpreting them. It is a very specific expression of power and is central to the production and maintenance of the myriad of social and power relations on the continent.

On the other hand, political violence designates physical acts of violence (such as assault, torture, terror, political repression, police brutality, paramilitary, insurgency and counter-insurgency violence, armed resistance, riots and so on) performed by and in the name of the state, political ideologies, revolutionary movements, armed insurgency groups and other such political organisms, either reinforcing the state or opposing it and contesting state power. Related to the active contestation over state power and the exercise of it, as well as responses to it, political violence, which has clearly identifiable subjects and falls within the subject-object dimension of violence, is among the most visible forms of violence. It is quick to elicit social alarm and moral outrage and attract revulsion and condemnation. In Africa, this type of violence is linked to the form and nature of the postcolonial state and its regimes of violence, paraphernalia of coercion, systems of repression and force, which are themselves structured and informed by (a) the violent structural legacies of colonialism (the colonising structure) and, (b) the relational logics and catastrophic consequences of contemporary processes of power, domination and resistance in the global political economy, which creates conditions for violence.

Anybody vaguely familiar with the nature of postcolonial governmentality in Africa would recognise the pervasiveness of this type of violence. Whether the state is a one-party state or is ruled by a military junta or a so-called democratic regime, the logic of the exercise of power is largely the same: it is arbitrary and easily lends itself to violence and abuse. In Sierra Leone, Nigeria, the DRC and elsewhere on the continent, one is likely to encounter the flagrant manifestation of power if you are within the reach of its exercise. This holds for relationships between the state and its citizens, the security forces and demonstrators, office secretaries and citizens seeking bureaucratic service, workers and their bosses, chiefs and their wards and so forth. A university professor can, with impunity, fail a student who refuses to sleep with him; bosses could get their female assistants fired for turning down their advances; police officers could arrest someone for refusing to pay a bribe. There are many examples of governments withholding much needed development projects as punishments for communities supporting the opposition.

Fela Kuti understood this reality well and depicted it in his numerous compositions, probably better than any political scientist ever will. It is in his work, which captures the multiple dimensions of postcolonial African political life and the quotidian violence it is stuck in, that one comes face to face with the contours and realities of postcolonial political violence, the nature of the pathologies of power, its paradoxes and violent inclinations. In 'Sorrow, Tears and Blood', for example, he paints a vivid picture of how police action, in response to ordinary protest action or oppositional politics, results in a state of despair, violence and death:

Everybody run, run, run
Everybody scatter, scatter
Some people lost some bread
Someone nearly die
Someone just die

Police dey come, army dey come
Confusion everywhere
Seven minutes later
All don cool down brother
Police don go away, army don disappear
Them leave sorrow, tears and blood
Them regular trade mark.

Here, Fela Kuti is drawing attention to the intimate violence that connects the postcolonial state and its hapless subjects, the way the coercive instruments of state are deployed to quell dissent and how this accentuates the atmosphere of violence, which in turn creates a 'culture of terror', transforming the postcolonial state into a 'space of death' (Taussig 1984). His context is, of course, postcolonial Nigeria, but he might as well have been referring to any other African state: apartheid South Africa, Jean-Bédel Bokassa's Central African Republic, Félix Houphouët-Boigny's Côte d'Ivoire, Kwame Nkrumah's Ghana, Sékou Touré's Guinea, Samuel Doe's Liberia, Mohammed Siad Barre's Somalia, Idi Amin's Uganda, Mobutu Sese Seko's Zaïre, Laurent-Désiré Kabila's DRC, Paul Kagame's post-genocide Rwanda and so on. Growing up in Siaka Stevens's Sierra Leone, for example, the anxieties of quotidian terror spearheaded by the state hovered over everyday life and accented the atmosphere of violence in that state. In order to consolidate power, Stevens maintained a police state that terrorised its citizens through judicial and extrajudicial measures, terror tactics and paramilitary violence spearheaded by the notorious Internal Security Unit (ISU), later renamed State Security Division (SSD) (unflatteringly derided as 'I Shoot U' and 'Siaka Stevens Dogs' respectively). The state's attempt to crush anyone who dared to challenge Stevens's authority, as in the case of protest actions organised by university and high school students, for example, played out almost exactly in the grotesque form that Kuti renders it in 'Sorrow, Tears and Blood' or 'Kalakuta Show'.

But political violence in Africa is not a *de novo* experience; it is, as Mudimbe reminds us, a function and signifier of the intermediate space and the colonising structure that creates and sustains it. A property of the colonising structure, the postcolonial state is a violent political machine that relies on regimes of force and systems of coercion to maintain its hold on society and keep its captive populations in subjection. But this violence is also productive, in the sense that it has the capability for reproducing itself and even structuring responses to it.

While violence can take on an independent character, it is always really informed by and dependent on its logic of emergence and thus feeds on itself. This is partly why the generic postcolonial state remains largely indistinguishable from the colonial state that preceded it, in terms of the logic of rule and relations of subjugation and domination. This is also partially why insurgency groups fighting to overthrow repressive regimes end up mimicking the very violence that pushed them to insurgency in the first place, reproducing in some other guise the very system of oppression they are fighting to overthrow. Kabila's post-Mobutu DRC, but more specifically, the Revolutionary United Front (RUF) insurgency group in Sierra Leone or the National Patriotic Front of Liberia (NPFL) illustrate this well. As the RUF itself admits in its published documents, it was the logic that informs the exercise of power in postcolonial Sierra Leone that would, in part, inform their conduct as an insurgency group during the Sierra Leonean civil war:

> Intimidation, violence and threats of violence were used to control and contain the anger and frustrations of the suffering people. The APC [All People's Congress] regime will intimidate the people by a show of force with guns to 'show the people where power lies.' It is this experience that has taught the suffering Africans of Sierra Leone that power lies in the gun and whoever controls the guns controls the means of suppression and the means to steal the wealth of the country (Revolutionary United Front 1995).

With guns and a war machine, the RUF organised and deployed the same violence they claimed to be fighting against and now that they had control over the means of repression, terror and death, they resorted to stealing the wealth of the country and in the process badly brutalised the very people on whose behalf they claimed to have engaged in insurgency action. In the end, they became a poor reflection of the state they were fighting to overthrow. In other words, their actions were not really very different from the logic of violence associated with the exercise of power in Sierra Leone that they were contesting; what was different was the fact that they took that logic to its furthest possible extremes.

This is one of the areas where Fanon's prescription of violence as 'the perfect mediation' and a tool for leaving colonial hell becomes a little wanting, for it underestimates, by not paying sufficient attention to it, the structuring power of violence. Even in states where anti-colonial liberation wars succeeded in overthrowing the colonial state – Algeria, Angola, Guinea-Bissau, Mozambique, Zimbabwe and even South Africa – there is ample evidence to suggest that the states that emerged were, in important ways, very similar to the colonial state they overthrew, so that the same violence that had dominated the colonial phase would continue to colour the post-liberation phase. This is precisely why unarmed miners protesting for better wages and conditions of service in post-apartheid South Africa, for example, would be gunned down in cold blood by the state security apparatus in a political violence reminiscent of the apartheid era. Mamdani (1996) understands this structuring power of violence well and has indeed posited the legacies of late colonialism as a possible explanation for its persistence in relation to the nature of post-independence governmentality in Africa. For Mamdani, resistance against the colonial state and efforts at reforming its structure in the post-independence era have been fraught with the difficulty of transcending the institutional and structural imprints of a bifurcated state structure and its logic of decentralised despotism, so that every reform effort ends up reproducing its logic of constitution in different guise. In other words, the logic of power that shaped the structure of the colonial state and its violent inclinations is the same logic that continues to inform efforts at reforming or rebelling against it in the postcolonial era. Part of the challenge has been transcending the condition of possibility of the postcolonial state, whose modalities, because of the colonising structure, remain stuck in its colonial genesis and antecedent. But as Mudimbe (2013) ponders, can anything, really, transcend its condition of possibility?

This leads us to the second axis of violence: structural and systemic violence – violence embedded in the structures of our political, economic and social systems and the catastrophic consequences they have for people, states and societies (Žižek 2008; Galtung 2009; Scheper-Hughes and Bourgois 2004; Bourgois 2001). Structural violence is a quintessential example of the second conceptual field of violence identified earlier, which is very difficult to grasp because it is linked, not to identifiable subjects committing the acts of violence, but to the generic 'system'. As Galtung explains: 'There may not be any person who directly harms another person in the structure. The violence is built into the structure and shows up as unequal power and consequently as unequal life chances' (2009: 83). This violence is rooted in macro-level structures that underpin not only the organisation and functioning of global and domestic political and economic systems, but also social and culturally defined attitudes, towards gender and sexuality, for example. The global capitalist system and its exploitative logic are expressed or manifested locally in exploitative arrangements that result in unmitigated misery and physical, psychological and emotional anguish, captured by the depressing indices, for example, of privation, extreme poverty, grotesque forms of inequality and conditions of marginality (Bourgois 2001; Fanon 1963).

Pierre Bourdieu's structural 'law of the conservation of violence' needs to be recalled here (Bourdieu 1998; see also Žižek 2008; Galtung 2009). To Bourdieu, the 'active violence of people' is really the expression of the latent or hidden violence of the functioning of our political and economic systems. This is to say that the structural and systemic violence that potentiates world order and that the functioning of global, as well as domestic political and economic systems need to thrive, ultimately manifests itself concretely in real spatial and temporal terms. Violence, Bourdieu tells us, can be displaced and disguised, but it cannot be cheated, for ultimately, every form of violence, whether inert, displaced or disguised, will be paid for in concrete terms and this has real and adverse consequences on people and societies. In the specific context of the ongoing neoliberal attack on the welfare state in Europe and the likely fallout from it (we have now seen ample evidence of this fallout in riots in Paris and London and especially in Greece, but also Spain, Portugal and elsewhere), he cautions:

> You cannot cheat with the law of the conservation of violence: all violence is paid for, and for example, the structural violence exerted by the financial markets, in the form of layoffs, loss of security, etc., is matched sooner or later in the form of ['active violence of people' seen in] suicides, crime and delinquency, drug addiction, alcoholism, a whole host of minor and major everyday acts of violence (Bourdieu 1998: 40).

This has relevance for the African context (as can be seen in Sierra Leone, Liberia, the DRC and elsewhere on the continent), where the most tragic expressions of structural violence are seen in extreme poverty, precarious living conditions, violent insurgencies, civil wars, armed conflicts, communal violence and so on. That the conflicts of the 1990s came in the wake of the decimation of African economies by structural adjustment policies spearheaded by the International Monetary Fund and the World Bank, for example, is telling of the catastrophic consequences of Africa's historical and contemporary experience with a violent and exploitative world order, characterised by a political economy of unequal access to power and wealth and dominated by the narrow interests of the dominant capitalist states.

Conflicts on the continent therefore are partly the flagrant manifestation of the 'inert violence' of these historical and structural realities of global political and economic systems and their attendant catastrophic consequence in 'the active violence of people' (Bourdieu 1997: 233). But even when these wars break out, they remain immersed in the contexts and configurations of a global political economy of unequal power and wealth (Žižek 2011).

The parasitic relationship between African states, which were constituted under concrete conditions of Western colonial domination, and the West, whose narrow geopolitical interests have always stood in the way of African self-determination – and these states have remained immersed in the politics of global economic and political orders of unequal power relations that produce wealth and affluence, on the one hand, and conditions of dependence and insecurities, on the other – is partly what explains the extreme poverty, economic distress, lumpenproletarianisation of urban spaces, demographic imbalances, development failures, abusive working conditions, depressingly low life expectancies, high infant and maternal mortality rates, social disintegration of African societies, political crisis and conflicts on the continent and so on. In discussing violence in the international sphere, Fanon makes a timeless observation: 'Europe is literally the creation of the Third World. The wealth which smothers her is that which was stolen from the underdeveloped peoples' (1963: 102). Fanon is, of course, referring to the structural relations of power, domination and exploitation, the violence it portends for Africa and other non-Western societies and drawing attention to the co-production of the West and the non-West, in that the structural power that produces Western power, wealth, affluence and identity is simultaneously that which reproduces non-Western wretchedness, poverty and insecurities.

I would like to integrate a third axis of everyday, interpersonal violence, which is rooted in micro-level practices that underpin everyday social and power relations. Everyday violence incorporates both 'peace-time crimes' and the 'small wars and invisible genocides' that plague poor people, communities and states around the world (Scheper-Hughes 1992, 1996, 1997), as well as the banality of everyday life and 'the routine practices and expressions of interpersonal aggression that serve to normalize violence at the micro-level such as domestic, delinquent and sexual conflict, and even substance abuse' (Bourgois 2001). Everyday violence is both the product of social orders, which define attitudes, for example, towards gender and sexuality, family and domesticity, as well as the symbolic, structural and political apparatuses (in terms of their specific manifestation in the everyday sphere of societal and interpersonal relations). It can be difficult to detect as having structural, systemic, or even political properties – in part because it is disguised (hence normalised) in the repetition and banality of the everyday, but also because it is often interpreted through behavioural and psychologising perspectives that see it as the pathologies of identifiable individuals (Bourgois 2001; Scheper-Hughes 1992, 1996, 1997; Bourdieu 1997; Wai 2012a).

There is an intimate relationship and obvious overlap between political and structural violence and everyday interpersonal violence and the symbolic processes through which it is normalised and legitimated. The 'peace-time crimes' that Nancy Scheper-Hughes (1997) writes about, for example, are partially the effect of state-perpetrated or state-sponsored violence, as well as the consequences of the conditions imposed by structural inequalities and systemic violence. In Sierra Leone, for example, during the Stevens years, the state did not only use its disciplinary and coercive instruments (in the form of the army and paramilitary forces) to quell dissent and keep its captive population in check, it also used *raray man* (lumpen) youth, themselves victims of the state and its marginal existence, to unleash large-scale violence on opponents on an everyday basis. In addition, the structural violence that creates conditions of physical and emotional distress colours the nature of social interaction in the form of everyday violence, in terms of existential struggles over access to resources, anger and frustration, all of which frequently manifest themselves, for example, in domestic abuse, substance abuse, communal and interpersonal violence, open conflict and so on.

Jamaica Kincaid's account of the ease with which an event turns into the everyday and the everyday into event in the Caribbean island state of Antigua is a telling illustration:

(Here is this: On a Saturday, at market, two people who, as far as they know, have never met before, collide by accident, this accidental collision leads to an enormous quarrel – a drama, really – in which the two people stand at opposite ends of a street and shout insults at each other at the top of their lungs. This event soon becomes everyday, for every time these two people meet each other again, sometimes by accident, sometimes by design, the shouting and the insults begin) (1988: 56).

This holds true for most African societies as well. My own experience growing up in Sierra Leone tells me that such events-turned-everyday and everyday-turned-events are not only frequent, but also usually go beyond the two people they originate from to include their friends and relatives and so forth, so that what begins as an accidental mishap can quickly develop into huge fights that draw in whole communities and in which people are injured and which invite police action. And these kinds of conflicts could linger on for years until an opportunity presents itself for their violent re-enactment. (For example, some of the violence during the Sierra Leonean and Liberian civil wars had nothing to do with the RUF or the NPFL per se, but arose out of the opportunity that their insurgencies presented for settling old scores and for overturning the old political and social orders that informed everyday power relations, which easily lend themselves to violence and abuse. Indeed, the conflicts fed not only into the nature of political violence, but also the routinised and banalised patterns of everyday interpersonal violence that preceded the war. Many rural youths joined the warring factions to gain the power to carry out their revenge on chiefs they saw as corrupt or to settle scores in family feuds. In many places, feuding families actually encouraged family members to join opposing warring factions and this led to tit-for-tat attacks and reprisals wherever the conflict spread).

When Fela Kuti sings 'Roforofo Fight', it is precisely about this everyday violence that often grows from inconsequential encounters and erupts from nowhere, but that can easily and rapidly engulf not only those involved in it, but also the onlookers, passers-by and bystanders that he refers to. In most places in Africa, as in the Caribbean and Latin America, daily social interactions and dialogues, whether in the private or public sphere (such as the local market, the office, the parks, the everyday street) could be very violent encounters. A man can be beaten to death for stealing mangoes in the local market. I know of cases where a child's hands were dipped in burning oil or had melting plastic poured on them for stealing candy. These everyday acts of violence may well seem like random acts of depraved individuals, but there is more to them than is usually acknowledged. They occur in concrete conditions of power and domination and are potentiated by the conditions imposed by socio-historical, structural, systemic and power-political forces.

The issue though, as Bourdieu reminds us, is that there is another kind of violence, what he calls symbolic violence, contained in speech and its forms, that makes the violence 'exerted against stigmatized populations' very difficult to talk about 'in an accurate and realistic way without seeming either to crush them or exalt them' (1997: 233). While those living under conditions of domination and constant exposure to violence tend to tragically direct that same violence against their companions in misfortune, these actions, as tragic as they may be, are shaped by historical, structural and systemic forces that structure such violent outbursts: 'The violence exerted every day in families, factories, workshops, banks, offices, police stations, prisons, even hospitals and schools . . . is, in the last analysis, the product of the "inert violence" of economic structures and social mechanisms relayed by the active violence of people.' Take, for example, the Sierra Leonean civil war, in which some of the worst atrocities and acts of violence and brutalities against defenceless civilians were committed predominantly by marginalised urban and rural youth who made up the bulk of the various armed factions.

While one may be tempted, as has been done by many who have tried to interpret that conflict, to pathologise them as depraved, thus crushing them under psychologising perspectives that depict them as innately violent, they were themselves victims of the structure of violence embedded in the state of Sierra Leone and the forces responsible for its marginal position in a global system of unequal access to power and wealth and the dangerous and precarious conditions that this creates for its marginalised populations. That the violence and brutalities they perpetrated during the conflict were targeted at ordinary people like themselves makes it particularly disturbing, but this is 'one of the most tragic effects of the condition of the dominated' that Bourdieu tells us about. And this does not and should not make them inherently evil, or less human than those seeking to understand their actions. It also does not negate the veracity of their own marginal existence and lived realities under conditions of domination, marginality and violence. As Uzodinma Iweala notes of his characters in *Beasts of No Nation*, they

> are not monsters. They are not psychopaths – at the very least not before war finds them. They, like the many children forced into combat and even the adults they fought alongside, are people with histories, hopes and visions of what life should [and could] be like. These histories and hopes are sometimes all that they have as a guide through the insanity of war. They are what make the violence and brutality they experience and inflict so tragic, so absurd (2005: 9).

The 'original sin' as foundational violence

Let us bring this discussion of violence to a close by incorporating Jean-Paul Sartre's conception of the 'original sin' as primary violence and its implication for violence in Africa. 'The best way to conceive of the fundamental project of human

153

reality,' Sartre tells us in *Being and Nothingness*, 'is to say that man is the being whose project is to be God' (1956: 724). However, this quest for omnipotence is threatened by the realisation of the existence of Others whose consciousness or perception of us we have no access to or control over. We come to awareness of the existence of the Other not through the Other's body, but through 'the look' of the Other, which makes us experience our own body as an object for the Other. With the gaze of the Other, our being-for-itselfness (our being as a sovereign subject, conscious of and in control of our own being) is transformed to a being-for-others (the object of the consciousness and gaze of Others that we have no access to or control over). It is with the Other's look that we realise our vulnerability:

> With the Other's look the 'situation' escapes me. To use an everyday expression which better expresses our thought, I am no longer master of my situation. Or more exactly, I remain master of it, but it has one real dimension by which it escapes me, by which unforeseen reversals cause it to be otherwise than it appears for me [. . .] The appearance of the Other, on the contrary, causes the appearance in the situation of an aspect which I did not wish, of which I am not master, and which on principle escapes me since it is for the Other (Sartre 1956: 355).

This encounter with the Other is not only a source of alienation – for it is with the gaze of the Other that we realise our own objecthood, which is also an alienating experience – but also a source of conflict and struggle for mastery. The terrifying awareness of being looked at produces an experience of shame or guilt that Sartre equates with the fall or original sin:

> It is before the Other that I am guilty. I am guilty first when beneath the Other's look I experience my alienation and my nakedness as a fall from grace which I must assume. This is the meaning of the famous line from Scripture: 'They knew that they were naked.' Again I am guilty when in turn I look at the Other, because by the very fact of my own self-assertion I constitute him as an object and as an instrument, and I cause him to experience that same alienation which he must now assume. Thus the original sin is my upsurge in a world where there are others; and whatever may be my further relations with others, these relations will be only variations on the original theme of guilt (Sartre 1956: 531).

In order to control our own subjectivity and freedom, Sartre contends, we must re-establish our being-for-itselfness by controlling the Other and his or her freedom and turning him or her into a being for us. This is done by returning the gaze and turning the Other into an object. Thus 'the objectification of the Other [. . .] is a defence on the part of my being which, precisely by conferring on the other a being for-me, frees me from my being-for the Other' (Sartre 1956: 359). It is through this retaliatory posture or act that we not only re-establish ourselves as pure subjects, but also constitute the Other as a pure object, existing for and through us.

This very act of constituting the Other as an object is an act of violence and Sartre posits it as the ontological and inescapable source of conflict anchored on the reality of existing with others in a world in which everybody wants to be God, for as Mudimbe explains, 'by positing ourselves as subjects, we alienate Others, who in turn cannot but alienate us, since they are subjects in their own right' (2013: 30). In such a situation, the world becomes an endless battlefield where the quest for omnipotence becomes a continual struggle for mastery over others and the drive to reduce them to objects is endlessly played out:

> We are always, no matter what attitude is adopted, in a state of instability in relation to the Other. We pursue the impossible ideal of the simultaneous apprehension of his freedom and of his objectivity. To borrow an expression from Jean Wahl, we are – in relation to the Other – sometimes in a state of *trans-descendence* (when we apprehend him as an object and integrate him with the world), and sometimes in a state of *trans-ascendence* (when we experience him as a transcendence which transcends us). But neither of these two states is sufficient in itself, and we will never place ourselves concretely on a plane of equality; that is, on the plane where the recognition of the Other's freedom would involve the Other's recognition of our freedom (Sartre 1956: 529).

Sartre's 'original sin' is the primary or foundational violence, which, while it can suggest the superfluousness of individual and collective identity and existence, hence highlighting 'the concrete experience of being-with-others in situations of solidarity', it does provide the key to decoding 'the everyday banality of the experience of existing and its dehumanisation' (Mudimbe 2013: 7) and thus can explain a whole range of violent relationships – colonial and imperial domination, wars, ethnic conflict, domestic and gender-based violence and so on – which emerge from the process of Othering and objectification and the continual impulse to appropriate, conquer and possess. Such then, as Mudimbe points out, is the locus from which social identity, but also conflict and violence can be thematised:

> It is a self-concept, borne with a progressively increasing sense of belonging to already constructed in-groups (a race, a gender, a religion) and gradually gaining access to freedom. In its affirmation in 'we-nesses' and facing out-groups, a social identity outgrows its genesis, asserts itself in a project, as that which, in concrete relations with others and in reference to itself, can identify with its own capacity, along with those of others, in the travail of transcendence (2013: 30).

I want to put this forward as a possible explanation of the violence at the heart of colonial modernity and the Western will to power and domination. It accounts for the impulse that drove the expansion of Europe and the accompanying monstrosities that continue to define global realities. In an earlier work, Mudimbe explained these monstrosities this way:

> The geographic expansion of Europe and its civilization then was a holy saga of mythic proportions. The only problem, and it is a big one, is that as this civilisation developed, it submitted the world to its memory; but, at the same time, it seemed itself to be sanctioned by and to produce the most unimaginable evils a madperson could have imagined. To focus only on the last five centuries, let us note three remarkable monstrosities which seem intrinsically part of Western history: the slave trade and its politics since the fifteenth century, colonialism and imperialism at the end of the eighteenth century and throughout the nineteenth, and fascism and Nazism in the twentieth (1994: xii).

Included in these 'monstrosities' are the genocidal and dehumanising violence against the original inhabitants of the Americas and Caribbean, colonial genocide in Namibia and Belgian Congo and, in the age of liberal internationalism and the current mutation of American empire, brutal colonial wars in places such as Afghanistan, Iraq and Libya, not to mention the epistemological, representational and systemic violence that continues to generate crises all over the world, which themselves are a property of the regimes of violence associated with the politics of European expansionism since the fifteenth century.

In this violent political reality, three historical moments can be identified: exploration, colonisation and globalisation. The first moment involves the politics of expansion, inaugurated by the sagas of oceanic exploration in the fifteenth and sixteenth centuries and the definition of the frontiers of the 'West' (and the 'rest') under signs of 'discovery', violence and conquest and the political, economic and cultural systems that it made possible (Mudimbe 1994; Hall 2006; Besis 2003). This can be regarded as the primary violence in the constitution of modern African societies and continent's tragic 'encounter' with the West: the slave trade would narrate itself accordingly and the same movement of reduction would progressively guarantee the gradual invasion of the continent, ultimately resulting in its colonial occupation in the nineteenth and twentieth centuries (Mudimbe 1994; Wai 2012a).

The second moment, more essentially, designates the upsurge of 'new imperialism' in the nineteenth century, which triggered the scramble for Africa and the arbitrary carving up and annexation of the continent into European colonial possessions. This moment of violence was built on the first moment in a continuum of violence, domination and exploitation that includes transatlantic slavery, the disruption of the continent's productive processes and its incorporation into the modern world system and the constitution of the colonising structure whose structural imprint designates the intermediate space. Completely disrupting the continent's own endogenous transformative processes and reconstituting social and political relations through violent appropriative mechanisms, the colonising structure accented and banalised violence in every social relation and this continues to define our systems of living and ways of life.

The third moment of violence corresponds with the current era of neoliberal globalisation, which has, since the 1970s and 1980s, seen the intensification of Western capitalist and imperialist domination of the world. Indeed, it has been through the neoliberal imposition that the African continent has been disciplined and impoverished through credit manipulation and debt-management mechanisms, encapsulated in structural adjustment policies, which destroyed economies and increased misery, poverty and violence on the continent. That civil wars in many African countries in the 1990s and beyond came in the wake of this decimation of African economies speaks to the fact that globalisation is not a neutral process of global connectivity, but a very violent process of power, domination and exploitation.

These moments (exploration, colonisation and globalisation) constitute three moments in the same historical movement of reduction that has progressively guaranteed European domination of the world, creating misery and wretchedness for the rest. To say this is not to imply that colonial modernity, itself a specific form of violence, invented violence in Africa. Nor does it mean to suggest that the continent did not have problems with ethno-identitarian difference and the banality of everyday existence before colonial contact. Indeed, Africa had its own problems with social identity and individual and collective existence long before any European set foot on African soil. However, the advent of colonial modernity and its monstrosities accented violence on the continent, not only distorting the violence inherent in its own indigenous social and political formations, but also disrupting its capacity for coping with, managing and displacing those regimes of violence. At the same time, it overwhelmed the African continent with the violence constitutive of colonial modernity and its exploitative material logics and politics of alterity, thereby transforming Africa into a site for the projection and displacement of modernist violence. What I have suggested throughout this chapter is that the current manifestations of violence in Africa are not a unique or inherent African pathology, but (a) the flagrant exemplification of the violence inherent in social and political systems that structure modes of living and ways of life; and (b) the actualisation and manifestation of the constitutive violence inherent in the historical and structural processes of colonial modernity through which the states on the continent have historically been produced and are constantly reproduced and reimagined.

Note

1. The ideas expressed in this chapter emerged out of conversations with Foday Mannah, Nathan Okonta, Bikrum Gill, Zahir Kolia and V-Y Mudimbe, who were also generous enough to read and comment on earlier drafts. I would especially like to thank V-Y for his friendship and support and Grant Farred, Leonhard Praeg and Kasereka Kavwahirehi for inviting me to be a part of the project that has made this publication possible. Needless to say, I alone am responsible for the content of this chapter.

References

Bayart, Jean-Francois. 1993. *The State in Africa: The Politics of the Belly*. London: Longman.
———. 1999. 'The "Social Capital" of the Felonious State or the Ruses of Political Intelligence'. In *The Criminalisation of the State in Africa*, by Jean-Francois Bayart, Stephen Ellis and Beatrice Hibou, 32–48. Bloomington: Indiana University Press.
Bessis, Sophie. 2003. *Western Supremacy: The Triumph of an Idea?* London: Zed Books.

Bhabha, Homi K. 1994. *The Location of Culture*. New York: Routledge.

Bourdieu, Pierre. 1997. *Pascalian Meditations*. Translated by Richard Nice. Stanford: Stanford University Press.

———. 1998. *Acts of Resistance: Against the Tyranny of the Market*. Translated by Richard Nice. New York: The New Press.

Bourgois, Philippe. 2001. 'The Power of Violence in War and Peace: Post-Cold War Lessons from El Salvador'. *Ethnography* 2(1): 5–34.

Chabal, Patrick and Jean-Pascal Daloz. 1999. *Africa Works: Disorder as Political Instrument*. Oxford: James Currey.

Fanon, Frantz. 1963. *The Wretched of the Earth*. New York: Grove Press.

Galtung, Johan. 2009. 'Violence, Peace and Peace Research'. In *Violence: A Philosophical Anthology*, edited by Vittorio Bufacchi, 78–109. New York: Palgrave Macmillan.

Hall, Stuart. 2006. 'The West and the Rest: Discourse and Power'. In *Modernity: An Introduction to Modern Societies*, edited by Stuart Hall, David Held, Don Hubert and Kenneth Thompson, 184–227. Oxford: Blackwell.

Hobsbawm, Eric and Terence Ranger (eds). 1992. *The Invention of Tradition*. Cambridge: Cambridge University Press.

Iweala, Uzodinma. 2005. *Beasts of No Nation*. New York: Harper Perennial.

Kincaid, Jamaica. 1988. *A Small Place*. New York: Farrar, Straus and Giroux.

Mamdani, Mahmood. 1996. *Citizen and Subject: Contemporary Africa and the Legacy of Late Colonialism*. Princeton: Princeton University Press.

Mbembe, Achille. 2001. *On the Postcolony*. Berkeley: University of California Press.

Mudimbe, V-Y. 1988. *The Invention of Africa: Gnosis, Philosophy, and the Order of Knowledge*. Bloomington: Indiana University Press.

———. 1991. *Parables and Fables: Exegesis, Textuality, and Politics in Central Africa*. Madison: University of Wisconsin Press.

———. 1994. *The Idea of Africa*. Bloomington: Indiana University Press.

———. 2011. 'For Fanon: A Meditation'. Thinking Africa Public Lecture, Rhodes University, Grahamstown, 6 July.

———. 2013. *On African Fault Lines: Meditations on Alterity Politics*. Pietermaritzburg: University of KwaZulu-Natal Press.

Patočka, Jan. 1996. *Heretical Essays in the Philosophy of History*. Translated by Ezrazim Kohák. Chicago: Open Court.

RUF (Revolutionary United Front). 1995. *Footpath to Democracy: Towards a New Sierra Leone*, available at http://www.sierra-leone.org/AFRC-RUF/footpaths.html.

Sartre, Jean-Paul. 1956. *Being and Nothingness*. Translated by Hazel E. Barnes. New York: Washington Square Press.

Scheper-Hughes, Nancy. 1992. *Death without Weeping: The Violence of Everyday Life in Brazil*. Berkeley: University of California Press.

———. 1996. 'Small Wars and Invisible Genocides'. *Social Science and Medicine* 43(5): 889–900.

———. 1997. 'Peace-Time Crimes'. *Social Identities* 3(3): 471–97.

Scheper-Hughes, Nancy and Philippe Bourgois. 2004. 'Introduction: Making Sense of Violence'. In *Violence in War and Peace: An Anthology*, edited by Nancy Scheper-Hughes and Philippe Bourgois, 1–31. Malden: Blackwell.

Taussig, Michael. 1984. 'Culture of Terror – Space of Death: Roger Casement's Putumayo Report and the Explanation of Torture'. *Comparative Studies in Society and History* 26(1): 467–97.

Wai, Zubairu. 2012a. *Epistemologies of African Conflicts: Violence, Evolutionism and the War in Sierra Leone*. New York: Palgrave Macmillan.

———. 2012b. 'Neo-Patrimonialism and the Discourse of State Failure in Africa'. *Review of African Political Economy* 39(131): 27–43.

Žižek, Slavoj. 2008. *Violence: Six Sideways Reflections*. New York: Picador.

———. 2011. *Living in the End Times*. London: Verso.

CHAPTER 8

Postcards from the Postcolony

Leonhard Praeg

> The objective was to situate the African between his people and the colonizers without completely reducing him to either side.
> — Nnamdi Elleh, *Architecture and Power in Africa*

27 April 2013

Dear Valentin—

It's been such a long time since I wrote to you. The reason for this, you may recall, is that I've not been well. When I told a friend about the misery of being burnt out, she responded, 'Well, then you should read Graham Greene's *A Burnt-Out Case*'! What a jolly assumption, I thought, to think that reading about somebody else's misery will make my own more bearable. Anyway, I'm quite sure I won't be able to contribute anything meaningful to our conference in August, not only because of the burn-out, but because it feels as if I just don't have anything left to say – not even to a friend. And why say something if you have nothing left to say? Isn't there enough of that in the world already?

This must seem very strange to you: I am writing to say I have nothing to write about. 'What a peculiar postcard!' you might exclaim, perhaps even with a gesture of exasperation. 'And what a character! Why doesn't he just *not* say it!' Alas, we both know that these moments are more complex than that, our choices infinite and relationships far less stable than the rules of logic would suggest. The narrator in *Le bel immonde* understood this well. Remember the letter he wrote to his lover in Chapter 2 of Part 2: 'My very dear friend, you told me the day before yesterday that you no longer wish to see me: you are not interested in me. Faced with the choice you have imposed upon me, I wonder if I have permission to question myself on something other than myself [in the German translation: *ob ich mir*

161

über etwas anderes als nur mich selbst Fragen stellen darf]. I have been forbidden to discuss your decision [*ich habe kein Recht*]; I cannot even do so, for in such a discussion I could only rebel or accept. If I were to do the former, that amounts in the final analysis to a violation of you; and if the latter, to question, once again, the attitude I have had towards you since the beginning. All of these would contradict the principle of availability [*verfügbar und bereit zu sein*] which I hold so dear.'

Indeed. Our lover has a dilemma, for he realises that to be active and question her decision cannot but violate the sovereignty (*Recht*) of her decision; on the other hand, to be passive and accept it will cast a shadow of bad faith over their relationship ('You mean you're not going to fight for me! For us?!'). What a conundrum. But our lover is more wily than this passage suggests because he exercises a third option, namely *to tell her about his conundrum*. While he is not actively trying to change her mind (*bereit zu sein*), neither is he merely being passive (*verfügbar*) by just letting it go. Instead, he articulates the tension, his own indecision or undecidability and, in so doing, he is neither active nor passive. You see then, my friend, there is more than meets the eye in the statement, 'I am writing to tell you that I have nothing to write about.' Sometimes the most important thing we can articulate is our indecision – which, of course, requires a decision in itself, et cetera. But enough of all that. I am very near the end of Cervantes's *Don Quixote*. What a truly magnificent novel! I would love nothing more than to find a moment at the conference to discuss it with you.

Until then, I remain your friend,
Leonhard

* * *

10 May 2013

Dear Valentin—

Thanks for your email of last week. I didn't immediately respond because I wanted to finish *Don Quixote* first. Your explanation of how Cervantes manages to make the reader smile for almost a thousand pages is, I believe, to the point. We are, indeed, as you put it, presented with the 'perfectly rational behavior of someone walking within a cultural configuration with an intellectual grid that is perfectly rational, but that belongs to a configuration governed by relations of similarities and analogies'. Your question, 'How did Cervantes manage such a magnificent invention?' is unnerving for what it promises: an answer. Because in order to produce an answer, wouldn't one need to account for Cervantes's intellectual grid in its totality and, in order to do that, for the totality of intellectual grids within which it appears as extraordinary as it does? Of course – but that would require an infinite number of postcards and an eternity to write them in and, even then, the complexity of a coherent answer would elude us!

We would do better, I think, by mapping the *relations of similarities and analogies within the grid of rationality itself*. After all, Cervantes's rational grid was not only undermined or relativised by an episteme of analogies that preceded it and continued to exist at odds with it; the grid within which he wrote also replicated within itself a set of similarities and analogies, the most salient of which must surely be the undecidability that constitutes sovereignty in terms of *a relation that is not a relation*: Descartes's *cogito* (*Discourse* (1637), *Meditations* (1641)) is/not in relation to the world; or rather, it can only arrive at itself by imagining itself, first, *in* relation to the world, only to suspend that relation in order to articulate itself as unrelated to the world. Similarly, Don Quixote imagines himself *in relation* to the world as Sovereign Knight, Righter of All Wrongs, but that relation is constantly suspended by Sancho Panza who shatters his illusion by constantly returning his Master (perhaps 'Master') to the interiority of madness and folly, a *cogito*/self not in relation to the world, closed in upon and lost to itself. Perhaps, then, what endears the Knight of the Sorrowful Face to us is the fact that he embodies both the aspiration to *and* the folly of sovereignty.

The literary value of the text lies in the exquisite manner in which Cervantes balances this tension in his central character(s). But the philosophical value, I think, lies elsewhere: for Cervantes is clear that for Don Quixote to become an executed sovereign subject in relation to the world, he would have to violently suspend every reminder of the very relationality that accounts for his being in the world as a historical subject: history ('Knighthood is a thing of the past'!), his friendship with Sancho Panza (as complicated as a master-servant friendship may be, as Diderot's master explains to his servant Jacques 'You don't understand the meaning of the word friend when it is used by his superior to his inferior'), every other self-appointed knight in the kingdom, everyone who dares question his belief in himself and so on – in short, history, fellowship, intersubjectivity, divine authority: the very violent suspensions that made possible the peace treaties of Osnabrück and Münster (1644–48).

Cervantes presents us with a vision of the violence of sovereignty as farce. Formulated differently, sovereignty – to paraphrase Kundera, one of 'the west's finest illusions' – is shadowed from its inception by the self-consciousness that calls it forth as a possibility, while condemning its very desirability. Would it be too much to suggest that *sovereignty* is the exact locus of an undecidability in our relation to the world; an undecidability that recognises violence both as the condition of being in the world (indispensable to the founding and perpetual regrounding of the social bond) *and* the total eradication of which lends purpose to being in the world? In this sense, 'sovereignty' is a border concept. It marks the entry into the world of a subject that will henceforth almost exclusively be concerned with eradicating the violence that was necessary for its own arrival in the world. And is this an aporia or a curse? If the former, do we try to think beyond the impasse or do we reconcile ourselves to finding ever more sophisticated ways of understanding the essentially inescapable, unchangeable aporia that is the numinous structure of violence? Is this even the right question to ask, that we should choose or argue this way or that? Or should the question rather be the historical: at what stage did the metaphysical assumption regarding the numinous nature of violence ('the wrath of a loving God') pass over into accepting the tension between generative and destructive violence as but a paradox at the heart of a normative discourse?

For Charles Taylor, the answer is relatively straightforward: it was a function of a disenchanted, rational world in which the old melody of self-purification through sacrifice continued in a new register of rational virtue (Robespierre). Perhaps we can also denote this as the moment when the twin assumptions of universal equality and the right to collective self-determination reconstituted violence, first and foremost, as a problem for thought (or impossible thought and, hence, for Cervantes, as farce). Perhaps one of the most acute manifestations of this immanent paradox is the aporia of the founding – in the case of Rwanda and many other postcolonial states, of *deferred* founding – as a moment of suspended anticipation: 'anticipation' because the promisorial structure of the founding projects the realisation of *belonging* in equality, justice and peace as an attainable, future goal; 'suspended' because the aporia that states, 'Every new order announces itself through a violation of what it stands for' demands sacrifices and the exclusion of historical *distinctions* in order to reimagine belonging in terms of republican distinctions.

Please do forgive me for rambling on like this, a belated and fatalistic *Jacques* with no apparent sense of purpose. But, as much as I would like to blame it on the fever, your question got me thinking and, in so doing, raised the spectre of one who frantically tries to gather dust. I sign off empty-handed, again. Well, almost. Seems as if we have at last settled on a theme for the August conference. I will write soon.

Trusting this card finds you well, I remain your friend,
Leonhard

* * *

21 May 2013

Dear Valentin—

As you will no doubt have gathered from the emails copied to you, we have at last settled on a theme for the August conference: 'Violence in/and the Great Lakes: The Thought of V-Y Mudimbe and Beyond'. I suspect much is going to be made of the ambivalence of the 'in/and', as well as the indecision or undecidability suggested by it. On the one hand, the preposition 'in' suggests violence contained within a republican form – albeit the 'Great Lakes' as supranational entity imposed over the demarcations of various sovereign states (Burundi, Rwanda, north-eastern DRC, Uganda, north-western Kenya, Tanzania) and an allusion to the reality of political forms that preceded colonialism – while, on the other hand, talk about violence *and* the Great Lakes seems to externalise violence by (also) placing it on the outside of this imaginary construct or *in relation to* it. In a sense, this tension between violence *on* the inside and violence *from* the outside articulates the general economy of violence, a tension between the *violence of the founding* (of domesticating violence within, and *as*, the generative source of authority in the state's various historical iterations as Kongo, Congo Free State, Belgian Congo, Republic of the Congo, Zaïre and so forth) and the *violence of reconstitution* that perpetually haunts the republic in the form of various coalitions and alliances at once internal *and* external to the republic – an economy quite clearly demonstrated by the manner in which the First and Second Congo Wars blurred the distinction between revolution and foreign invasion.

I wonder how much this oscillation between *in* and *and*, between the violence of the founding and the perpetual movement of violent reconstitution through 'negative forces', contributes to the undecidable relationship the rest of the world

165

has with this war, a world that can conceive of it neither in terms of space nor war – or when it does, of a 'war' that dedifferentiates into 'conflict' and a space that unfolds into 'region' or 'district' – generalities, significant as they may be, that have also become the condition of the possibility of various forms of resignation. On the one hand, the war is said to be constitutively transnational (not one that spilled over sovereign borders) and, as such, undermines traditional categories of analysis that distinguish between internal and external forces, regression and repression, local and global and so on, the result of which is a dedifferentiation that is wholly a function of the dynamic nature of time and space in war networks. The war, it is argued, is so complex, the number of players so multiple, the 'changing web of political, military, and commercial ties' (Carayannis) so intricate that it is impossible to have a relation with either the geographical space or the violence that perpetually reconstitutes our perceptions of it. Although the epistemic a priori of such a quasi-scientific complexity analysis was well documented in the later part of the *Gulbenkian Report*, the existential and ontological question it leaves unanswered is: how does one empathise with subjects constituted by networks that constantly destabilise, even invert, the opposition between victim and perpetrator (of which the child soldier can be said to be metonymic)? On the other hand, even where this opposition is relatively stable, we find a certain empathy fatigue reproduced through the sustained and seemingly endless oscillation between constituted and constituting power.

True and understandable as both these responses may be, they seem already to speak (or *refuse* to speak) of an encounter anterior to the act of naming the war as 'complex' or the result of an 'oscillation between constituted and constituting power' – an encounter that calls for (and forth) a mediation of the passage from that which I momentarily want to refer to as 'bare life' (Agamben) and its (re) codification in various political forms. Of these codifications, the 'republic', the 'iteration of founding violence' or 'its perpetual deconstruction' by 'the movement of reconstituting power' and so on, are already but iterations of well-worn categories that mask an encounter with bare life as both the *conditio sine qua non* and *conditio per quam* of political life, both the *condition for* the possibility of the political, as well as the condition *through which* we conduct the political, both the condition *for* and *of* politics. (What if the end were always already contained in the beginning, the logic of the failure already prefigured in what made it possible?) If we were to say anything about this war, shouldn't our starting point be an attempt to understand this condition of 'bare life' and any glimpse into the postcolonial condition it could afford us?

I will have to think more about this. For now, as I ponder our conference theme and the shameful lack of outrage this war has produced worldwide, I cannot but wonder: is it conceivable that the undecidable relation of the world to this war is a function of the fact that it presents us with bare life *as a movement*, at once the deconstruction of political forms and the condition of their possibility? Where would one even begin to circumscribe such a movement? I look forward to hearing from you.

In the meanwhile, I remain, as always, your friend
Leonhard

*   *   *

25 May 2013

Dear Valentin—

Sometimes I despair; I'm not always sure how one is meant to 'hold it together' in the postcolony. I'm not just thinking of the burn-out – which I have come to think of as a disease of purpose, contracted by one whose existence has become too much driven by purpose and as such, a teleological malady (L. *ill* + *habitus*) – but also about a recent existential interlude, an act of violence that caught me 'off guard', as it were. I arrived on the scene after the fact, so I got it all second-hand, but apparently a white man had beaten up a young, black car-guard in the High Street – in self-defence, he claimed. Now, to appreciate the implausibility of this claim to self-defence, one must bear in mind that car-guards are not thugs; in fact, they are seldom criminals; they don't intimidate and, in small towns such as Grahamstown, they are never racketeers – all of which makes the man's claim of 'self-defence' ludicrous, to say the least. And yet and yet . . . On occasion, I have also sensed in myself an impatience, perhaps even a violent discomfort, with these so-called car-guards. It is not in my nature to actively express such anger or discomfort, but neither can I passively let it be, so please bear with this postcard.

Car-guards: for a variety of well-known reasons, both general to postcoloniality and specific to South Africa, the state does not provide adequate security to the vast majority of its citizens. As in many other parts of the world, a consequence of this has been the privatisation of security. A lesser-known phenomenon, and one probably peculiar to the developing world, has been an additional 'informalisation' of security, that is, a situation in which security services are provided by individuals who make their living in and through the shadow or informal economy. Car-guards are, by and large, poor and/or homeless people who have somehow managed to obtain the most basic accoutrements of a 'security service provider' – most notably a luminous orange or green vest – in order to pose as protector of one's vehicle wherever it is parked. Because they are neither mandated by the state/municipality to provide a security service nor does their service, in most instances, have any real market value, their very presence has become the embodiment of a fascinating legitimacy crisis typical of interfaces between the formal and informal economies – that is, where individuals in the informal sector seek to be inducted into the formal sector as legitimate providers of services usually considered 'of value' by those whose exchanges are limited to the formal economy. Typically, a car-guard resolves the problem of providing a service that has no legitimacy and little value through appeals articulated in one of four discourses. The two primary discourses are, firstly, a pretence, nonetheless, to have the right/authority to collect parking tax; secondly, if ignored, an economic appeal premised on the quasi-contractarian assumption that a service has value because it was rendered, irrespective of whether or not it was needed. These are supplemented by appeals derived from two further, secondary discourses. The first resembles a discourse on aid and development ('At least I'm trying/I'm not doing crime/I'm trying to pay rent/school fees', et cetera), while the second reveals the existential bottom line of the car-guard's existence: having thus far failed to be 'compensated', s/he will drop all pretence at providing a legitimate/useful service and, through a discourse of charitable giving, become indistinct from a beggar.

Oh, forgive me for boring you with the minutiae of life in the postcolony, but the car-guard often reminds me of Salvatore, the monk/vagabond in the Benedictine abbey of Umberto Eco's *Il nome della rosa*; he, writes Eco, whose gaze is undecidably either innocent or malign, who has a nose that is not a nose and a mouth that is not a mouth, whose speech is and is not a language because he 'spoke all languages, and no language. Or, rather, he had invented for himself a language which used the sinews of the languages to which he had been exposed . . . taking words sometimes from one and sometimes from another.'

In the case of the car-guard, and please bear with me as I begin to circumscribe my own occasional violent discomfort, the question is this: what is the effect of being confronted by a person/vagabond/monk who speaks all languages and therefore none? All four of the discourses appealed to by the car-guard constitute intersubjectivity in a specific way, either by rearticulating *distinction* (between ruler and ruled, taxer and taxed or between developed and developing, wealthy and poor) or *belonging* (reciprocity and equality in contracting services or, simply, a shared humanity). However, when the car-guard speaks all these languages and therefore none in particular, s/he also presents as all these subjectivities and therefore none in particular. This is not to say that s/he is therefore not human; quite the opposite, it is to say that in that instant s/he is present *only* as human, that is, as human being prior to our codification into a range of political subjectivities. Further, given the logic of intersubjectivity, if one pole in any of the above distinctions (ruled, taxed, developing, poor) collapses into every subjectivity and therefore none, so does the other (ruler, taxer, developed, wealthy). Here, it seems to me, we get a glimpse of bare life *as a movement*, of being as at once the deconstruction of political forms and the condition of their possibility. The car-guard draws one into a violently shifting movement or force of deconstructed and reconstructed subjectivities so that one eventually recognises oneself as Salvatore, vagabond/citizen – *banned* as outsider, outlaw, no longer a political subject nor subject to the Law. Therein lies the source of the violence that intrigues me: who wants to be a human if you can be a subject? Humans don't have power, subjects do.

As I sign off today, I cannot but wonder if this little incident does not suggest a possible passage from existential to ontological reflection. Is an incident such as this one not in many ways a synecdoche of postcoloniality as such, an interaction that discloses something specific about the citizen *as* vagabond, a political subject without the *habitus* of political form – one for whom, by way of example, the imposed/inducted liberal democratic nation-state as a political form, with its implied subjectivity, always remains but 'one of the languages we speak' and in that precise sense, always yet-to-come (in a more acute manner than it always does)? And is this deferral not evident in the gaping abyss between the 'We' of the Constitution and where 'we' are actually at, always a vagabond/monk in the Abbey of democracy – a tension that perpetually shines the light of self-consciousness on a political form that *therefore* remains arbitrary and *therefore* easily discarded, reinvented and adopted in an endless series of reconstitutional crises, invariably led by those who claim to speak on behalf of true democracy: Alliance des Forces

Démocratiques pour la Libération du Congo (AFDL), Reassamblement Congolais pour la Démocratie (RCD) and so on?

I'm excited by the possibility of tracing this thought-way in the direction of a postcolonial ontology of sorts, but that will have to wait for another day.

Trusting you are well, I remain your friend,
Leonhard

P.S.

I thought I was done with thinking for today, but clearly thinking wasn't yet done with me. It appears that in this description of the postcolonial condition as one in which we speak all languages and therefore none, there is already at work what we can refer to as a first-order, universal or general economy of transcendental violence (Derrida), in addition to which, or layered over which, a second-order, epistemological violation of Africa. As for the first, I refer to it as 'first-order' precisely because it is inescapable: the process through which bare life is inducted or codified again in order to become the subjectivity of this or that political form is a violent process because all singularity is lost in the name of a general, universal master trope, such as 'constitutional democracy' or 'the Republic'. But it is *transcendental* violence exactly because that violation is the condition for the possibility of some such dialogue, human interaction or the political to occur *überhaupt* (at all). For Africans, this universal tragedy of speech is complicated by the additional fact that the signification established through this *archē*-violence – in speech, discourse, political forms and institutions – *precisely because it has always been such a poor reflection of our/their lived reality*, remains forever visible *as* violence. We/they live in a world that is named violence.

We also know, historically, that there have been two major responses to this: one, to discard in its entirety this alien virtual reality of signification imposed on us/them; two, to accept as irreversible the fact of this imposition and to explore various ways of overwhelming its virtuality (Quayson) with 'more appropriate' or 'proper' significations – the 'symbolic violence [that] ultimately turns into nationalism and subsequently leads to a political struggle for liberation', as you commented in *Invention*. Which of these may be the more viable response is not my concern here. What does intrigue me is the necessary incompleteness of both: whether conceived as starting over, from the beginning as Fanon urged, or as overwhelming the virtual by the proper, the latter will always contain within itself traces of the virtual that was the reason for the negation; the beginning is given to us, again, in the end, with the 'end' postulated as perpetual new beginning and so forth. In other words, postcoloniality is, and will forever remain, driven by a residual desire that cannot find its true articulation (as effect) in the same system that generated it (as cause).

This is my question, then: what does it mean to be (Being) in a world where the passage of *archē*-violence remains unredeemed by the specific forgetfulness that is a condition for the transformation of virtual speech into 'real' speech, virtual institutions into 'real' institutions and so on? Is postcoloniality not perhaps a condition in which *archē*-violence remains forever visible, in which it is never a matter of remembering and/or returning (in order to recollect, contest and dispute the transcendental violence at the source of the political), but rather a condition in which the passage from bare life to the political, from a multiplicity of forms to the subject(ivity) of, say, the liberal democratic nation-state, remains forever visible *as a passage* (in a more acute sense than it always does)? Is postcoloniality not a condition, in fact, that constitutes the *subject as self-conscious passage* from one to the other, a passage that never ends or culminates in form – or when it does, restlessly so (as in the so-called neo-patrimonial state)?

This is not all bad news. For, is the subject conceived as self-conscious passage not the subject proper of any and all humanist discourses? Is 'the human' *qua* conduit of constitutive violence not, properly speaking, the quasi-transcendental concept of *the human* at the root of all humanisms? I write 'properly speaking' because what is the -*ism* but a fatal and futile attempt to arrest this restless passage, to announce its cessation in the constitution or founding of a political subject called, named, 'the human', and therefore already a form of resignation – as if the human so named in human*ism* represents all that we are ever capable of being? The reason, I believe, it has been so difficult to give substance to what it means to be a postcolonial subject, to flesh out this subjecthood in ontological terms, is because the question requires from the answer a certain pretence to forgetfulness, as if the nameless had successfully passed over into the named – that is, 'postcolonial subject', as if the passage were over, dialectically (through an act of recognition) *aufgehoben* (sublimated) in its own forgetfulness. This is simply not possible for a subject who is constitutively a passage. In other words, a subject constituted as the passage from the nameless to the named can never name itself other than 'as passage' (*from* the nameless *towards* the named). For this subject, home is unhomely; *heimlich zu sein, heisst unheimlich zu sein* (to be at home means not to be at home) – a doubling back onto itself in an inversion Freud recognised when he noted that '*heimlich* is a word the meaning of which develops in the direction of ambivalence, until it finally coincides with its opposite, *unheimlich*. *Unheimlich* is in some way or other a sub-species of *heimlich*.'

As for the man who attacked the car-guard: would not anybody who thought of themselves as the cessation of violence, as having survived the middle passage between the nameless and the named, only to be told that they have remained a vagabond, outside or prior to all political forms, lash out at the world? Has violence not always been *pharmakon* in the precise sense of being that which makes home homely (*heimlich*) by unhomely (*unheimliche*) means; that which 'has the power to bind together completely isolated individuals and . . . by doing so . . . isolat[ing] these individuals even further' (Arendt)?

I end this postscript with a peculiar discontent. It feels as if I've barely scratched the surface of what it *means to be* a postcolonial subject: to be; *zu sein*, Being; *Sein*. Is it too late to address this subject as a question about being, as *Seinsfrage*? Or may some rudimentary grafting of our question onto *Being and Time* yet be the only way to comprehend the postcolonial subject in relation to the question of violence that seems to constitute it as passage? You know what it's like: the more precise the question, the more impossible the answer. To get a glimmer of a thought means already to find (*to be*) oneself being thought. *Being*, a restless passage.

I remain, I hope,
Leonhard

*   *   *

1 June 2013

Dear Valentin—

It is as if the car-guard episode afforded me a glimpse into some understanding of the existential place of violence in everyday postcolonial life, how violence illuminates something important about the way we are 'tempted to exist' (to paraphrase that immortally beautiful title of Cioran's). But I have been haunted by the nagging feeling that the story contains more, perhaps a clue to something more fundamental, something ontological; a clue to what it might *mean to be* (postcolonial) *überhaupt*. Despite myself, I keep returning to the sloppy inversion hinted at in my last email: son-father; first Derrida, then Heidegger. *Muß es sein?*

*   *   *

3 June 2013

Dear Valentin—

I have not heard from you in a while, probably because you've been travelling again. You seem to do a lot of that. As for myself, my thinking seems to have taken me further and further away from the topic I am supposed to be thinking and writing about. At the same time, it feels as if I've never been so close to an understanding of the questions we have to ask if we want to begin thinking about violence in/and the Great Lakes *and beyond*. (What is this 'beyond' but an allusion to a never-ending passage? And what if this endless *passage* were the most fundamental characteristic, not of being in general, but of postcoloniality in particular, an *auseinadersetzung* (grappling) with, which is presupposed by what we propose to consider as political *problematique?*) Do you see what I mean when I say that I feel at once very far removed *and* unimaginably close to the theme that has inspired all these little postcards of the last weeks? And isn't this experience typical of any engagement with the historic a priori? The question is: How to start excavating that experience in order to shed light on our conference theme? The episode with the car-guard seemed to have opened up into a domain where *bare life*, as conceived here – being as a self-conscious passage of unredeemed transcendental violence – could receive its proper ontological treatment. Isn't being-violated so conceived, that is, living in suspended anticipation of being safe in the world, what Heidegger would have called an existential or mode of existence – alongside guilt, death, conscience, understanding – from the perspective of which we can understand the very structure of Being (postcolonial)?

I returned to sections 12–13 of *Being in Time* today. The parameters seem clear enough: the analytic presents the various a priori existentials that, once analysed from a transcendental perspective, will illuminate *what it means to be* (Being). First caveat: Heidegger does not claim to have analysed all existentials (including 'love', 'joy', et cetera). Second caveat: The existentials that do receive attention are analysed in a specific order, from that which affords a *general* awareness of our existence (being-in-a-world), to the specific existential that reveals to Dasein the factical nature of its own existence (care). As for being-in-a-world, the preposition 'in' is the locus of the difference between the ontic and the ontological meaning of the phrase. The ontic meaning is not a priori, but a posteriori, or the result of experiencing myself *in* the world. On the other hand, to be in the world in an ontological sense refers to a feeling of familiarity with the world, of being at home in the world, of belonging: *dwelling*. Third caveat: dwelling does not exclude the possibility of sometimes feeling estranged or alienated in the world. *For to be a stranger in one place means that there is another place where one is at home, even if one can't find it or doesn't know where it is* (Gelven). To dwell, then, on the horizontal plane that is the world, to be in the world, encompasses both the possibilities of the homely *and* the unhomely, of feeling familiar and estranged. The latter is encompassed in dwelling exactly *because the former is possible*. In other words, dwelling, being-in-a-world, is possible on a horizontal plane of possibilities, if not *here* then *there*.

Much has been written about J.M. Coetzee's *Disgrace*, about the stark reality of violence in the postcolony and the brittle forms of forgiveness and reconciliation engendered by it. But, to my knowledge, nobody has as yet commented on what strikes me as its most disconcerting sign of postcolonial violence: David Lurie and his daughter Lucy are attacked on the farm where they live (incidentally, very close to our conference venue). David is hit over the head, dragged across the kitchen floor and left unconscious in the bathroom. When he regains consciousness, his first thought is of Lucy: '"Lucy!" he croaks, and then, louder: "Lucy!" He tries to kick at the door, but he is not himself, and the space too cramped anyway, the door too old and solid. *So it has come, the day of testing.* Without warning, without fanfare, it is here, and he is in the middle of it' (emphasis added).

Again, as the expression would have it, the devil is in the detail, in the third person singular pronoun 'it'. For, what is the 'it' in 'So *it* has come . . . '? The 'it' is clearly not an object of the world that arrived on their doorstep. David's first thought is not the ontic, '*They* have come for us', but the ontological, ' . . . *it* has come, the day of testing'. 'It' refers to the anticipation of being-violated into not-being, of not-being-in-a-world, a possibility that now, finally, discloses itself, not as a mere possibility that always shadowed being-in-a-world as a possibility yet to come, but as that which had always been more real than reality itself. 'It' reveals something important about the structure of existence on a vertical plane of being and not-being: of always anticipating being violated and because of that very anticipation, as always-already-having-been-violated (note: not 'of', but *as* always-already-having-been-violated. 'Of' suggests a pre-existing subject who is violated, while 'as' suggests a subject existing *as* violation).

Is dwelling possible for a subject who is always already violated? Or is there a tipping point where the probability of death (of expecting it any moment of every day so that when 'it' comes, the experience is, conflictingly so, also one of relief that the waiting is over) radicalises the meaning of death beyond, what would then appear to be, 'mere' *Sein zum Ende* (Being-towards-the-end)? Where the probability of death is higher than the probability of living – North Kivu and South Kivu as a metonymic expression of various places in contemporary Africa come to mind – I sense an inversion that I struggle to name. What I do know is that in *that* moment David recognises that existence, being, was only ever a momentary exception, a temporary reprieve from another, more permanent state of affairs, formulated negatively: that being was only ever the unrealised reality of not-being.

Sections 45–53: Being-towards-Death. The awareness of the meaning of death is one of the ways in which Dasein can arrive at an authentic and ontological awareness of itself and the meaning of being because it can 'focus one's attention on the self *as it belongs to* the individual Dasein'. Such awareness is the ground of authentic existence because what it means *to be* is determined, in part, by what it means *not* to be. An inauthentic way of understanding the meaning of death means emphasising its actuality over its possibility, when we think of death in terms of the *actual* death for someone who has *actually* died as a way of not focusing on death as a real *possibility* for ourselves. In this way, death is turned into an object or future event we come to fear. The mood or state of mind that accompanies an authentic realisation of the inevitability of death, however, is not one of fear or anxiety or even terror, but *dread* (*Angst*): dread, the occasional uncanny estrangement from life itself discloses to me what it means to-be-going-to-die. Whereas fear is always directed at some thing, dread is function of *nothing* in particular; nothing*ness*, or the strangeness induced by the awareness of our finitude, of being thrown into a world and, hence, of being-able-not-to-be, so that we can say: 'To dread death . . . is to be uncannily aware of one's own *possible* dying', not as future event, but as possibility. This is a fragile difference: an inauthentic view of death is one of a future actuality, but an authentic view of death is being-towards-a-possibility. How can one retain thinking of death as meaningful possibility without thinking of its future actuality? Heidegger's answer is the distinction between *expecting* and *anticipating* death, succinctly summarised by Gelven: 'To look forward to death as an *actuality* is to look forward to no longer being possible, *and hence is to draw away from one's being-able-to-be*. But to look forward to death, not as an actuality, but as a *possibility*, is to *focus on one's being-able-to-be*' (emphasis added). In other words, concludes Gelven and I suppose this is the crux for me, in the authentic confrontation with the possibility of non-being, there is an awareness of the ground for being, rather than not-being. Living with the awareness, not of my *actual* (non)existence, but my *possible* (non)existence, means I am living with ontological awareness.

This, by any account, is moving thought – not only thinking as movement, but thinking that moves one. That said, if the place of 'time' in *Being and Time* is not simply as another phenomenon to be analysed, but rather *the* ontological perspective from which to contemplate the meaning of being, I am left somewhat restless by the absence of a temporality that would signify appreciation of the difference between the *possibility* of dying and constantly living with the *likelihood* and *probability* of dying. Consequently, the difference the latter would make to one's awareness of death and, hence, if not the meaning of being and Being (on this Heidegger is clear), then at least on the status of the *concept* of being and being-in-a-world in relation to not-being. Somewhere between the inauthentic *actuality* of death and the authentic *possibility* of being-possible-not-to-be, I want to see the *probability* that contracts time itself, so that reflecting on death is not Dasein's authentic choice, but a *consciousness forced upon it*; a death-awareness or consciousness woven into the very fabric of life that causes the *distinction* between being and not-being to become indistinct, so that a curious inversion emerges (not unlike the negative development of a positive photographic image), an image of Dasein, not as a subject who contemplates death as the possibility *nicht-mehr-sein-zu-können* (not to be able to be), but rather as a subject for whom being, *sein*, remains possible only as *hätte-sein-können* (might have been).

Does living the probability of death (living as if being were merely a possibility) not radicalise Heidegger's observation that contemplating not-being affirms the possibility of being-able-to-be, so that in our case we should rather speak of a subject who, by contemplating death, is not affirmed in being, but rather violated-unto-being? This is violation or death, not as the realisation of a possibility or the 'end', but as *archē*-violence (having-always-already-been-violated), in the light of which life appears as a temporary reprieve. To live with this consciousness, a consciousness that is a function of the probability (quantity) and not the actuality or possibility (quality) of death, is for me the most acute expression of the postcolonial condition, of Being as unrealised not-being. When this subject is eventually subjected to 'real' violence, the moment will assume the form of a self-recognition peculiar to this logic of inverted negativity: an encounter with what had always been more real than reality itself, that is, with the not-being that only ever temporarily violated itself into/as Dasein. '*So it has come, the day of testing. Without warning, without fanfare, it is here, and he is in the middle of it.*'

Perhaps violated-unto-being compels us to recognise being-in-a-world as a border concept, a concept of the limit, an undecidability or even, to adopt yet another image, a Möbius strip that, in certain contexts and under certain conditions, reveals a dreadful estrangement from life so fundamental as to be more real than reality itself – a revelation always understood as a recognition (L. *re-*, again + *cognosco*, know), (not)being as an interface of *it* (being) with 'it' (not-being). This would clarify a curious tension: on the one hand, postcolonial being as shadowed by the *destructive* possibility of not-being (an unfortunate metaphor: are objects more or less real than their shadows? Plato, et cetera), in which Being is constitutively violated; on the other hand, the very recognition of Being constitutively violated as *generative* exactly because it accentuates or 'brings to mind' and thereby actualises life or the *factual* nature of existence, of being alive, of being not-yet-violated, of not-yet-not-being. Is this tension between the destructive and the generative not the reappearance, in the language of hermeneutic phenomenology, of the numinous structure of violence? And is the subject conceived as interface of *it* and 'it' not also the vagabond of my earlier musings, s/he who is at once the object of so much violence, as well as the subject that so violently deconstructs every political form along with its implicit subjectivity?

Now to explore that would be a project for someone with a capacity for the useless, somebody who does not live and work under the sign of not-being and its institutional translation into an urgency that shadows philosophy in the postcolony: *Violence: Being in Time*. Alas, I'm not that person. In fact, having just dutifully completed Graham Greene's *A Burnt-Out Case*, I am more inclined to follow him to a leperosie in the heart of a fictitious Congo, there to follow my boy into the woods and to cover him with my body in search of an apophatic gesture that signifies nothing, not even nothing. Did Querry find absolution in that moment? And is absolution for a lapsed Catholic the same as exonerated empathy for a lapsed Protestant? Can one be violated (active) by/through empathy (passive), by/through 'understanding' (active/passive) as a form of auto-violation?

Christ. I just looked at that sentence: It reads like one of Derrida's obscure postcards. I better stop there/here, as/if by melancholy/irretrievable loss; thoughts pass through me oblivious of being (*canned laughter*).

I remain, for now,
Leonhard

P.S.
I take the laughter to suggest that it is already too late (*passé*) to play with the ontology of writing like that; that doing so belonged to a phase we went through, a momentary anti-imperialism that was allowed to test our patience because it had to demonstrate a point by now well taken. But is that it? Is it just me who is out of touch with the social networking world or are they, in fact, droning over us again, even as I write?

*   *   *

7 June 2013

Dear Valentin—

I'm writing this time to say that I could have sent this particular postcard to any of a number of people, but in the end I decided to send it to you because most people would have found it either insignificant or simply strange. Only the reader of my previous postcards to you would be able to make sense of the strangeness I'm about to narrate to you – the full significance of which, I must confess, still eludes me. I had a very strange and menacing dream last night. Two policemen were dragging off a man who was doing everything in his power to resist them. While he was kicking, twisting and turning against the force of law, he was also shouting something incomprehensible at me. I thought he was addressing me, specifically, me in particular and not just me as a witness to the injustice of his arrest, which seemed to imply that I had somehow been complicit in his arrest and that I had one last opportunity to prove his innocence and set him free. I rushed over to help him, or at least to hear what he was screaming, only to notice that he was a mute. With what was left of his tongue, he was producing the most awful, gargling and menacing speech imaginable. I must have cried out in horror because both policemen stopped and turned around. Neither of them had hands, only stumps; they were mutilated lepers and both had only dark holes where their eyes were meant to be. Shocking as this sight may have been, the thought that startled me and woke me from this terrible nightmare was this: if they knew they couldn't see me, why did they turn their heads in my direction? Was it pure malice? What am I to make of such a strange dream? What does it mean? Was it a warning – a reminder, perhaps, that every war, however ideologically overdetermined, contains moments that terrify precisely because they do not signify, acts of violence that mean nothing? I'm sorry to leave you with such an image.

I remain your friend,
Leonhard

*   *   *

12 June 2013

Dear Valentin—

Since I last wrote I have been thinking about how to describe in more detail the life that becomes visible only as interface of *it* with 'it', being and not-being, of being-in-a-world and violated-unto-being. We are clearly at some kind of limit here, undecidably poised between the political and the exclusion from the political: the subject as bare life, at once the passage or point of intersection between not-being or surplus produced by the present political and the condition of possibility of the future political. But I have become suspicious of this phrase 'bare life' – mainly because I am sympathetic to Laclau's critique of Agamben's central thesis that the original political relation is the ban. The ban involves abandonment in the sense that those reduced to bare life are left outside any communitarian order. In this way, claims Agamben, the ban holds together bare life and sovereignty and, as such, can be interpreted always to have been at the source of sovereign power. But, argues Laclau, at work in this argument is an untenable generalisation that assimilates *all* situations of being outside the law to the logic of the ban. In order for this to be true, he claims, Agamben needs two further presuppositions: one, of 'sheer separatedness', according to which the banned outsider is dispossessed of any kind of collective identity or communitarian *belonging*; two, a 'radical indefension', which leaves the outsider wholly vulnerable to the violence of the city/sovereign. For Laclau, neither of these presuppositions is true, as a consequence of which, the 'ban' cannot function as a master trope of sovereignty and/or the political. The outsider finds him/herself, not outside all law, but outside *the specific law of the city*. Laclau references Fanon's description of the march of the lumpenprotelariat in *Wretched of the Earth* – the 'pimps, the hooligans, the unemployed, and the petty criminals [who] throw themselves into the struggle like stout working men'. These outsiders are not beyond the law as such – they merely march to the drum of a *different* law (that comes from elsewhere, the past, the future or even a Higher Law) taken as 'starting point for a new collective identification *opposed* to the law of the city'. Far from a binary opposition between sovereignty and bare life, connected via the umbilical cord of the ban, we are presented with a de facto contestation of one law by another, of the march of one collectivity against sovereignty as a political abstraction of another, so that we end up, not with 'lawlessness as against law, but two laws that do not recognise each other'. The result, Laclau argues, is the *relation* of a mutual ban as *archē* of the political, 'for it is only in that case that we have a radical opposition between social forces and, as a result, a constant renegotiation and re-grounding of the social bond'.

I think it is to some such understanding of the political as different conceptions of the law that do not recognise each other, of a constant agonistic regrounding of the social bond and of differences that always seem to remain antagonistically irreducible, that we have to turn in order to circumscribe the ontological indeterminacy or undecidability of the postcolonial condition. Here, I'm thinking of Arendt's elaboration in 'On the Nature of Totalitarianism' of the distinction Montesquieu introduced in Book III of *L'esprit des lois* between the form of government and the principle that animates action in it. The former refers to what makes a form of government recognisable as, and here Montesquieu follows the classic classification, republic, monarchy or tyranny. The republic is a constitutional government in which the people hold sovereign power, a monarchy, where sovereign power resides with one person and tyranny, a government that is lawless because everyone is subject to the arbitrary will of one person. In each of these, the principle of government or what animates and guides all actions, is different. In a republic, it is virtue expressed as the love of *equality*; in a monarchy, honour expressed as the passion for *distinction*; in tyranny, it is *fear*. These principles guide the actions of both rulers and the ruled and are, as Montesquieu admitted, political principles that pertain to the public life of citizens, not the private lives of individuals; the domain in which, 'I am a citizen like all other citizens, and [not] personal life, in which I am an individual unlike anybody else' (Arendt). Montesquieu never considered that these principles might also contain clues to judging or creating what is right or wrong in the private sphere. Instead, he advanced the idea of a common ground from which both structure and principle sprang, a shared ontological root of both the private individual and the public citizen, suggesting that at the root of each cultural or historical form of government lies an *archē* or 'common ground which is both fundament and source, basis and origin' (Arendt). The common ground upon which hierarchical forms of government, such as monarchy, are premised and which guides the actions of their subjects, is *distinction*. This articulates an experience inherent in the human condition, namely the recognition that humans are distinct from each other by birth. Likewise, the fundamental human experience that is the common ground for republican law and action is living together with and *belonging* to a community of equally powerful human beings. It is only because we recognise the equality of power that we do not feel alone in the world. As is to be expected, the common ground of structure and action in tyranny is the inverse of this: fear is the expression of an anxiety (a panic, I would say) we experience when we feel utterly alone in the world. Arendt writes: 'The dependence and interdependence which we need in order to realise our power . . . becomes a source of despair whenever, in complete *loneliness*, we realise that one man alone has no power at all but is always overwhelmed and defeated by superior power' (emphasis added). In this sense, fear as a principle of action is a contradiction in terms because, rooted in a despair over the impossibility of action, it can only be destructive or 'self-corrupting'. And further, 'Out of the conviction of one's own impotence and the fear of the power of all others comes the will to dominate, which is the will of the tyrant . . . Tyranny, based on the essential impotence of all men who are alone, is the hubristic attempt to be like God, invested with power individually, in complete solitude.' For Arendt, following Montesquieu, these three forms of government are authentic exactly because the common ground represented by each – distinction, belonging, loneliness – are constituent elements of the human condition and, as such, representative of primary, universal human experiences.

To these three forms of government, Arendt adds a fourth, totalitarianism, because it is unprecedented and defies comparison. If law, or in the case of tyranny, lawlessness, is the essence of monarchy, democracy and tyranny, the terror deployed in order to manifest the laws of History or Nature is the essence of totalitarianism and the principle, not of action, but of a world-historical *movement* that culminates in the establishment of 'a desert of neighborlessness and loneliness'. In other words, the defining characteristic of totalitarianism is that 'no guiding principle of action taken from the realm of human action – such as virtue, honor, fear – is needed or could be used to set into motion a body politic whose essence is motion implemented by terror'. Instead of a principle of action, what this form of government requires is an ideology that dominates human beings 'to the point where they lose, with their spontaneity, the specifically human unpredictability of thought and action', a world in which everything is permitted and everything is possible, which takes 'the utter impotence of the individual for granted and provides for him either victory or death, a career or an end in a concentration camp, completely independent of his own actions or merits'.

From a postcolonial perspective, it would be tempting to continue along this pre-scientific trajectory of classification of forms of government and the principles of action that animate them by adding the patrimonial and/or neo-patrimonial state. But the patrimonial state is not unprecedented, in the sense that the modern Westphalian state was invented precisely to solve – by means of the autonomous and anonymous law before which we all act as equals and 'in concert' – the problems generated by all pre-modern, patrimonial states. The neo-patrimonial state, as the name indicates, is only distinct in that it combines elements of the patrimonial state and the modern, constitutional state. To me, this seems to suggest that any circumscription of the human condition exemplified by the neo-patrimonial state and that which makes of it an authentic expression of the human condition must depart, not from the assumption of a singular and therefore unique principle of action emanating from it, but rather from the legacy of colonialism as a radical interruption of endogenous processes of socio-political movement, which resulted, not in the gradual mutation of political forms and their associated principles of action, but in *the simultaneous manifestation or coincidence of various political forms that seamlessly blend into or alternate with each other*. What is most specific about the human condition so conceived is the coexistence in time and *therefore* the relatively random deployment of principles of action that sometimes reinforce and sometimes work against each other as conflicting attempts to reground the social bond in equality, honour *and* fear.

Of these oscillations in principles of action, the most disturbing figure must surely be the child soldiers that Kabila recruited to join the AFDL, who thought of him as father-like figure (*Mzee*) and who formed a 'quasi-familial relationship with his officers' (Prunier) in the long march towards true democracy, only to end up contributing to the replacement of one form of tyranny with another. If we were to take these tropes – 'quasi-filial relationships' (honour), 'the fight for democracy' (equality) and 'tyranny' (fear) – as expressive of a dimension of the human condition (distinction, belonging and loneliness), what figure would better capture their abstract unity than Salvatore, who 'had invented for himself a language which used the sinews of the languages to which he had been exposed . . . taking words sometimes from one and sometimes from another' (Eco)? And once we have conceived of their abstract unity in these terms, are we not then well placed to delimit a domain in which the 'it' that posits life as violated-unto-being, appears *in* and as a function *of* the fault lines caused by the perceived randomness with which these principles of action were/are deployed – a randomness all the more terrifying for constantly mimicking the arrival of a new *nomos*?

Perhaps the phrase 'bare life' is inadequate to denote this condition; on the other hand, perhaps it is still a useful way to circumscribe a condition that can only come about as the result of an exclusion from one conception of the political, while functioning as condition of the possibility of another – both the *conditio sine qua non* and *conditio per quam* of one conception of the political, the condition *for* its possibility, as well as the condition *through which* we conduct another, past or future, conception of the political; a condition that, in this particular case, is constantly reproduced, contrary to Laclau, not by the clash between contrasting conceptions of the law that do not recognise each other, but when actions animated by one principle of action are executed in conflict with actions animated by another: honour *and* equality *and* fear.

If this is indeed the case, we are left with an extremely ambiguous understanding of postcolonial sovereignty – an ambiguity perhaps rooted in the originating self-consciousness that will forever haunt it with a conception (or memory?) of interdependence most magnificently exemplified by the relationship between Don Quixote and Sancho Panza. And with that, we seem to have come full circle. I find myself back at the beginning, but differently so. I shall write again soon.

I remain, as always, your friend,
Leonhard

* * *

19 June 2013

Dear Valentin—

I'm going to have to stop sending you these postcards – if only so that I may have something left to say at the conference. For now, perhaps only this: as much as I appreciate Agamben's work, I think Laclau is right: the ease with which the former moves from *genealogy* to *origin* becomes particularly problematic when he posits the 'ban', not only as an important historical constituent of sovereignty, but as *archē* of the political as such. The resulting demand – to work towards 'a political theory freed from the aporias of sovereignty' – would then, as Laclau claims, condemn us to nihilism. But this question is not to be settled in a little postcard. That said, I wonder if it may not, after all, be useful to consider sovereignty, neither as articulation nor un-articulation, but rather as *dis*articulation of the human plenitude at the source of the political?

Perhaps a clue to the difference between Agamben and Laclau lies, neither in accepting as foundational the aporetic structure of sovereignty in relation to the 'ban', nor in seeking to transcend the aporia as a condition for the true political by hypostasising one force of law into a multitude of forces of law, but rather in remaining attentive to the manner in which each of these forces functions as a principle of action that mobilises one dimension of the plenitude of the human condition (*distinction*, *belonging*, *loneliness*) as a critique of all others.

Sovereignty has only ever been a myth underwritten by the force of violence as its sole guarantor: not simply as its condition of possibility, but as a movement that accompanied it from its inception, first as the violence needed to enforce it, to make it Law and, subsequently, as the violence that continued to haunt it as a spectre in the form of a self-conscious enforcement of the law. Perhaps it is true, as Kafka argued, that Cervantes's wisdom consists in suggesting that Sancho dreamt of being Don Quixote, much like Don Quixote dreamt of being Descartes's self-enclosed and heroic *cogito*: that Sancho is to Don Quixote as Don Quixote is to Descartes – a venerable Chain of Being beyond becoming. Perhaps the dream that continues to inspire sovereignty has always been one of completion, of being the embodiment of human plenitude itself in order that we may become complete subjects, that is, truly capable of suffering in the world. Corresponding to this figure of the subject as embodiment of human plenitude, of the human *as* subject and the subject *as* human, would there not then also be an additional figure of 'sublime empathy' that can only come about once and *because* we have inducted the complete human into the political, that is, in response to having received the subject, however briefly and in all its plenitude, as the cessation of violence and no longer as born of violence and therefore the continued source of violence?

We seem to have arrived at our final undecidability: on the one hand, empathy, without which life itself seems unimaginable and a sign of a necessary failure of just such a complete induction; on the other hand, the promise, the dream that seems so terrifyingly heterogenous to life itself, of existing without being haunted by the very violence that makes subjectivity possible. To phrase this differently, and paraphrasing that other Jacques (often vilified for his fatalism), is this decision not both before us, still to come, *as well as* more ancient than memory itself?

I remain your friend,
Leonhard

P.S.

I finished the page proofs of *On African Fault Lines* today. I lingered a little longer on 'Within Silence: Haiti' because I suspect that, of all the meditations in this collection, it may turn out to be the one most reluctant to yield its secret to the reader. This is not unexpected because, in my reading of it, the essay is fundamentally concerned with the moment we come to speech – that is, the moment just before we start to speak, fully confident that we will be able to convey the very thought that precipitated speaking. Perhaps its central concern is neither with silence nor with breaking silence and where violence is concerned, neither with 'it' (life as violation-unto-being) nor with the violent redemption of 'it' into politics, but rather with the moment of temptation, the precarious moment when the promise of simultaneously honouring silence *and* signifying it, of acknowledging both the *archē* status of violence and the imperative to resist violence, generates a self-consciously endless, post-secular eschatology in which we can neither bury 'it' in silence nor redeem 'it' in signification because ultimately, these are just two different ways of disarticulating the world.

Note

A version of this chapter first appeared in German (translated from English by Martin Ross) in *Polylog* 31 (2014): 43–62.

References

Epigraph
Nnamdi Elleh. 2002. *Architecture and Power in Africa*. Westport: Praeger.

27 April 2013
Mudimbe, V-Y. 1982. *Auch wir sind schmutzige Flüsse*. Frankfurt am Main: Verlag Otto Lembeck.
———. 1989. *Before the Birth of the Moon*. New York: Simon & Schuster.

10 May 2013
Cervantes, Miguel de. 2003. *Don Quixote*. Translated by Edith Grossman; introduction by Harold Bloom. New York: Eco.
Diderot, Denis. 1999. *Jacques the Fatalist*. Oxford: Oxford University Press.
Kundera, Milan. 1990. 'The Depreciated Legacy of Cervantes'. In *The Art of the Novel*. London: Cox & Wyman.
Praeg, Leonhard. 2008. 'The Aporia of Collective Violence'. *Law and Critique* 19(2): 193–223.
Taylor, Charles. 2002. '*Gewalt und Moderne*'. *Europäische Revue* 23. Also available as an audio file: 'The Sources of Violence, Perennial and Modern' at http://archiv.iwm.at/index.php?option=com_content&task=view&id=365&Itemid=496.

21 May 2013
Agamben, Giorgio. 1998. *Homo Sacer: Sovereign Power and Bare Life*. Translated by Daniel Heller-Roazen. Stanford: Stanford University Press.
Carayannis, Tatiana. 2003. 'The Complex Wars of the Congo: Towards a New Analytic Approach'. *Journal of Asian and African Studies* 38(2): 232–55.
Mudimbe, V-Y (ed). 1996. *Open the Social Sciences: Report of the Gulbenkian Commission on the Restructuring of the Social Sciences*. Stanford: Stanford University Press.

25 May 2013
Arendt, Hannah. 1994. 'On the Nature of Totalitarianism: An Essay in Understanding'. In *Essays in Understanding: 1930–1954*. New York: Schoken Books.
Derrida, Jacques. 1981. *Writing and Difference*. Translated by and with introduction by Alan Bass. London: Routledge & Kegan Paul.
Eco, Umberto. 1984. *The Name of the Rose*. London: Picador.
Freud, Sigmund. 1955. 'The Uncanny'. In *The Standard Edition of the Complete Psychological Works of Sigmund Freud, Vol. XVII (No. 17) (1917–1919)*. Translated under the general editorship of James Strachey with Anna Freud. London: The Hogarth Press.
Mudimbe, V-Y. 1988. *The Invention of Africa: Gnosis, Philosophy, and the Order of Knowledge*. Bloomington: Indiana University Press.
Quayson, Ato. 2002. 'Obverse Denominations: Africa?' *Public Culture* 14(3): 585–88.

1 June 2013
Cioran, E.M. 1998. *The Temptation to Exist*. Chicago: University of Chicago Press.

3 June 2013

Coetzee, J.M. 1999. *Disgrace*. London: Vintage.

Gelven, Michael. 1970. *A Commentary on Heidegger's* Being and Time. New York: Harper & Row.

Greene, Graham. 1974. *A Burnt-Out Case*. New York: Heinemann.

Heidegger, Martin. 1962. *Being and Time*. New York: Harper & Row.

12 June 2013

Agamben, Giorgio. 1998. *Homo Sacer: Sovereign Power and Bare Life*. Translated by Daniel Heller-Roazen. Stanford: Stanford University Press.

Arendt, Hannah. 1994. 'On the Nature of Totalitarianism: An Essay in Understanding'. In *Essays in Understanding: 1930–1954*. New York: Schoken Books.

Eco, Umberto. 1984. *The Name of the Rose*. London: Picador.

Laclau, Ernesto. 2007. 'Bare Life or Social Indeterminacy?' In *Giorgio Agamben: Sovereignty and Life*, edited by Matthew Calarco and Steven DeCaroli, 11–22. Stanford: Stanford University Press.

Montesquieu, C. de Secondat, Baron de. 1823. *The Spirit of Laws*. London: Collingwood.

Prunier, Gérard. 2009. *From Genocide to Continental War: The 'Congolese' Conflict and the Crisis of Contemporary Africa*. London: C. Hurst & Co.

19 June 2013

Derrida, Jacques. 1994. *Specters of Marx: The State of the Debt, the Work of Mourning & the New International*. London: Routledge.

Laclau, Ernesto. 2007. 'Bare Life or Social Indeterminacy?' In *Giorgio Agamben: Sovereignty and Life*, edited by Matthew Calarco and Steven DeCaroli, 11–22. Stanford: Stanford University Press.

Mudimbe, V-Y. 2013. *On African Faultlines: Meditations on Alterity Politics*. Pietermaritzburg: University of KwaZulu-Natal Press.

CHAPTER 9

Debitores Sumus . . . On Ways of Exhausting Our Question on Violence

V-Y Mudimbe

I

To a question of mine about what kind of clean, ethical language to use in order to express the unspeakable, two intellectual daughters have responded, independently, by using the concept of 'singularity'. One is Canadian. She is black. In French, she focuses on the victimisation of women and refers to a complex history of violence in the past and the present, mentioning Jewish, Polish, Russian women and referring to the 'comfort women' in Asia. In anger, a question from Gertrude Mianda: 'How to face three apparently interrelated factors, which, referring to the Great Lakes, might be linked, an international indifference, violence and its best manifestations in practices of appropriating female bodies as politically strategic and economic instruments?' The second daughter is Portuguese. She is white. She, Catarina Gomes, invited me to face Paula Rego's 'Dog Woman', adding a question: 'Does the recognition of humanity depend on the recognition of a singularity that cannot be possessed or objectified?'

One consults a different history. One remembers that the traditional priest, after observing the missionary and the efficiency of his action, decided to dissociate himself from his own cult. He joins the new faith, transfers and adapts his own beliefs. The traditional priest has integrated the community of those who can see differently, the Christians. They differentiate themselves from the pagans, now named in the local language as those who belong to the devil. The distinction has reactualised what in the tradition was signified in a metaphor opposing 'the visually impaired', prisoners of the phenomenal world and the 'strong', those who could see, those who know what others do not. This note from Patrice Mufuta's *Le chant kàsàla des Lubà* (1969) echoes an anecdote from J.D.Y. Peel's *Religious Encounter and the Making of the Yoruba* (2000). During the missionising period, a Church Missionary Society official heard this in a village: 'There is not a day past . . . in which we never call the name of [Olorun], the living God, but the book people [Christians . . .] take the matter of God too much upon themselves, as if they only know him' (Mufuta 1969: 181).

II

In the conclusion of *Discovering Religious History in the Modern Age*, apropos the difference between German and French scholars' views on the 'history of religions and modernity', Hans G. Kippenberg states:

> Encompassing a view of modernity within a view of the history of religions formed the pragmatic side of the new paradigm of the history of religions, and explains the modes of the descriptions. Past and remote religions were described to counteract the claims of modern society for a complete renunciation of religions (2002: 195).

This point concludes a masterful study that begins with a contextualisation of the debate on the nature of discourses on religion. The introduction to the American edition usefully situates it by invoking a number of references, including the illustrative arguments of Jonathan Z. Smith in *Imagining Religion* (1988) and Russel T. McCutcheon in *Manufacturing Religion* (1997). The first dwells on the part of the scholar in the invention of religions; the second correlates scholarship, teaching religion and politics. These are statements in the history of a discipline.

Two viewpoints organise the issue, that of the historian and that of the missiologist, both considering how Christian Africa is and this is a point that cannot bypass the new forms of presence of Christianity and Islam. Any problematisation of interactions between these two religious systems and the local traditional expressions faces the fact of incomparable grammars. The Africanisation of Christianity or Islam designates also different processes. For instance, in East Africa, Swahili Islam offers many angles and, historically, in terms of the first Islamic migration to Ethiopia, the 614 AD *Hijrah*, and the coexistence of Islam and the Coptic Church. And, centuries later down the coast, the 1505 confrontation in Mombasa between Christian Portuguese and Swahilis. Thousands of African Muslims are converting now to Christianity, each year. The other way around, too, it seems. In both cases, pious propaganda defines grounds to protect against competition. Possibly a similar reason would have motivated Catholics to remember a timely rediscovered symbol. With *The Martyrs of Mombasa* (1997), Malachy Cullen resurrects a major mediation, death in the name of faith.

Always part of the imperial convoy and of the colonial enterprise, to invoke again the catechists' mediators, they are the necessary mediations by which the mission identifies with its aim. They are, first, efficient go-between auxiliaries of the missionaries and the culture to convert; second, servants of the letter called upon to inhabit the new culture through the metamorphosis of traditional rituals; third, they are living testimonies of the mutation of an original place into a Christian space. In this individual, three mediations – a body, the letter, a testimony – are firmly interrelated within a transcending fellowship.

As of today, let us refer to paradigmatic breakdowns. Here are statements on African affairs, from three angles. To begin with, from Thomas P.M. Barnett's *Great Powers*, first, what seems like an innocuous observation: 'China once had all the same problems that Africa suffers today: warlords, civil conflict, unending war, corruption, tyrants, and an imperviousness to past Western efforts to shape events there. And how did China pull itself together economically' (2009: 193)? And, indeed, the following suggestion: 'As Deng's famous maxim put it: "it doesn't matter whether the cat is black or white, as long as it catches mice." Most of what ends up working in Africa will probably come as a surprise, just as it did in China'. And finally, a realist position, presented in the same book: 'Economist Paul Collier, for example, estimates that 40 percent of military spending in Africa is made possible by official developmental aid flows, and that many military coups are nothing more than periodic "profit-taking" exercises' (192).

To reflect this from a statement that celebrated years before this influential book in political economy, here are the main lines of the official declaration of a pan-African meeting of Third World theologians that took place in Accra, Ghana, on 17–24 December 1977. It faces the success story of Christianity and, at the same time, accents what is presented as the 'ethnicity of Africa'. From this basis, the document evaluates the Christian presence in Africa. A brilliant synthesis is given by Fabien Eboussi Boulaga in his acclaimed *A contretemps: L'enjeu de Dieu en Afrique* (1991); the emergence of Christian African theological practices, as expressed in relation to three axes.

One, African traditional religion is perceived as a stepping stone of the Gospel. It is a critical engagement with the Bible and black liberation theology from South Africa. The declaration affirms five interacting references: the Bible and the Christian tradition, African anthropology, traditional religion, African Independent Churches and, finally, what it calls 'African realities' that include references to socio-economic factors, colonialism and racism, sexism and other forms of cultural alienation. As surprising as it might seem, a concept articulates the apparent coherence of this declaration. It is used; it is 'singularity'.

It cannot be accidental that such a concept seems to be a key to different approaches. From Latin, the singular or *singularis* is what cannot be confused in the reality that the Latin language, for instance, denotes under *ambo*, the designation of two, or in plurality expressions.

And finally, one might try to face the singularity issue from the identity issue that it supposes by its own particularity. In terms of questions of method, and taking into account the contribution from Laura Kerr in this volume, and going back to a normative reference: what is normal and what is pathological? The question refers to Georges Canguilhem's book (1991). From a syllabus that has been guiding a meditation of more than 40 years, here are three entries, preceded by a quotation from Lewis Carroll:

> I wonder if I shall fall right through the earth! How funny it'll seem to come out among the people that walk with their heads downwards! The antipathies, I think . . . but I shall have to ask them what the name of the country is, you know. Please, Ma'am, is this New Zealand? Or Australia (1948: 190)?

Three lines can qualify the quotation, that is, the problem, and where it is. It is in a tradition that is French and that implies the reconceptualisation of an approach to anomaly and disease, the normal, abnormal and pathological, norm and average, the value of error and any individuality as a strategic defence problem. With, in retrospect, issues on anxiety, fear, defence, resistance and conflicts (Anna Freud).

A second entry is Canguilhem's focus on 'Epistemology without Subject' (Iwele, Kerr and Mudimbe 2007: 182) versus the notions of *subject* and *identity* in Martin Heidegger's *Identity and Difference* (1974: 146). They demand an attention to at least the following issues: first, to understand error and the pathological not in terms of deviation, but in terms of necessity? The importance and pertinence of the notion of infraction? And finally, to face the opposition between the philosophy of the *cogito*, a philosophy of the Concept, that is, of *a way* of existing as human being.

And finally, a third entry, in time, in retrospect of Sigmund Freud's *Civilization and Its Discontents*, Goethe: 'He who possesses science and art also has religion; but who possesses neither of those two, let him have religion' (in Freud 1961: 127).

191

III

Three Christian witnesses from the twentieth-century dynamics:

John V. Taylor, the general secretary of the Church Missionary Society (1963–73) and Bishop of Winchester (1974–84), is the author of *The Primal Vision*. Reflecting on the African religious experience, he observes that 'ethnologists haven't yet been able to agree as to what place God occupies in the African worldview' (2001: 52). In this statement, one has a judgement on anthropological knowledge, as opposed to the expected spiritual motion represented in a missionising process:

> Only the practice of the presence of a God in sacrament and meditation in a steady, painful flowering of sensitivity to all presences, can restore and integrate so that even–ness can be maintained. 'Compassion' is the final operative word to define what the way of presence really means. It sums up the listening, responsive, agonising receptivity of the prophet and the poet (Taylor 2001: 137).

Second, the Belgian Franciscan, Placide Tempels, also a missionary, the well-known author of *Bantu Philosophy* (1969). In a reflection of the process that legitimised *Bantu Philosophy*, measuring its limits, he refers to his own conversion:

> I used to believe that after discovering the Bantu personality, I would become again the pastor, the chief, the doctor, now recognised as a master of a technique, of an adapted language 'to teach' Christianity. I suddenly understood in this encounter, person to person, soul to soul, being to being, that we had moved from a reciprocal knowledge to a situation of sympathy; in brief, of love, and that precisely Christianity had been born again and recommenced (1962: 19).

And finally, from an African priest, Jean-Marc Ela, an academic with doctorates in theology and sociology, who chose a pastoral commitment in rural areas of north Cameroon. His testimony, entitled *Ma foi d'Africain*, circles on itself in a comment on the 'great challenge to faith and to theology in Africa [which] is our historical situation that snatches Christianity out of meaninglessness' (1985: 182). Ela has a question: 'How can the Easter message once again become a well where Christians and churches can draw strength to lead ahead, "O Death, where is thy victory?" That is the question I ask myself in *My Faith as an African*, as the third millennium draws near.'

These testimonies are statements in two traditions, Christian and African. They tell of a manner of existing in a story of a revelation and in relation to a will to truth. They attest also to the pitfalls from conflicts of existing in a language of faith detached from a disciplinary objectivity. The assessment on ways of converting needs another viewpoint.

The Abrahamic Lord is a jealous one, mediated in many visages, all worked out in lines often removed from human restrictions. Can one be Christian, accept African prescriptions on ancestorship and attend Islamic prayers? The banality of the question in Mombasa or in Dakar may seem horrific elsewhere. Yet, accommodations could meet the repertory of public virtue. Indeed, common sense, believers might disagree on ways of dissensions about rules. Says the Qur'ān (Pickthall 1938: 2, 286): 'Allah tasketh not a soul beyond its scope.' This concerns all. Its practical meaning, decoded in the language of the scholar, the one about whom it is written elsewhere in the Qur'ān (25, 20): 'We never sent before thee any messengers but lo! they ate food and walked in the markets. And We have appointed some of you a test for others: Will ye be steadfast? And thy Lord is ever Seer.'

Patrick Ofori's *Islam in Africa South of the Sahara* (1977) and Samir M. Zoghby's *Islam in Sub-Saharan Africa* (1978) have collected entries to an ignored field of scholarship and, importantly, in cultural identity and faith. To say the least. Within the same landscape, other voices had been addressing the issue otherwise. In West Africa, some of the best-known masters in spiritual direction, Tierno Bokar and Amadou Baba, had a rule: 'Brother in God, you, who come to our *zawiya*, this space of ours, are you absolutely decided to sing the hymn to the only truth?' René Luc Moreau annotates the invitation in *Africains Musulmans* (1982) by norming it in the specificity of an African Islam. From its initial inspiration, he writes, quoting Maxime Rodinson, 'in Islam there is always a betrayed revolution and always a revolution to recommence'. The Islamic task retraces its African actuality to foundational markers of the Qur'ān: monotheism versus animism, the dynamics of the word and the symbolics of demonology and spirits.

The concept of an appointment in the service of the truth has been doubling the task of revisiting what both the politics of knowledge and missionising have damned, i.e., that which is put under animism.

A new zone of testimony sets a place of faith at the intersection of the burden of traditions and arguments of Christianity and Islam. With the upsurge of the prophetess all around the continent, one documents in the most literal sense a bold Christian favour along judicative veneration for the letter. One does not know exactly how many assemblies led by prophetesses exist today in Nairobi. There are hundreds of them throughout sub-Saharan countries. In common, they present three main features: an extreme faithfulness to the Abrahamic faith, a careful ministering to the members, doubled by healing liturgies, all stipulated by rules of initiation. In their own language, the quest states a combat. A notable case, because it became missionary, has been studied by Julie Ndaya Tshiteku in her 'Prendre le bic' (2008).

There is something else to be invoked: cultural confrontations that Christian trends induce. In the 1980s, the dynamics of the Pentecostal movement proved it. Fortifying a globalist imagination, the Christian fundamentalism, initiated by the German Reinhard Bonnke, based its action on an absolute faithfulness to scriptures. On the other side, mainstream Protestant denominations and Catholicism were advancing, in the sense of cultural inculturations. Pentecostalism, globally, was indeed conservative on social issues, its project being strictly a concern for 'taking the continent for Jesus'. Fundamentalist evangelism has been inspiring new independent churches more attentive to the integration of Christianity in their own imaginary, whereas mainstream denominations tend to promote a Christian humanism.

Addressing the implications of connections between Christian symbols and political activism, in *Questioning the Secular State*, edited by David Westerlund, Paul Gifford who has carefully detailed the problem in a number of studies, writes:

> This slow and belated awakening of the mainline churches is of some importance for the future of the fundamentalist churches. In Latin America . . . the evangelical churches have been forced to address political issues because 'their great ideological rival', liberation theology, has made this political agenda inescapable. It is probable that the lack of liberation theology in Black Africa has helped the evangelical churches resolutely avoid this step (Westerlund 1996: 214).

The signs are visible, indicative of a postcolonial Christian panorama. The conversion of black Africa, which is a success story of both Christianity and Islam, is also the cause of a latent confrontation with traditional practices. On the west coast, for instance, Dean S. Gilliland quotes Musa Gotom, past general secretary of Church of Christ in Nigeria, who declares that 'African religion has declined considerably and is still on the decline. One would say African religion preexists, however, as a worldview; and, as such, is still active in both Muslim and Christians without their realising it' (1986: 173). And, immediately after this, follows the opinion of an academic who holds that 'very educated Nigerians pay regular visits to the priests of African religious shrines to obtain material objects and concoctions. It is simply amazing the way intelligent Africans visit fortune tellers'. The observation manifests a key to an approach of an African religious climate.

Here is a statement that makes one reflect. From Etienne Gilson's *God and Philosophy*, this statement makes one think at least twice:

> Abstractly speaking, the early Greek philosophers could have immediately brought the evolution of Greek natural theology to its close; but they didn't, because they didn't want to lose their gods. Our first reaction is naturally to blame such a lack of philosophical courage; but there might be less courage in following abstract logic than in refusing to let it play havoc with the manifold of reality (2002: 14–15).

IV

The title of Louis-Vincent Thomas and René Luneau's book – *La terre africaine et ses religions* (1980) – is a good case. It refers to the African continent as '*terre*', to be understood as a locus. This *terre*, designated by the adjective 'African', localises a place, straightening it and its religious practices as a theoretical space. Ali Mazrui is right when, in *Africanity Redefined*, he quotes Melville Herskovitz, who suggests that Africa is a geographical fiction: 'It is thought of as a separate entity and regarded as a unit to the degree that the map is invested with an authority imposed on it by the mapmakers' (2002: 43). From the viewpoint of those inhabiting concrete cultures in East, Central or West Africa, this entity is an abstraction. Their testimonies are not. One accepts this invention as it reflects a spatial coherence that reflects the sense of a place. About this African space and its religious practices, Thomas and Luneau, for instance, situating themselves as critical eyes, observe this '*monde étrange*' (strange world) from two viewpoints. They describe, first, its time of certainties, which has been followed by the history of transformations that opens a new world in mutation. A picture may signify what is out there: processes in the reconfiguration of myths, rituals and religious traditional practices vis-à-vis dynamics induced by Islam and Christianity. In sum, three references are depicting contextualised models and the way they portray, on the one hand, in the word or in the letter, what warrants the evidence of an absence and a presence and, on the other hand, what certifies conceptions about linkages of certainties to rituals that organise human life.

In these considerations, a sign of respect for the witnesses and, after the theologian Paul Tillich's correlation method, signs and symbols are met in the manner they are given, interconnected with others on the basis of similarity and accepted in the designations and figures that join them in narratives. From Tillich's *Dynamics of Faith*, a guiding idea: 'There is no substitute expressing the reality to which the term "faith" points' (2005: xxi):

(a) At the historical and political level, these signs function as liberation movements from foreign oppression and as forces of progress against alienating relations represented by capitalist bureaucratic systems;

(b) at the level of sign, they use symbolic codes, rituals and beliefs, issued forth from the local milieu and a regional social order; and

(c) at the level of individuals, they are part of half-affective and rationalised responses to an existential anguish whose roots are deep within the collective unconscious.

Politicians may understand the phenomenon better than clerics. In *Non-Bourgeois Theology*, Joseph G. Donders, a professor of philosophy at the University of Nairobi, reports the case of Jomo Kenyatta, the first president of Kenya, and that of his successor Daniel Arap Moi, who followed his *nyayo*, footsteps:

> One Sunday he went to an Evangelical Brotherhood church, another Sunday to the Catholic cathedral, another time to the Bahai meeting, and so on. In most places he was asked to say something. Kenyatta's preaching – always religious and political – made the same points. We are, notwithstanding our religious differences, all children of the same God, we are brothers and sisters and we should live accordingly in peace, love, and unity. He always added that we should forgive and forget whatever had happened in the past (1985: 112).

Apologising for the division of believers in a faith that transcends a locality, Kenyatta was hitting home by fusing the political and the religious in his body and in his speech. At a different level, another ironic mingling in Donders's observations, namely: 'If [John] Mbiti were to write a new book on the religious condition in Kenya . . . the title might be "African Religious Denominations and Philosophy," or, perhaps more to the point: "African Religious Denominationalism and Religion"' (1985: 111).

Valeer Neckebrouck (1988), a doctor of anthropology and of theology, suggests an original etiology of contemporary trends from what he calls a 'schismatogenesis' context:

(Classical thesis) versus (the case of Za-Krestos)
Western church versus Eastern church
Protestant/Catholic versus Orthodox
Missionary leadership versus autochthonous leadership
Western cultural model versus inculturated Christianity

A critique of the primacy of entries on the left, usually admitted as the condition for new churches, Neckebrouck's hypothesis raises questions differently. For example, the Za-Krestos case in Ethiopia contradicts the usual explanation. In *Théologie et culture*, Neckebrouck presents his double hypothesis that extracts itself from past categories:

(a) A known observation since Barrett's study: African independent churches proceed generally from Protestant denominations and are marked by a wish to cultural difference;

(b) the stronger the structuration of a church (Anglican and Catholic), the more articulated is its hierarchy and the more centralised its organisation, the less accented are trends towards separatism;

(c) the less integrated and less hierarchical the formal structures, a characteristic of Calvinist and Evangelical constitutions, the more the tendency towards separatism.

The hypothesis should be taken seriously. It presents the advantage of going beyond criteria that would oppose branches of the same church. This grid that belongs to social sciences presents a credibility based on its functional capacity. Confirming the hypothesis, African initiated churches are producing their own schismatic branches and prophetesses lead observable new assemblies.

V

Debitores sumus non carni ut secundum carnem vivamus

— Romans 8:12[1]

Here is a symbolic key to the unthinkable. It is a technicality that could be referred to in terms of 'Fluxion Wars', that is, an idea of 'tending to . . .'. In his *A Brief History of Infinity* (2003), Brian Clegg has a phrase that has nothing to do with the cultural testimony that this chapter has been facing. Here is a statement about the deaths of millions of people. For sure, between seven and ten, by now. The statement is grave and cannot be negated, unless checked. The 'tending to . . .' such a figure is a moving away from something. Here, one faces this. One thing, mathematics. In the idea of 'tending to . . .', another thing, the incredible despair of humanists in facing what such an idea might imply when referring to fellow human beings.

There must be a truth and its objectivity, as it can be testified by the senses. Accepted or rejected in speech or behaviour, the perceived or the affirmed or the rejected can be qualified as good and bad in relation to the only objective criterion we can invoke: the uniqueness of any human being.

Cultural or religious initiation: what is its proof and its ethical values against the 'tending to . . .' quotation? Initiation is a generality. It designates a variety of institutions, spaces of discontinuities and interactions, transitions and recommencements. A major entry to explication of religious practices, it has no adequate name. Labelled animist or pan-vitalist, anthropocentrist or cosmocentrist, its activity escapes the logic of definitive classifications. At least, one problem stands as a necessary precaution. It concerns the value of concepts needed in relation to social science, in order to designate symbolic layers that initiations activate between the visible and the invisible, the immanent and the transcendent, apropos ways of perceiving such cultural economies from a rationalist angle. At the outset of *La religion spontanée* (1997), Henri Maurier uses the expression *'l'insinuation raciste'*. The rationalist can find good reasons to take for granted whatever grid can be bestowed on such a difference. On the other hand, the same presuppositions could justify as an essence of the very thing imprisoning the difference in a fictitious web of symbols.

Recently issued from an international conference organised at the Catholic University of Louvain, on 10 March 2005, a special issue of *Histoire et Missions Chrétiennes* is centred on the question 'Is African religion rehabilitated?' (2007:

3). A subtitle specifies the way of a question, or the 'changing perception on the African religious fact'. From the contributions, here are a few directions. First, the connections between European and African perceptions of the return of African religion; thus, a fundamental question: what is this return? Second, interrogations on the religious in concrete expressions chosen – suffering in the Great Lakes region; religion and politics in South Africa; beliefs in ancestors and Christian practice in Madagascar; manifestations of the divine in mythical narratives, legends and proverbs among the Lubas; thus, a fundamental question: how to read this African religious modernity? Third, from the editors' position, an objective: to reflect on the visibility of traditional religion; thus, a fundamental question: what is it today?

In this incomprehensible situation of violence in the Great Lakes region, one thing imposed itself upon my mind. It is a question mark. Thinking of a friend, the late Richard Rorty, who in *Contingency, Irony and Solidarity* (1989), wrote about the limits of expression of the 'language game of one's time'. From a methodological agnosticism, this is the only thing that seems more or less certain. What is negated in the Great Lakes' violence is not only human dignity, but might also be the mysterious and unique humanity of the gift of life.

The title of this meditation, '*Debitores Sumus*', was, and is, an invitation to face the unspeakable, which is 'tending to . . .' the unspeakable that religious systems seem to have failed. Or, have we failed the systems?

Notes

I would like to acknowledge, for their contribution to this text, Trip Attaway and Elsie Bell – the first for administering the project and typing the manuscript and the second for editing it.
Unless otherwise indicated, all translations are by the author.
1. 'So then, brothers and sisters, we are debtors, not to the flesh, to live according to the flesh' (*New Revised Standard Version of the Bible*).

References

Barnett, Thomas P.M. 2009. *Great Powers: America and the World after Bush*. New York: Berkeley Books.

Canguilhem, Georges. 1991. *The Normal and the Pathological*. New York: Zone.

Carroll, Lewis. 1948. *Alice's Adventures in Wonderland*. Wellesley: Branden Books.

Clegg, Brian. 2003. *A Brief History of Infinity: The Quest to Think the Unthinkable*. London: Robinson.

Cullen, Malachy. 1997. *The Martyrs of Mombasa*. Nairobi: Paulines Publications Africa.

Donders, Joseph G. 1985. *Non-Bourgeois Theology: An African Experience of Jesus*. New York: Orbis Books.

Eboussi Boulaga, Fabien. 1991. *A contretemps: L'enjeu de Dieu en Afrique*. Paris: Karthala.

Ela, Jean-Marc. 1985. *Ma foi d'Africain*. Paris: Karthala.

Freud, Sigmund. 1961. *Civilization and Its Discontents*. New York: W.W. Norton.

Gay, Peter. 2006. *Freud: A Life for Our Time*. New York: W.W. Norton.

Gilliland, Dean S. 1986. *African Religion Meets Islam: Religious Change in Northern Nigeria*. Lanham: University Press of America.

Gilson, Etienne. 2002 [1941]. *God and Philosophy*. New Haven: Yale University Press.

Heidegger, Martin. 1974. *Identity and Difference*. New York: Harper & Row.

Iwele, Godé, Laura Kerr and V-Y Mudimbe (eds). 2007. *The Normal and Its Orders*. Ottawa: Editions Malaïka.

Kippenberg, Hans G. 2002. *Discovering Religious History in the Modern Age*. Princeton: Princeton University Press.

Maurier, Henri. 1997. *La religion spontanée: Philosophie des religions traditionnelles d'Afrique noire*. Paris: L'Harmattan.

Mazrui, Ali Al'amin. 2002. *Africanity Redefined: The Collected Essays of Ali A. Mazrui, Volume I*, edited by Ricardo René Laremont and Tracia Leacock Seghatolislami. Trenton: Africa World Press.

McCutcheon, R.T. 1997. *Manufacturing Religion: The Discourse on Sui Generis Religion and the Politics of Nostalgia*. New York: Oxford University Press.

Moreau, René Luc. 1982. *Africains Musulmans: Des communautés en mouvement*. Paris: Présence Africaine.

Mufuta, Patrice. 1969. *Le chant kàsàla des Lubà*. Paris: Julliard.

Ndaya Tshiteku, Julie. 2008. *'Prendre le bic': Le combat spirituel congolais et les transformations socials*. Leiden: Le Centre d'Études Africaines.

Neckebrouck, Valeer. 1988. *Théologie et culture: Mélanges offerts à Mgr Alfred Vaneste*. Louvaine-la-Neuve: Noraf.

Ofori, Patrick E. 1977. *Islam in Africa South of the Sahara: A Select Bibliographic Guide*. Nendeln: Kto Press.

Peel, J.D.Y. 2000. *Religious Encounter and the Making of the Yoruba*. Bloomington: Indiana University Press.

Pickthall, Mohammed Marmaduke. 1938. *The Meaning of the Glorious Quran*. Hyderabad-Deccan: Government Central Press.

Rorty, Richard. 1989. *Contingency, Irony and Solidarity*. Cambridge: Cambridge University Press.

Smith, Jonathan Z. 1988. *Imagining Religion: From Babylon to Jonestown*. Chicago: University of Chicago Press.

Taylor, John V. 2001. *The Primal Vision: Christian Presence amid African Religion*. London: SCM.

Tempels, Placide. 1962. *Notre rencontre I*. Limete-Léopoldville: Centre d'Études Pastorals.

———. 1969. *Bantu Philosophy*. Paris: Présence Africaine.

Thomas, Louis-Vincent and René Luneau. 1980. *La terre africaine et ses religions: Traditions et changements*. Paris: L'Harmattan.

Tillich, Paul. 2005. *Dynamics of Faith*. New York: Harper Collins.
Westerlund, David (ed.). 1996. *Questioning the Secular State: The Worldwide Resurgence of Religion in Politics*. New York: St Martin's Press.
Zoghby, Samir M. 1978. *Islam in Sub-Saharan Africa: A Partially Annotated Guide*. Washington: Library of Congress.

Violence and the Sublime

Leonhard Praeg

> Our metaphysical faculty is paralyzed because actual events have shattered the basis on which speculative metaphysical thought could be reconciled with experience. Once again, the dialectical motif of quantity recoiling into quality scores an unspeakable triumph.
>
> — Theodor Adorno, 'After Auschwitz'

The question of responsibility raised in the introduction to this volume, which returns in many different articulations in the essays that follow, presupposes some clarity on two related questions. In the first instance: who is the 'we' in the injunction 'we have a responsibility' and, in the second instance: what is the nature of responsibility – 'our' responsibility – in relation to what appears in so many ways and for so many reasons to be incomprehensible? It seems that the question of responsibility arises or becomes thinkable only as the result of a meta-reflection on both the addressee of the injunction and on what it means to assume responsibility in the face of the unspeakable. Such a meta-reflection could be construed, perhaps somewhat obtusely, as having to take responsibility for responsibility – if, by that doubling into meta-reflexivity, we understand an interrogation of the conditions for the possibility of responsibility, that is, what it means to think through the nature and possibility of ethical community in the face of the sublime, in the sense of being unspeakable and incomprehensible.

The first question can also be formulated as: what are the historical fault lines in 'our' responses to this war? It is a truism to say that for any critical humanism (does the very plurality of humanisms, their demarcation in cultural traditions, not already mark the origin of the necessary failure of all humanisms?), every conflict and every war is or should be the responsibility of humanity as such. But the translation into the political domain of this quasi-spiritual insight – whether derived from Abrahamic or non-Western traditions, such as African humanism – is never seamless. We know that only through some wars (not all) are victims constituted who, more readily than others, invoke 'our' sympathy and 'our' empathy. Nowhere is there a clearer indictment of the very idea of humanism than the manner in which certain victims, certain categories of people who belong to certain cultures and certain religions, get lost in the translation between the quasi-spiritual notion of the 'human' and the politics of humanity. Before we can assume responsibility for the victims of the war that has been the subject of the conversation represented by this collection of essays, our originary responsibility consists in interrogating this political matrix (best represented perhaps by the synecdoche of 'racialised Western modernity') that politicises in order to generate the very language of responsibility and irresponsibility, what 'having empathy' means, what it means to witness with pathos (from the Greek *pathêtikos*, suffering).

But this question regarding that which seems truly outrageous, namely a 'politics of empathy', according to which there are political conditions for the possibility of empathy, presupposes clarity on, and our having taken responsibility *for*, a question even more fundamental namely: how can 'we' – however this 'we' is construed, interrogated and critiqued and its seeming impossible unification under the sign 'all of humanity' lamented – act responsibly in the face of what appears sublime? In his *Critique of Judgement*, Immanuel Kant argues that there are two types of object that resist the totalising grasp of the imagination and as such constitute the unimaginable or the incomprehensible, namely the mathematically and dynamically sublime (2007: 78, 96). Violence, such as we have witnessed in the history of the Democratic Republic of the Congo (DRC) war, offers examples of both. The mathematically sublime is encountered in statements such as 'between 7 and 10 million people have died in this war' because, once individual suffering is multiplied to that extent, we are no longer able to grasp the meaning of suffering and death (in as much as we ever do). Similarly, while we can understand the qualitative dynamic of murder in many forms, our encounter with sexualised slaughter in the DRC war ('They cut off her left breast and put it in her hand . . . She was crying but finally she died. She died with her breast in her hand') is accompanied by the 'restless movement' Kant reserves for an encounter with this sublime, the uncontrollable oscillation between the recognition that our capacity for understanding is being violated and our attempt, nonetheless, to comprehend, in its totality, that which violates our understanding. Perhaps we can simplify Kant's terminology somewhat and refer to these manifestations of the sublime in the modes of *quantity* and *quality* – their combined manifestation in the *Shoah*, which, to paraphrase Adorno, scored 'an unspeakable triumph' over humanity.

To the modes of quantity and quality in relation to the sublime, we can add two further modes relating to *complexity* and *temporality*. These modes also signal something of the limits of comprehension and, in as much as comprehension is a condition for the possibility of empathy, will either – depending on one's politics and how one positions oneself in relation to the possible 'we' of the injunction to take responsibility – absolve one of responsibility or compel one to rethink the nature of the ethical in relation to the sublime.

By the mode of *complexity*, I refer to the general recognition that this has never been a local war, but rather the conflict of glocal interests, a fact expressed as much by its undecidable description ('DRC war' and/or generalised 'conflict in the Great Lakes region') as by the manner in which the First and Second Congo Wars blurred the distinction between internal revolution and external invasion. Add to this, the ever-changing flux in the web of political, military and commercial ties – both national and multinational – and a picture of complexity emerges that defies any totalising attempt at understanding. Dovetailing with this complexity is the sublime in the mode of *temporality*: where or how is this war/conflict to be demarcated, its beginning and cause located in time? Any easy classification that derives from the arbitrary distinction between 'colonial' and 'postcolonial' is subverted by Ngwarsungu Chiwengo, who in Chapter 5 reminds us that 'the cycle of violence in post-independence DRC is, ironically, not limited to our era, but has its genesis in the Congo Free State', that is, it spans, without being reducible to, at least the period 1904–2006. The temporal dimension of an event, which defies the totalising grasp of our understanding, subjects the event (and therefore, perhaps, *every event*, although this implication cannot be explored here) to that 'restless movement' we recognise as an encounter with the sublime.

The common denominator in the four modes of the sublime suggested here – *quantity, quality, complexity* and *temporality* – becomes evident in the light of Kant's description of the limits of the imagination:

> For if the apprehension has reached a point beyond which the representations of sensuous intuition in the case of the parts first apprehended begin to disappear from the imagination as this advances to the apprehension of yet others, as much, then, is lost at one end as is gained at the other, and for

comprehension we get a maximum which the imagination cannot exceed (Kant 2007: 82).

Every encounter with the sublime – irrespective of the mode of its manifestation – is a 'liminal experience' (Praeg 2010), an experience of being and thinking (at) the limits of human imagination. How we respond to such liminal experiences cannot but have implications for the way we think about community, that is, the way we think through questions of responsibility and ethics.

A recurring thematic in the discourse on the conflict in the Great Lakes region has been the articulation of a fault line that clearly fingers 'the West' for its lack of responsibility, empathy, intervention or simply for failing to 'pay attention' to the nature of this war and it casualties, for consistently having failed to empathise or respond to the brutal slaughter, torture, rape and massacre of millions of men, women and children. The simplest explanation of this failure invokes the operation of the 'economy of the Manichean allegory' (JanMohamed 1986) at the heart of racialised Western modernity. True as that may be, for the sake of exploring what it means to take responsibility for 'our' responsibility, one could, from a more generous perspective, argue that every trope invoked by this *imaginaire* to account for its irresponsibility derives to some extent from one of the four modes of the sublime articulated here: the conflict involves too many people who are difficult to identify with because they are not so much citizens of sovereign states as they are subjects of obscure and atavistic, quasi political formations, clans, ethnic groups, kingdoms and the like (*quantity*); much of the violence is too brutal, unspeakable and inhumane to provoke as a matter of course the logic of sustained humanitarian intervention – which also accounts for the ever-recurring Conradian notion of an 'essentially brutal Congo' (*quality*); the conflict is too glocal and therefore too complex and it is unclear whose responsibility begins and ends where (*complexity*); in addition to being a war with no clear cause and therefore no beginning and possibly no end (*temporality*). Everywhere, 'the parts first apprehended begin to disappear from the imagination as this advances to the apprehension of yet others [so that], as much, then, is lost at one end as is gained at the other', a relentlessness we recognise at the root of the West's melancholy 'empathy fatigue'.

We can say at least two things about the status of this invocation of the *problematique* of the sublime in relation to the DRC war: one, it tells us something not about the West's failure to act responsibly but rather, given the fact that it invokes the limitation of the human imagination, something about humanity's failure to respond responsibly. There is no easy distinction here between an irresponsible West and an Africa that readily assumes responsibility – a fact clearly demonstrated by South Africa's own corporate interests in the outcome of this war; two, while we may invoke the *problematique* of the sublime as a way of explaining our collective inertia and irresponsibility, doing so never quite adds up to an excuse. It just does not follow and to understand why not, it may be useful here to bear in mind Jean-François Lyotard's notion of the 'immemorial' as

> that which can neither be remembered (represented to consciousness) nor forgotten (consigned to oblivion). It is that which returns, uncannily. As such, the immemorial acts as a kind of *figure* for consciousness and its attempts at representing itself historically. The prime example is Auschwitz, which obliges us to speak so that this event remains an event, so that it does not become something that happened, among other things (Readings 1991: xxxi).

Lyotard attributes the responsibility of bearing witness to the immemorial to the avant-garde in its manifold realisation – poets, artists and, in *The Differend*, the philosopher. For both the novelist and the thinker or philosopher, the *archē* or originary responsibility, the responsibility that precedes all others, resides in the obligation to make visible and comprehensible that which is constituted as opaque in the various modes of the sublime. On this point a distinction emerges, however vaguely, that may be more useful and interesting than the irresponsible distinction between Western inertia and African innocence, a distinction that emerges from Lyotard's attribution of responsibility, which suggests the configuration of the ethical in two distinguishable *imaginaires* – two 'complex systems of presumption . . . that enter subjective experience as the expectation that things will make sense generally' (Vogler 2002: 625) – in a way that interfaces while remaining irreducible to the Africa/West binary. One the one hand, there is the *imaginaire* of the individual artist or philosopher who responds to the transcendental yet aporetic imperative to speak about the unspeakable, to bear witness to that which cannot be imagined or represented to consciousness. This is a responsibility *despite* and we are offered a very eloquent expression of it in relation to the sublimity of the temporal, perhaps unsurprisingly, by Marcel Proust in *Remembrance of Things Past*: 'A "real" person, profoundly as we may sympathise with him, is in a great measure perceptible only through our senses, that is to say, remains opaque, presents a dead weight which our sensibilities have not the strength to lift' (1985: 91).

Yet, far from delivering us, irresponsibly so, to resignation in the face of the sublime, the opaque, suffering individual compels us differently, for as Proust continues:

> The novelist's happy discovery was to think of substituting for those opaque sections, impenetrable to the human soul, their equivalent in immaterial sections, things, that is, which one's soul can assimilate . . . [In this way, the novelist] sets free within us all the joys and sorrows in the world . . . the most intense of which would never be revealed to us *because the slow course of their development prevents us from perceiving them* (1985: 92, emphasis added).

In the second *imaginaire*, the ethical is not primarily configured as an aporetic imperative pivoting on the tension between the imagination and the event in order to perpetually strive to represent to consciousness that which cannot be represented to it, but first and foremost in relation to an intersubjective Other, who similarly finds him or herself at the mercy of this aporia. Here, the ethical precedes any fidelity to the transcendental 'truth' and the *problematique* of the in/adequacy of our representations. If the conceptual axiomatic of the first *imaginaire* is the solitary, individualised avant-garde, the second *imaginaire* is the conversation or the dialogue, the intersubjective praxis of making comprehensible.

Those who participated in the conversation 'Violence in/and the Great Lakes: The Thought of V-Y Mudimbe and Beyond', as well as the readers of this volume, have and will continue to encounter what it means to take responsibility in both senses. On the one hand, Mudimbe's *oeuvre* – novelistic, philosophical, historical – stands as lasting testimony to the individual artist and philosopher's recognition of the imperative to take responsibility in the face of the sublime and to bear witness to the immemorial; on the other hand, dialogue among friends and colleagues bears testimony to a different truth: responsibility is, first and foremost, not a concept or an idea, but a praxis constitutive of humanity in the precise sense that were I the sole remaining human being in the world, the statement 'I have a responsibility' would be as meaningless as the claim 'I am free'.

References

Adorno, Theodor W. 1973. 'After Auschwitz'. In *Negative Dialectics*. Translated by E.B. Ashton, 361–65. London: Routledge & Kegan Paul.

JanMohamed, Abdul R. 1986. 'The Economy of the Manichean Allegory: The Function of Racial Difference in Colonialist Literature'. In *'Race', Writing, and Difference*, edited by Henry Louis Gates Jr and Kwame Anthony Appiah, 78–107. Chicago: University of Chicago Press.

Kant, Immanuel. 2007 [1790]. *Critique of Judgement*. Oxford: Oxford University Press.

Praeg, Leonhard. 2010. 'Of Evil and Other Figures of the Liminal'. *Theory, Culture & Society* 27(5): 107–34.

Proust, Marcel. 1985. *Remembrance of Things Past, Vol. 1*. London: Penguin.

Readings, Bill. 1991. *Introducing Lyotard: Art and Politics*. London: Routledge.

Vogler, Candace. 2002. 'Social Imaginary, Ethics, and Methodological Individualism'. *Public Culture* 14(3): 625–27.

Notes on the Contributors

Justin K. Bisanswa received his Doctorate en Philosophie et Lettres from l'Université de Liège (Belgium). He teaches African Literatures at l'Université Laval (Québec, Canada), where he holds the Canada Research Chair in African Literature and Francophonie. His recent publications include: *Conflits de mémoires: V.Y. Mudimbe et la traversée des signes*, *Roman africain contemporain*, *Dire le social dans le roman francophone* (with Kasereka Kavwahirehi) and *Entre inscriptions et prescriptions: V.Y. Mudimbe et l'engendrement de la parole*.

Ngwarsungu Chiwengo, professor of English and director of Black Studies at Creighton University in Omaha, Nebraska, is a native of Congo (DRC). She obtained her Ph.D. at SUNY/Buffalo and taught at the University of Lubumbashi for nine years, where she also chaired the English department. During the Mobutu transition, she was federal and vice-president of the Democratic Christian Social Party (PDSC). Her book *Understanding 'Cry, the Beloved Country'* analyses the novel's literary and historical background.

Grant Farred is professor of Africana Studies at Cornell University. His most recent book is *In Motion, At Rest: The Event of the Athletic Body*. His other works include *What's My Name? Black Vernacular Intellectuals*, *Phantom Calls: Race and the Globalization of the NBA* and *Long Distance Love: A Passion for Football*. He served as general editor of the Duke University-based journal, *The South Atlantic Quarterly*, from 2002 to 2010. He is the editor of the series 'Thinking Theory Now' (Stanford University Press). His forthcoming works include *Conciliation*.

Olga Hél-Bongo is professor of Francophone Literatures at l'Université Laval and a research fellow at the Research Chair of Canada in African Literatures and Francophonie. She has written numerous books and articles, including '*Nos songes valent mieux que nos discours': La rêverie dans les* Essais *de Montaigne*, *Société et énonciation dans le roman francophone* (with Mbaye Diouf) and '*Les* *enjeux de l'essai dans l'œuvre romanesque de V.Y. Mudimbe'* in *Entre inscriptions et prescriptions: V.Y. Mudimbe et l'engendrement de la parole.*

Kasereka Kavwahirehi is professor of French at the University of Ottawa, Canada. He is a specialist in francophone literature, with interests in postcolonial studies and African philosophy. His recent publications include: *V.Y. Mudimbe et la ré-invention de l'Afrique, L'Afrique: Entre passé et futur* and *Le prix de l'impasse.* He is also the co-editor of *Dire le social dans le roman francophone contemporain* (with Justin Bisanswa) and *Beyond the Lines: Fabien Eboussi Boulaga, a Philosophical Practice* (with Lidia Procesi).

Laura Kerr is a mental health scholar (Ph.D., Stanford University) and a marriage and family therapist registered intern (MA, Pacifica Graduate Institute), specialising in the treatment of trauma, with an interest in Jungian psychology. Prior to becoming a psychotherapist, Dr Kerr taught at Stanford, including a graduate course with V-Y Mudimbe on the phenomenology of madness. With Mudimbe and Godé Iwele, she edited *The Normal and Its Orders: Reading Georges Canguilhem.* You can find out more about her at http://www.laurakkerr.com.

V-Y Mudimbe teaches at Duke University in North Carolina, United States of America. Among his publications are *The Invention of Africa, The Idea of Africa, Tales of Faith: Religion as Political Perfomance in Central Africa* and *On African Fault Lines.*

Leonhard Praeg is associate professor in the Department of Political and International Studies at Rhodes University and the author of, most recently, *A Report on Ubuntu* and co-editor (with Siphokazi Magadla) of *Ubuntu: Curating the Archive.* He is series editor of the Thinking Africa Series, published in collaboration with University of KwaZulu-Natal Press.

Zubairu Wai is associate professor of Political Science at Lakehead University, Thunder Bay, Ontario, Canada. He is author of *Epistemologies of African Conflicts: Violence, Evolutionism and the War in Sierra Leone,* winner of the ATWS Toyin Falola Africa Book Award for 2013. His research adopts critical theory and postcolonial perspectives to address questions of power, knowledge, identity and representation in the discourses and political economy of violence, conflicts, security and development.